"Simply outstanding – I will have no hesitation in using it in any future course I may teach on leadership. I cannot think of any book on leadership with the potentially life-changing impact of the author's call to lead like we really mean it."

Professor Joseph Wallis
School of Business, American University of Sharjah

"…Thankfully, this book goes far deeper than the standard management texts. The author argues convincingly that you cannot, to quote him, 'lead like you mean it' if you don't ask deep questions about the power of integrity, thinking for yourself, and the compelling need for education and personal growth. The book is a provocative and penetrating exploration of the historic and philosophical roots of the postmodern leadership crisis. He takes us into the very foundations of understanding human nature and the development of character."

David Hodes
Systems Thinker, TOC Expert, and founder of Ensemble Consulting Group

"An outstanding book that gets down to the core of the leadership challenge globally throughout history; relevant now and in the future. Brilliant!"

Dr. Lehan Stemmet
Organisation and Personal Development

"A very important book. To a generation of leaders standing on the quicksand of individualism and relativism this book offers purpose and confidence. Read it!"

Greg Fleming
CEO of the Maxim Institute

Copyright © 2010 Andre van Heerden, All Rights Reserved.

Except for the purpose of reviewing, no part of this publication may be reproduced or transmitted in any form or by any means, electronic or mechanical, including photocopying, recording or any information storage or retrieval system, without the written permission of the publishers. Infringers of copyright render themselves liable for prosecution.

Disclaimer: Every effort has been made to ensure this book is as accurate and complete as possible, however there may be mistakes both typographical and in content. The authors and the publisher shall not be held liable or responsible to any person or entity with respect to any loss or damage caused or alleged to have been caused directly or indirectly by the information contained in this book.

ISBN: 9780986459856

Published by The Power of Integrity, Auckland, New Zealand

www.powerofintegrity.com

Design by Dannie Jefferies, GreatDesigns

LEADERS AND MISLEADERS
THE ART OF LEADING LIKE YOU MEAN IT

ANDRE VAN HEERDEN

To Cheryl — for showing me the true meaning of leadership

Contents

	Introduction: Why this book?	7
1.	Leaders and misleaders	13
2.	What's gone wrong?	27
3.	Leading like you mean it	43
4.	The power of integrity	59
5.	Thinking for yourself	75
6.	Education and personal growth	99
7.	Understanding human nature	117
8.	Building character	135
9.	Building fulfilling relationships	157
10.	Leaders unleash creativity	179
11.	Quo Vadis?	203
	About Andre van Heerden	227
	Bibliography	228
	Index	233

INTRODUCTION
WHY THIS BOOK?

"If you are on the wrong train, it does not help to run down the corridors to the back." Dietrich Bonhoeffer

In a world full of books and devoid of leaders, will another book on leadership make any difference? It might, but only if it can show the reasons why what we are doing is not working.

In the leadership workshops I run, I usually ask participants the question: "What percentage of leaders in all walks of life do you believe are really effective?". Over the years, the responses have reflected a familiar pattern: most people — and my sample covers a very broad demographic sweep — are of the opinion that fewer than ten percent provide leadership that really makes a positive difference. Over the past forty years, working as a teacher, a soldier in the Rhodesia War, a creative director in advertising, a marketing strategist and more recently as a corporate consultant and leadership mentor, I have had wide first-hand experience that tells me the 'less than ten percent' judgment is fairly generous. And the alarming anecdotal evidence regularly provided by friends, business associates and the media strongly reinforces this commonly held opinion that leadership is seriously lacking at all levels of Western society.

There are a great many obvious symptoms of the leadership crisis at the national and international levels: the ravages of endemic war and seemingly intractable geopolitical tension; economic disarray resulting from gross mismanagement, corruption and greed; the all-too-visible waste and degradation of human potential and natural resources; the ever-growing catalogue of calamitous social dysfunction; the failure of vastly increased funding to deliver improved health and education services; and the pseudo-celebrity antics of politicians and would-be world leaders — these are some of the more serious symptoms of the problem of leadership failure in 'higher places'.

In the workplace we encounter disillusionment, demoralisation, cynicism, and despair. The treatment of people in the workplace as dehumanised functionaries rather than as human beings, the high incidence of dysfunctional relationships, and the almost total absence of loyalty on either side of the management–employee divide are all symptomatic of the leadership crisis. Leaders shape culture, for better or worse, and statistics clearly signal the decay of corporate culture around the world: in 2004, the percentage of employees in the US who said they were truly "engaged" in their work was just 29 percent. An astonishing 54 percent put themselves in the "not engaged" category and 17 percent of employees noted that they were "actively disengaged." (The *Gallup Management Journal*'s semi-annual Employee Engagement Index 2004)

The phenomenal commercial success of the Dilbert cartoons, the runaway French best-seller *Bonjour Paresse,* and the British television comedy series *The Office* provide damning, if entertaining, evidence of the debilitating lack of leadership in the workplace today. The galley humour employed is built on the profound irony that all of the incidents portrayed and the ideas lampooned are easily recognisable as being inspired by actual workplace experiences.

All of this tallies with the stories I receive daily, from the United States, Europe, South Africa, Australia, Canada, or New Zealand, about leadership that is either perverse or incompetent, or both; and I have no reason to doubt that this scarcity of effective leadership is a global phenomenon.

How can this be? There has never been as much dedicated literature on the subject of effective leadership: the management and leadership shelves in bookstores and libraries are overflowing with compelling titles on how to mass-produce leaders and solve all the problems facing an organisation in just a few easy steps. Tertiary courses in leadership proliferate as universities and business schools cash in on the obvious deficiency, and the corporate world spends ever more money on leadership development. Even schools are now providing special programmes to nurture nascent leadership potential. We have never been busier trying to produce leaders, yet we are still desperately short of good leadership.

The harsh reality is that it puts the future of our whole society in jeopardy. The cumulative effects of poor leadership across all sectors will lead inexorably to societal collapse, as it has done throughout history. The current crisis of democracy all over the Western world is a leadership crisis, and it was predicted with remarkable accuracy by prescient writers eighty and even one hundred and eighty years ago.

I believe this leadership crisis is intimately related to a cultural development in Western society that has accompanied the emergence of the post-modern mindset, with its radical scepticism and its ambivalence to the concept of truth. Public discourse in politics, the professions, business, and the arts has become superficial and sterile, and is rightly viewed with a measure of distrust. This has been a disaster for personal relationships generally, and the social, political, and economic consequences are clear. Inevitably, leadership has been a major casualty, because the demise of trust destroys the foundation on which it is built.

It is impossible to build or maintain a free, democratic society on deceit, and if the free market needs democracy and a sincerely dedicated civil society to function as it should, we are already in serious trouble. Deceit has become institutionalised. Consider just a few of the verbal commitments heard in the workplace every day, and the reality of the behaviour that contradicts them:

- We say we believe in honesty, but we question the meaning of truth.
- We say we believe in open communication, but we practise political correctness.
- We say we believe in empowerment, but we prefer to retain control.
- We say we believe in creativity, but we stifle ideas and questions.
- We say we believe in teamwork, but we promote selfish individualism.
- We say we believe in work/life balance, but we keep increasing workloads.
- We say we believe in confidence, but we actively encourage cynicism.
- We say we believe in change, but we never make the distinction with progress.

- We say we believe in core values, but we are dismissive of morality.
- We say we believe in loyalty, but we only look after ourselves in a crisis.
- We say we believe in strategy, but we have a short-term focus and pursue the quick fix.

And, of course, we say we believe we can make people effective leaders by simply giving them the right skills, despite being confronted daily by irrefutable evidence to the contrary.

This all betrays either an impoverished understanding of, or a manipulative disregard for, human nature, and a basic lack of empathy with real people that makes it all but impossible to inspire them and get the best out of them in pursuit of a common cause. In short, it seems clear to me that we have a fundamentally flawed understanding of what leadership is, and consequently have been trying to develop leaders by using methods that simply do not work.

This book seeks to explain how we have gone wrong and to propose an alternative approach to leadership development. While I would not suggest it is a quick fix — it is, in fact, very much about long-term development — it has been a source of deep satisfaction to note the rapid gains made by people who have committed to the principles of the philosophy of leadership proposed in the pages that follow.

For more than a decade I have been working with organisations, large and small, on issues such as vision, strategy, corporate culture, attitudes and character, teamwork, communication, creativity and relationships. I called the programme of workshops I developed *The Power of Integrity*, because every topic ultimately came back to an insistent demand for personal and corporate integrity.

When the success of *The Power of Integrity* persuaded a large corporate organisation to ask me to develop a leadership programme for one hundred and twenty of its managers, I wrote one which I entitled *Leading Like You Mean It*. Working with successive groups of ten managers, we ran 360-degree assessments, intensive workshops, one-on-one mentoring sessions and personal development plans over a period of six months for each group. Since I operate a one-man business, I was intimately involved right from the start with every aspect of the development and delivery of the programme, and had the privilege of accompanying the many individual participants on their own personal leadership journeys. As the programme (as a whole or in part) has been adopted by other organisations over the years, I have had the pleasure and the extraordinary benefit of working with hundreds of leaders from an exceptionally wide demographic mix.

The most frequent feedback comments received from people who have participated in the programme are those I most sincerely hoped for when constructing and shaping the content: for example, "It was completely different to what I expected", "What I have learned is applicable not only to my work, but to my life as a whole", and "It has inspired me to make some immediate changes in how I work with people".

Many of these people have become good friends, and a greater number stay in touch on a casual basis, providing me with insights, information, and anecdotes that inform my own thinking on leadership and on the challenges involved in relating to people as experienced by all human organisations and communities. *Leading like you mean it* has consequently evolved to the point where I now believe it forms the basis of a book that can make a significant contribution to the whole question.

Leaders and Misleaders

CHAPTER 1
Leaders and misleaders

"Medieval men thought of the king as ruling 'sub deo et lege', rightly translated, 'under God and the law', but also involving something atmospheric that might more vaguely be called 'under the morality implied in all our institutions.'" G. K. Chesterton

THE COST OF LEADERSHIP

In the cynical, post-modern cultural milieu of the Western world, heroism is under siege. The protagonists of popular books and movies are often criminals and other social deviants, and the genuine heroes from the past or the present are assailed by the ever-growing ranks of the debunkers, who know there is money to be made either by exposing the human failings of supposedly perfect people, or by simply peddling lies. Hence, even people like Lincoln, Churchill, and Mother Theresa have been targeted — ironically all in the name of truth, which many of the debunkers profess not to believe in anyway. The great tragedy is that these heroes provide precisely the models of leadership we so desperately need, standing as they do in stark contrast to the shallow hedonist celebrities who attract most of the public's adulation today.

One hero of the past who has come under attack was a popular example of political leadership for five hundred years. Sir Thomas More, beheaded on the orders of Henry VIII in 1535, was the subject of Robert Bolt's play and the 1966 movie *A Man for All Seasons*, which unashamedly paid tribute to him as a man of principle ready to stand by the dictates of conscience even in the face of death. Post-modern revisionists, believing human beings are motivated only by self-interest, have seized upon More's worldliness and wealth, his political acumen, and his penchant for savage and often scatological invective, to cast doubt on his reasons for opposing Henry.

This betrays a very superficial understanding of human nature and is emblematic of the cynical nihilism which has gathered strength among academics and artists since the end of World War II and which seeks to relegate the rich heritage of Western culture to the scrapheap. Damning a person because they fall short of perfection is to give up hope in human potential and civilised standards, and to open the door to the moral confusion and psychological distress so prevalent today. More was susceptible, like the rest of us, to temptation — sexual, financial, professional, and political — but it is far better to have standards which you struggle to live up to than no standards at all. That, after all, is the basic test of civilisation. In the end, a contrite hypocrite is preferable to a callous cynic. As the Duc de la Rochefoucauld said:

"Hypocrisy is the homage vice pays to virtue."

As a devout Catholic, More contemplated taking holy orders, but his desire for a wife and family took his life in another direction and a career in politics opened up for him. In 1523 he became Speaker of the House of Commons and six years later was appointed Chancellor of England, the first layman to hold the position.

The heresy laws of England under King Henry VIII sound most severe to modern ears. As Chancellor, More applied them with compassion but firmness, and it is significant in the context of those violent and intemperate times that only four people paid the ultimate penalty during his period of office. This seems wholly consistent with his commitment to the principles of justice and charity, and the profound respect he enjoyed among his contemporaries.

Within a year of being appointed as Chancellor, More tendered his resignation when a royal proclamation required all members of the clergy to acknowledge the king as Supreme Head of the Church in England. Henry refused to accept it; the lines were drawn for a contest between one man acting on expediency, and another, acting on principle. More knew better than most that Henry was a dangerous man to oppose and that in addition to the obvious costs of principled action (More stood to lose not just power, prestige, and the favour of the king, but also most of his income and estates) death was a real possibility. Henry's primary reason for making himself Head of the Church in England was so that he could divorce Katherine of Aragon and marry Anne Boleyn. More steadfastly opposed the move, which enraged Henry further, and when the Chancellor offered his resignation again in 1532, it was quickly accepted.

Robert Bolt, an agnostic, wrote *A Man for All Seasons* as a celebration of one man's heroic commitment to following his conscience. It is clear that martyrdom was the last thing More wanted. He retired quietly into seclusion at Chelsea and used his considerable skills as a lawyer and a politician to ensure the Crown had no legal grounds to harass him further. But his silence gave no peace to Henry, who wanted the open approval of More, who was a popular figure. The pressure placed on More culminated in his incarceration in the Tower of London, where — despite the pleas of family and friends — he refused to acknowledge Henry as head of the Church, and so was beheaded in July 1535.

The publication of his book *Utopia* was delayed until fifteen years after his execution, mainly because of his outspoken account of the socio-economic conditions in England. His description of government as "a conspiracy of rich men procuring their own commodities under the name and title of a commonwealth" was hardly crafted to earn him support among the rich and powerful.

Sir Thomas More can be challenged on many of his political, social and religious standpoints, but his principle that there was a limit even to the king's power was a stand against tyranny. He emphatically embraced the truth that might is not right, and that there is a law higher than that of the state. It is the principle on which democracy and civil society are built.

It is instructive to consider who the real leader was in this tragic episode: Henry VIII or Sir Thomas More. Five hundred years on, Henry, the Machiavellian Renaissance ruler, is remembered mostly for his six wives and the frequency with which his executioner wielded the axe; Sir Thomas More, by contrast, continues to inspire people across the political spectrum through the sacrifices he made in standing firm on the principle that the king is not omnipotent and that wrong cannot be transformed into right by means of legislation. Hitler and the Nazis provided another epic example of this truth after they had achieved power in Germany through entirely constitutional means: everything they did from then on was perfectly legal, but egregiously immoral. The implications for leadership are compelling.

DEFINING LEADERSHIP

To understand how to create effective leaders, we have to start by defining what we mean by leadership. The dictionary on my computer indicates that: '*A leader is a head, a manager, a person in charge, an organiser, a principal, a chief, a boss, a director, or a guide. And that leadership is management, control, guidance, headship or direction.*'

Although useful, these dictionary definitions are inadequate in promoting a proper understanding of the nature of leadership in politics, business or any other arena. Three significant, if somewhat contradictory, definitions from well-known management thinkers provide a better understanding.

Abraham Zaleznik noted in his essay in the *Harvard Business Review* of May/June 1977 that '*Leadership inevitably requires using power to influence the thoughts and actions of other people*'.

Michael Feiner, in his book *The Feiner Points of Leadership*, says that leadership is something you do '*by enabling, by teaching, by coaching, and by helping your people to excel*'.

And John Kotter, in his analysis of business leadership, *Leading Change*, emphasises that '*Leadership defines what the future should look like, aligns people with that vision, and inspires them to make it happen despite the obstacles*'.

Zaleznik's definition would fit people popularly considered to have been great leaders in history, and also most current heads in business, politics, the professions, and other areas of society. Feiner's definition, on the other hand, would seem incongruous if applied to Alexander the Great, Napoleon or Elizabeth I, and while it employs words commonly used in our post-modern milieu, the reality is that there is little evidence of them being widely applied in the workplace. But in spite of their limited applicability, both definitions are nonetheless valuable because they express essential truths about the nature of leadership.

Kotter's definition seems to me to capture more cogently what leadership is: it fits as comfortably with a Napoleon as it does with a Mother Theresa and also encapsulates precisely what is required of a leader in the business world or any other field. However, over the years I have developed a particular view of leadership — one that all people who head teams or organisations can be measured against. This is the view that underpins the whole approach to developing leaders that I describe in this book.

DEFINING REALITY

Let me explain that view. In the workshops I run, one of the first challenges I confront participants with is to explain the thinking behind the statement by businessman Max De Pree, in his book *Leadership is an Art*, that '*the first responsibility of a leader is to define reality*'.

Most people readily affirm that 'defining reality' is 'telling it like it is', and are equally in agreement that leaders need to define reality to themselves, then to their team, to their own leader, to their peers, and to everybody else they deal with — customers, suppliers, the general public, and so on. (There are, of course, a few participants who challenge the notion that human beings can tell it like it is, claiming that truth is relative and largely a matter of opinion; this view is addressed in later chapters.)

Workshop participants are always amused by Josiah Royce's euphemism, quoted in Mortimer Adler's *How to think about the Great Ideas*, which defines a liar as: '*someone who wilfully misplaces his ontological predicates*'.

But it is more than amusing; it is also highly instructive. Our ontological predicates are the verb 'is' and its negative 'is not'; when someone knowingly says that something is, when he knows it is not, or vice versa, he is telling a lie. He is being untruthful. Human discourse and relationships can have no meaning whatever without the reality of objective truth and the ability of human reason, limited and fallible though it may be, to reach it in part at least. And the implications for leadership are crucial.

In my late forties I worked for a newly established specialist advertising agency that had the backing and the prestigious brand name of a major multinational group. I understood that my career in an industry ravaged by restructures, realignments, and the impact of new technology was under serious threat. Like several other senior staff members who had fallen on hard times in the ailing industry, I lacked any meaningful vision of the future, and was focused primarily on putting bread on the table. The promise made by the CEO that we would all share in the projected success of the agency sounded good, but the prospect seemed too remote to have any real motivational efficacy with seasoned and cynical advertising professionals.

Within two years, however, as a result of our expertise, experience, and excessive workloads (the agency was a proverbial sweatshop), this new operation had done exceptionally well, even at a time when the other agencies in the local group were underperforming badly. The multinational group then increased its share-holding in our fast-growing organisation, promising senior members of staff, including myself, shares in the group in a plan they intended to roll out over the next few years. Our own remarkable success and the promise from one of the world's largest advertising conglomerates encouraged all of us to view the future with rather more confidence.

Unfortunately, several people above us had beenced wilfully misplacing their ontological predicates for some time, and the next major development, eighteen months later, caught everyone off guard. Despite our awareness of the declining fortunes of the group's other agencies, our own growth and the appointment of our CEO to head up all three agencies suggested a likely turn around for them. It was not to be. A deal was struck which amounted to a regional takeover of the ailing multinational's operations by another group, and our CEO was a key player in the coup. The promises made to us were broken and when two of my closest associates — decent, dedicated professionals who had made huge contributions to the growth of the agency — lost their jobs in the subsequent restructure, the only reality I could define about my employers was that they readily used the lives of others as a means to their own ends. Although I was promoted, I resigned and hard as the following years were, I never once regretted leaving an organisation which was clearly not to be trusted. They have since been swallowed in another merger.

That was one of many personal experiences that led me to reflect on the nature of leadership, and it is interesting to measure it against John Kotter's definition: the agency leadership certainly defined what the future should look like, but they were lying. They certainly aligned us with the vision, but they did so dishonestly; and they inspired us to make things happen in spite of very significant challenges, by misleading us from beginning to end.

LEADING AND MISLEADING

My use of the word 'misleading' is deliberate. The dictionary defines 'misleading' as "deceptive, ambiguous, confusing, false, disingenuous, and untruthful"; To mislead is therefore to lie or to deceive someone. And you cannot define reality to yourself or anyone else if you resort to deception. I wholeheartedly endorse Max De Pree's injunction that to define reality to oneself and to others is the first responsibility of a leader, and leaders are challenged to do so hundreds of times each day, in meetings, over the phone, via e-mail and in personal reflection. When they seek advantage or refuge through dishonesty, they cease to be leaders and become instead misleaders.

Taking the negative of 'to lead' to be 'to mislead'', the logical conclusion is that leadership stands or falls on personal integrity. This is why I believe we should not even use the popular distinction between good leaders and bad leaders; we should simply acknowledge that people in positions of authority are either leaders or misleaders, with the inevitable shades of grey tinting all of us, because we are all fallible human beings. This more accurate distinction enables us to understand the whole concept of leadership more profoundly.

For example, Hitler was obviously not a great leader, but rather a notorious, and temporarily successful, misleader. In my workshops I have had people (albeit only a few) who have proposed Hitler as an example of a great leader, obviously appealing to success as the criterion. It is also significant that as prominent a scholar as Peter Drucker should have made the claim that the only three great leaders produced by the twentieth century were Hitler, Mao, and Stalin. This standpoint, however, does not bear even mild scrutiny.

Hitler may have enjoyed some stunning successes after coming to power in Germany, but his "thousand-year Reich" lasted only twelve years, and left his country devastated physically, emotionally and spiritually. Such genuine support as he enjoyed sprang from blind receptivity to his lies by a people humiliated by defeat in World War I and the Versailles Treaty that followed; for the rest, support was motivated primarily by fear — the Nazis used violence and intimidation to achieve their ends. Hitler's was a gangster regime, a haven for petty criminals, dishonest people on the make, and psychopaths. Hitler's goal was success at any price, as articulated in his assertion that *the winner will never be asked if he told the truth.*

Mao and Stalin were cut from the same cloth, and their legacies are equally shameful.

Significantly, Drucker has also said that "leaders have followers". Hitler, Mao, and Stalin never had followers — they only had the bribed, the broken, the beguiled ... and the bad.

The inescapable reality is that coercion, intimidation, exploitation, and manipulation of people is the very opposite of leading because it involves forcing or tricking people into doing what you want, using them as a means to your own ends. People in authority who resort to the lie do not lead others — they mislead them.

The limitations of John Kotter's otherwise excellent definition of leadership now become clear. Hitler, disdaining the truth, defined his vision of the future and aligned vast numbers of people with that vision, using lies and violence to inspire them to make the nightmare happen. The fact that his successes were transient is not the issue; some very worthy leaders often fail as well. The issue is plainly that his vision, alignment, and inspiration were all built on the denial and distortion of truth. We need a definition of leadership that stands on honesty, consigning lies and violence to misleaders.

A MORE DECISIVE WAY TO THINK ABOUT LEADERSHIP

The humanity of Teddy Roosevelt was shown in his declaration that America wouldn't be a good place for anyone, unless it was made a good place for all, which encapsulated the essential virtues of true leadership: respect for the dignity of all people and the honest dealings that exemplify that respect. To craft a vision that will see some people disadvantaged or even brutalised, and then to conceal such ugly realities behind falsehood, is to violate the justice, compassion, and pragmatism expressed in Roosevelt's words. And the implied mutual responsibility is also clear: the country, the enterprise, the many, must be good for the individual, and the individual must be good for them.

In the light of the distinction between leaders and misleaders, together with Roosevelt's simple guidelines and Kotter's insights, the following definition seems to afford a better understanding of what we should aim for when developing new leaders:

> *'Leadership inspires people to be the best they can be in mutual pursuit of a better life for all.'*

This definition cannot be made to fit Napoleon because although many of his achievements were meritorious, he built his empire on deceit and violence. He was one of the greatest military minds of all time and an administrator of genius; he had the undeniable ability to inspire others — his marshals, the men in the ranks and the French people en masse; but his sixteen-year regime left a Europe torn apart by war and, for a very long time after, pathologically fearful of French aggression. France itself was condemned to one hundred and fifty years of unstable political and social experimentation, and a long infatuation with military dictatorship. Napoleon had all the skills to be a great leader, but his attitude to himself was megalomaniacal, his attitude to other people was tyrannical, and his attitude to the world at large was contemptuous.

George Washington, on the other hand, fits this last definition of a leader. True, he was no military genius, and the intellectual and motivational power behind the American Revolution and the constitutional arrangements that followed is correctly credited to other great leaders — to Franklin, Hamilton, Jefferson, Marshall, and Adams. But he was a steadfast general who provided the newly born United States with a strong government that worked in the best interests of the country. Washington's leadership showed his sincere concern for the people he served and for the nation he was helping to build. Like the Roman general Cincinnatus, he put the country's needs first and refused the offer of long term power.

The essential difference between Washington and Napoleon was one of attitude — to themselves, their people, and the world in which they lived. That difference was decisive for the leadership they provided. The former was not perfectly good, and the latter was not utterly bad — they were both complex, unpredictable human beings, as we all are. But the one espoused liberty (albeit imperfectly), while the other exemplified tyranny. Washington was the leader, Napoleon the misleader.

The imperfections we are all burdened with and the fact that life is a journey mean that no cut-and-dried division between leaders and misleaders is possible; instead leadership can be seen as a continuum from the ideal leader to the ultimate misleader (see Figure 1.1). This continuum challenges us to strive daily to grow towards true leadership. No human being could ever be the perfect leader in every situation, but we are all capable of instances of great leadership; by multiplying the number of those instances the net outcome is leadership rather than misleadership. Any in-depth study of history's movers and shakers reveals few perfect leaders, but the unrecorded history of ordinary people would reveal a high degree of commitment to the ideal among parents, teachers, and spiritual and community leaders.

Of course, misleaders do not measure their effectiveness against any criterion other than their own self-aggrandizement; but anyone who is serious about inspiring people to be the best they can be must be prepared to reflect on their own position on the continuum on a daily basis. To take a simple example, imagine your teenage son falling behind on his studies and hanging out with a group known to be on drugs. Your every response will be fraught with danger and will inevitably move you one way or the other on that continuum. Leadership from you will save your son; abdication or misleadership will almost certainly result in disaster.

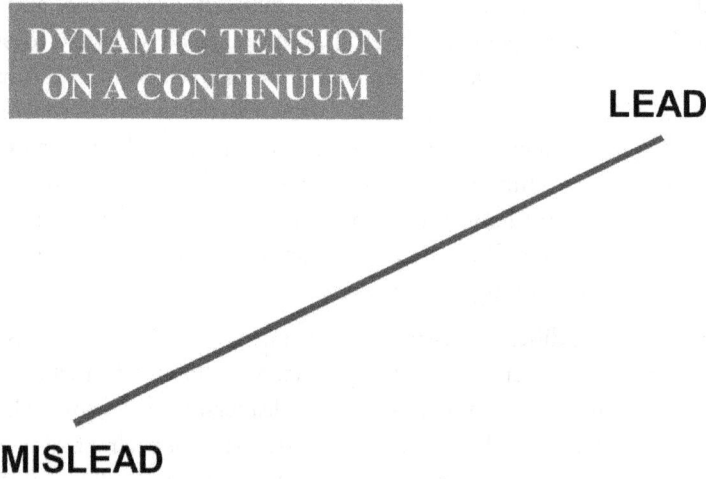

Figure 1.1

LEADING LIKE YOU MEAN IT

I call my leadership programme *Leading Like You Mean It* because leading is less about skills and ability than it is about attitude and character. Skills and ability are important, but they are not sufficient for effective leadership - they can be misused or left unused, depending on a person's attitude or character. This is precisely what makes leadership so demanding and so difficult to sustain.

Attitudes and character are not set in concrete; they are dynamic, developing qualities determined by ongoing personal choices. As anyone who has experienced armed combat will tell you, the line between courage and cowardice is a thin one, and courageous leadership in one instance is no guarantee against a cowardly response in another. Sound judgment in one crisis does not preclude the possibility of serious miscalculation in another. Leadership happens in the present moment, and depends on the attitude you adopt and the strength of character you demonstrate in that present moment. To be an effective leader, you have to resolve to lead like you mean it, taking up the challenge afresh in every developing situation.

Although the attitudes and character required for effective leadership are difficult to maintain consistently, we witness them daily — for example, in the activities of loving parents — and we can all develop them in ourselves by shaping our attitudes and character through our own free choices.

This leads to two further points. First, people become effective leaders by being themselves, not by trying to be like others. We all have unique qualities that enable us to provide leadership in ways that others would struggle to emulate. Secondly, in order to bring out the best in others, leaders must first bring out the best in themselves, which in turn requires self-knowledge and ongoing reflection. Leadership has to start with self-leadership (self-discipline, self-mastery, self-control — call it what you will).

In terms of age, gender, ethnicity, education, career, and personality, the participants on my programmes are diverse. The only common qualities they have are in their attitudes and characters (the distinction between personality and character is crucial and will be discussed later). The same holds true in any survey of the great leaders of history; for example, Socrates, Confucius, Marcus Aurelius, Joan of Arc, Abraham Lincoln, Mahatma Gandhi, and Nelson Mandela were from diverse cultures, but all displayed the qualities of great leadership as defined earlier.

LEADERSHIP IS ABOUT PEOPLE

This fact, that leadership is about people, seems to be a forgotten truth in a post-modern world driven by individualism, technology, and a pragmatist attitude that focuses on 'what works' rather than on 'what is right'. Typically, people in positions of authority are obsessed with reaching targets, improving systems, and promoting productivity and profitability, when they should be primarily engaged in getting the best out of the people they employ to achieve all those goals.

It is in this light that the distinction between management and leadership can be best understood. There was a time when I considered the distinction to be academic flummery, believing that managers were essentially required to be leaders. However, the analysis of thinkers such as Warren Bennis and John Kotter, together with my own experiences in working with leaders from many different fields, has shown me that the distinction can be highly instructive and meaningful for many in management positions. Although I maintain that managers need leadership qualities, their focus may well be on impersonal matters much of the time. In a sense, managers should be seen, as was suggested to me by a long-serving scientist, to be the undergraduates of leadership, only some of whom will continue with post-graduate and post-doctoral work.

The following distinction between management and leadership, for which I am mostly indebted to Warren Bennis, contributes to our understanding of what leadership is:

- While a manager focuses on systems, a leader focuses on people.
- While a manager is operational, a leader must be visionary.
- While a manager thinks tactically, a leader thinks strategically.
- While a manager fosters routine, a leader drives change.
- While a manager is conservative, a leader must be creative.
- While a manager seeks to control, a leader seeks to inspire.
- While a manager is replicable, a leader is unique.
- While a manager requires training, a leader requires education.

A persistent complaint that I hear from managers and putative leaders is that they are constantly interrupted by other people and are consequently unable to concentrate on their own operational responsibilities. That complaint is the surest evidence that they are not leaders, and perhaps do not want to be. Leadership is emphatically about people and about building constructive relationships — within the team and the organisation, with clients, with suppliers, regulatory bodies, the media, the general public, and so on. A leader requires a constant stream of communication from the complex network of relationships it is his or her responsibility to nurture.

TO LEAD IS TO INSPIRE

While a misleader will seek to confuse, coerce, and control, a genuine leader will be intent on inspiring people to commit themselves enthusiastically and of their own free will. Inspire is the key word in the proposed definition of leadership.

Significantly, Winston Churchill as a wartime leader drew inspiration from his illustrious ancestor John Churchill, Duke of Marlborough, who, for his part, was animated by the works of William Shakespeare, who in turn found his own inspiration in the stories of the Greek biographer Plutarch. These sources of inspiration, which exemplify the essential qualities of leadership, form a chain that stretches across two millennia. In four simple steps we can trace the origins of one man's great leadership. Why have we forgotten or consciously rejected the lesson contained in this outline of Churchill's personal development?

I always ask my workshop participants to identify the leader who most inspires them. Over the years, their answers have been remarkably consistent: the most common answers are listed in Table 1.1. It is significant how slender the influence of history and literature is among people today, but it is equally significant that they look so strongly to their parents and teachers as the great inspirations in their lives. I have included the list I would have made forty years ago as a young teacher with a passion for military history, and the list I would give today based on the understanding of leadership proposed here. It is interesting to note that the most recent list is comprised for the most part of teachers.

WHO INSPIRES YOU MOST IN TERMS OF LEADERSHIP?

40 years ago I would have answered:	Most common answers from the leaders' program:	Today I would answer:
Alexander the Great	Gandhi	Moses
Julius Caesar	Churchill	Socrates
Justinian	Mandela	Plato
Charlemagne	Shackleton	Aristotle
William Wallace	The Prime Minister	Confucius

Frederick the Great	Mother or father	Jesus
Napoleon	Grandparent	Aquinas
Lincoln	Teacher	Joan of Arc
Robert E Lee	Coach/instructor	Lincoln
Churchill	Former boss	Mother Theresa

Table 1.1

What is even more revealing is the answers that programme participants (of widely diverse ages and cultures, and both genders) give when asked to identify the qualities they admire most in the people they see as their inspirational leaders. Every single group has provided a list that includes integrity, honesty, respect, wisdom, confidence, compassion, vision, courage, perseverance, fairness, humility, and self-control. As will be demonstrated later, what they admire most, and presumably aspire to themselves, are precisely the qualities that are essential in making effective leaders; in other words, leaders are inspirational by exemplifying the qualities that the participants in the workshops keep holding up as their ideals. The central importance of inspiration in leadership means that it will figure in everything that follows, particularly in relation to motivation.

PROGRESS DEMANDS A DECISION

If one does agree with the proposed definition of leadership as *inspiring people to be the best they can be in mutual pursuit of a better life for all*, then this understanding of leadership should logically be applied to people in authority in every walk of life — to parents, teachers, business executives, community heads, professionals, and politicians. And it provides a criterion by which they may be assessed as being either leaders or misleaders — not according to their success or failure, but rather in line with their will to improve the lives of all people concerned.

This book is not so much about making better leaders, because we cannot do that until we know how to make leaders in the first place. Only when we are sure we are developing leaders rather than misleaders, can helping them to be better leaders become a practical proposition.

CHAPTER 2
What's gone wrong?

"Where everybody thinks alike, nobody thinks very much."
Walter Lippmann

The unexpected leader

The struggle between leadership and misleadership is as old as history itself, manifested not only in national and international affairs, but in every sphere of human activity. The ebb and flow of the ancient contest continues. Alongside the many tragic failures of humanity — tyranny, slavery, violence, and destruction — there are also many remarkable triumphs — democracy, freedom, reconciliation, and the arts and sciences. Interestingly, when great leadership emerges, it often comes from unlikely sources, and therein lies a clue as to why the post-modern world's dedicated efforts to produce leaders are meeting with so little success.

It may seem ironic to select an example from the history of one of the most wretched nations on earth, but just as neither Gandhi nor Churchill should be blamed for the failure of their successors, so Toussaint L'Ouverture deserves no censure for the reprehensible developments in his homeland following his death. The once prosperous country of Haiti in the Caribbean achieved its independence from France as a result of the first and only successful slave revolt in history, and though the final victory was won after his death (by a man who had served under him), it was only made possible by the accomplishments of the ex-slave Francois Dominique Toussaint L'Ouverture.

Haiti occupies the western third of the island, named Hispaniola by Columbus in 1492. The eastern two-thirds are today the Dominican Republic. In 1791, when the slave revolt erupted, what is today Haiti was the French colony of St. Domingue, and the Dominican Republic was the Spanish colony of Santa Domingo. The French, in just under a century, had developed a thriving plantation economy on the back of slave labour imported from West Africa, the original Native American culture having been destroyed by Spanish and French colonialism. The profitability of the sugar plantations had seen the number of slaves rise rapidly to five hundred thousand, about seven times greater than the combined coloured and white populations (the whites themselves being divided into the wealthy 'grand blancs' and the less well-to-do 'petit blancs'). It was a typical colonial society with a volatile class and ethnic cocktail. Order was maintained by brutal violence and the fear it inspired. Slaves for the most part lived a miserable existence, and suicide, abortion, and infanticide were common; life expectancy for plantation workers was abysmally low.

These unfortunate people only wanted, initially, to improve the conditions of their servitude, but the ideas and example of the American Revolution and then the French Revolution convinced the few who had received at least some education that they might demand much more. Toussaint was one of these.

At the outbreak of the revolt Toussaint was about fifty years old, a remarkable age for a black person who had grown up in slavery on St. Domingue. He had gained his freedom some seventeen years earlier, but this had changed only his legal status, not his social status. Nonetheless, through the support of the man who freed him and his own efforts, Toussaint became quite prosperous, acquiring land and slaves of his own. (Whilst scandalous to our post-modern sensibilities, it must have been the obvious career path for an enterprising ex-slave in eighteenth century St. Domingue.) Given all the other evidence, it seems probable his slaves were treated far more humanely than most.

A physically unimpressive and often sickly man, well past his prime and with a significant economic investment in the status quo, Toussaint swiftly seized the opportunity to lead his oppressed people out of slavery. There were many other potential leaders of the revolt, but Toussaint was the one who successfully negotiated the complex game-board, cluttered as it was with the socio-economic and political ambitions of French metropolitans, the neighbouring Spanish, grand blancs, petit blancs, people of mixed race, slaves, and free blacks, all of whom were impacted in one way or another by the ideas and events of the French Revolution that was tearing Europe apart. There were naturally also major implications for other slave-economies in the British West Indies and in America.

Toussaint rose above the other commanders of the various slave armies. It was not that they lacked his skills, but they did lack his knowledge and character. He had been educated by the Jesuits and was apparently well read in the classics, including Epictetus and Machiavelli, and the campaigns of Caesar and Alexander. Although steeped in the voodoo practices of his people and sensitive to their influence over most of his followers, he seems to have been a sincere Catholic. He was committed to fighting for a free, multi-racial society, and from the start he showed a unique concern for his troops. The disciplined force he built subdued the opposing armies and held both the British and the Spanish at bay, enabling Toussaint to make himself Governor-General and to seek the endorsement and support of Napoleon when the latter became First Consul in France in 1801.

Napoleon, however, sent a powerful army to defeat Toussaint, who was imprisoned in France, dying there in 1803. But the forces that Toussaint had marshalled and equipped were, as he had predicted, too much for the colonial power, and one of his generals, Jean-Jacques Dessalines, finally expelled them. With Toussaint off the stage, the savagery of this final phase of the conflict reached appalling proportions on both sides, and ominously for Haiti, Dessalines installed himself as emperor of the new state. In *Toussaint L'Ouverture*, Madison Smartt-Bell refuses to give credence to the conflicting myths that portray Toussaint as either a saint or a monster, but does concede the greatness that might have been:

'Appalling as it may have been, Dessalines' course of action was nothing if not logical. When Toussaint had tried to incorporate the white property owners into his vision of a new reformed society founded on universal recognition of the Rights of Man, the whites had done nothing but betray him. By comparison with Toussaint, Dessalines has often been denounced as a savage. Where the conciliatory Toussaint liked to say "Dousman alé lwen" (The gentlest way goes the furthest). Dessalines snarled a harsher order: "Koupé têt, boulê kay!" Cut off their heads and burn their houses!)'

Toussaint's remarkably compassionate and constructive leadership had emerged in a time and place where civilisation had been cruelly corrupted. He brought hope for a better future for all the inhabitants of Haiti, while Dessalines and others set the course that led inexorably to the gangster government of Papa Doc Duvalier. In our own time of crisis today, this lesson on leadership demands reflection.

"Follow the formula!"

In a world searching for answers to the seemingly intractable problems associated with the environment, the economy, and living together peacefully at home and abroad, leadership has become the central issue. The responses to these ongoing challenges have hitherto produced little more than a lingering smog of propaganda, cynicism, and suspicion, and a lot of verbal abuse. This pattern is repeated in businesses, communities and homes throughout the Western world as we all wrestle with smaller-scale conundrums that appear equally resistant to resolution.

The glut of new books and training programmes providing allegedly fool-proof formulae for effective leadership provides evidence of the need to fill the leadership void that mocks the most scientifically and technologically advanced civilisation in history. Yet to date these efforts have failed to produce the leaders required to address these troublesome and often dangerous issues. So what has gone wrong?

Quite simply, our society is labouring under the delusion that training people in skills that they can apply in the manner of a mechanical procedure will create effective leaders. The trainers promise, and the trainees demand, simple solutions to complex problems — the catch-cry is "No thinking involved, just follow the formula!".

Science and Utopia

Given the perversity of human nature, it is perhaps not surprising that humankind's most obvious prowess is also a spur to our greatest folly. The astonishing advances in science and technology over the past two hundred years have enabled most people living in countries with a free-market economy to enjoy nutritional and material benefits previously unimaginable to even the rich and powerful. We take for granted our clean tap water, the abundance of staples and delicacies on supermarket shelves, and the personal mobility provided by the motor car and air travel. Advances in medical and dental technologies and the ubiquitous hand of the 'nanny state' have further contributed to the complacency and sense of entitlement so pervasive in the West. Thus, in spite of all the evidence to the contrary — wars, terrorism, torture, slavery, drug-abuse, crime, social decay, environmental degradation, and economic uncertainty — the idea of producing 'scientific formulae' to resolve all our socio-political and economic problems remains an article of faith for many people.

The blind hubris of believing that such 'scientific formulae' will provide fool-proof social systems and perfectly modulated human behaviour that will usher in a utopian age is not just unscientific; it is also an insidious denial of human dignity: it carries the smell of the murderous, totalitarian social engineering of the last century, threatening to suppress the very qualities that make us human. J. R. R. Tolkein understood the danger, and also the true calling of humankind, giving them classic expression in *The Lord of the Rings*:

'It is not our part to master all the tides of the world, but to do what is in us for the succour of those years wherein we are set, uprooting the evil in the fields that we know, so that those who live after may have clean earth to till. What weather they shall have is not ours to rule.'

Notwithstanding Tolkein's enduring popularity, this wise counsel is for the most part ignored as people dream about social and organisational perfection instead of focusing on the personal responsibility and individual development essential to true human community. Inexorably, our brave new world of 'scientific solutions' is producing the maladies foretold by many of Tolkein's and Huxley's contemporaries, with leadership one of the main casualties.

THE GREAT LIE ABOUT LEADERSHIP TRAINING

Having once been a creative director in advertising, I am painfully aware of the human proclivity for making statements that subordinate factual accuracy to self-interest. Making seductive claims that played rather fast and loose with the truth in order to promote products and services was something I quickly learned to do. Old habits die hard and I acknowledge with some embarrassment that I must now exercise constant vigilance to prevent myself from slipping into hard-sell mode. This potential culpability conceded, I must now address the great lie about leadership training.

Though hundreds of organisations and best-selling books make the claim, it is simply meretricious to say that a particular programme or course will create leaders. The majority of people on my programmes initially express cynicism about attending "another programme" because they have been through leadership training before, often more than once, without their leadership capabilities making any real progress. It is therefore heartening to witness their post-programme attitudinal change and their enthusiasm for building on their refocused development as leaders, but I still make no claim to having an infallible method of 'making' leaders.

Leaders have to make themselves. It is irresponsible wishful thinking to believe that merely teaching people what to do in given circumstances and arming them with an arsenal of new skills will turn them into leaders. A dishonest person, a weak person under pressure, or a self-centred person can turn those skills to their own advantage, and in any event most people would struggle to use them even-handedly across all relationships. Being a leader is less about "what you can do" than about "what sort of person you are" — and only you can make the decisions and the ongoing choices that will determine that particular outcome.

THE BLIND FAITH IN SKILLS TRAINING

If leadership is essentially about people and how to get the best out of them in pursuit of a common vision, then there are certainly many important skills that are necessary to those ends: motivational skills, team-building skills, communication skills, conflict resolution skills, and delegation and empowerment skills. These and many others clutter the syllabuses of leadership development courses, as their marketers frantically repackage their wares in a never-ending campaign to create something apparently new and different.

Over the years, I have been approached by people in leadership positions at all levels who wanted quick-fix answers on how to run more effective meetings, how to improve personal time management, how to become better at making decisions, how to develop their strategic thinking ability, how to encourage greater creativity in their teams, how to manage excessive workloads, and many other issues that confront leaders in the workplace. I have furnished them with brief, bullet-point plans that I was confident would work, provided they were put into practice with the proper measure of respect due to all the people involved. From feedback received, in every case these short, tightly packaged mini-training sessions were immediately effective, and in some cases the gains were ongoing.

So the essentials of developing and utilising certain skills can be communicated quickly and simply, and more often than not the aspirant leaders discover they already have a reasonable grounding to start with. However, the real challenges in exercising some skills (for example, coaching upwards, as opposed to downwards, for one's team, or sideways for one's peers – a skill that many managers feel a need for) are the quality of the relationships involved, and the culture of the organisation. No amount of skills training can enable anyone to cultivate these successfully, regardless of what the proponents of people skills might assert. Love, respect, compassion, empathy, patience, and all the other requisite qualities are not skills to be learned but attitudes to be developed — with perseverance over time.

I once worked with a highly respected professional who produced internationally acknowledged work in nutrition, but who treated the team-building and business development aspects of his work with some disdain. Martin entered my leaders' programme with an open mind and an apparent willingness to improve both his own performance and that of his team. I was delighted when, just one week after the first workshop, he e-mailed me to say that a strategy template I had given the group had helped him, in conjunction with his team, to produce his best ever annual business plan. In picking up quickly on a simple piece of skills-training, Martin had proved to be a model student. His progress, unfortunately, never continued much beyond that point.

Martin had intelligence, an ability to communicate effectively, the respect and even the affection of his colleagues, as well as operational knowledge and experience that few could equal. Yet he did not actively use these skills and abilities to address the serious issues of underperformance and poor morale that plagued his team and the wider business. He was as aware as any of the other managers that their workplace was characterised by endemic inefficiency, lack of cooperation, and vindictive conflict. The corporate culture was a morass and Martin had all the skills to make a major difference, but he lacked the judgment and the will. It took others to provide the leadership that finally turned the business around.

Martin was the product of a system that believes leadership is a mechanical exercise that can be programmed into people through simple formulae and skills training. Leadership programmes all over the world package and market these skills in such compelling ways that most people blindly accept the prevailing 'wisdom', never stopping to ask why the results are so meagre. In reality, these much vaunted skills are little more than organisational or relationship processes — all rather easy to learn, but usually more difficult to put into practice in our daily lives, especially when we are stressed, angry, frustrated, or anxious. And the difficulty stems from the fact that we are not automatically ready to be programmed to behave in particular and predictable ways.

LEADERSHIP IS MORE ABOUT ATTITUDES

The private and public sectors are full of highly intelligent managers with all manner of technical qualifications and the sincere desire to head up a high-performance team, but they fail on a daily basis to promote the individual motivation and harmonious relationships on which the effectiveness of any team ultimately depends. Having attended skills training courses to no apparent avail, most of them now despair at the procession of recalcitrant misfits and malcontents who cause disruption in their teams.

This raises a significant point: anyone who is cynical about human nature is unlikely ever to be an effective leader — because cynicism, by definition, cannot inspire people, and inspiration, as noted in my definition of leadership, is the prime imperative. The question is: Can we teach aspirant leaders a skill that will make them more positive about the capacity of their people to change for the better? Alas, cynicism about human nature is part of a worldview developed, presumably, over many years and no amount of skills training is likely to change the overall attitude one has towards life. In an article in *Standpoint* in March 2009, the political commentator Kenneth Minogue refuted the lie that there are easy, skills-based solutions to all our problems. Speaking of young mothers, he said:

"Politicised compassion leads to multiple absurdities. One such is the belief these young mothers "lack parental skills". The term "skill" in our narrowly practical times means knowledge that gives you power. The Government is very keen on having everybody taught skills — parental, relationship, cooking — and successive ministers have "guided" schools into providing courses to supply the deficiencies. But this whole manner of speaking is obviously corrupt. The ordinary person, for example, who is on terms with many people, ranging from acquaintances and colleagues to friends and lover(s) does not have "relationship skills". Such a person has a particular kind of character, one that is capable of valuably relating to other people on many levels, and such a life only very marginally involves the exercise of teachable skills. A talent for love and friendship is generally acquired early in life. It results from involvement in the disciplines of family life. To talk, then, as if "relating" were a form

of skill to be acquired in some training programme is not only absurd: it is to cheat people by suggesting that the world is a great deal more manageable than it actually is. So-called "parental skills" are similarly elusive. They are learned in family life, and no amount of teaching in schools or drip-drip of peer group communication can create them."

Similarly, skills can never be enough to resolve the leadership crisis. Leadership is a state of mind, not a catalogue of skills. Leadership is built on the stance you take to the whole of reality — you yourself, other people and the world at large. In other words, leadership is built primarily on attitudes, and no amount of skills can compensate for the wrong attitudes. So, precisely what attitudes are required for effective leadership?

We will look more closely at attitudes in a later chapter on character, but for the moment we should identify the key attitudes needed by leaders by referring to the definition of leadership arrived at earlier:

'Leadership inspires people to be the best they can be in mutual pursuit of a better life for all.'

This understanding of leadership carries some clear implications. Firstly, it demands *respect* for all people, which in turn implies respect for the environment that sustains them. Next, it suggests *aspiration*, hope for a better future, and the *confidence* that it can be achieved through a coordinated and concerted effort. It also calls for *discernment*, a thoughtful and properly informed approach to the challenges presented, and the *courage* to do what is required and to persevere in the face of hardship, danger, frustration and disappointment. Finally, it makes plain the need for *fairness* in dealing with all people, and the *self-control* which is the custodian of a leader's integrity.

These seven key attitudes — respect, aspiration, confidence, discernment, courage, fairness, and self-control — cannot be acquired through skills-training; they are seeds that have to be planted, cultivated, and brought to fruition. They are the fruits of education.

ONLY GENUINE EDUCATION CAN PRODUCE LEADERS

A genuine education provides four elements essential for leadership — knowledge, strength of character, sound judgment, and a humane worldview, all of which are dependent on a person developing positive and constructive attitudes.

Training can be short and sweet, targeted to remedy a specific inadequacy, providing the quick-fix that has become almost mandatory in our post-modern society. It asks the question: "What can you do?", and tries to provide the skills needed to deal with the problems identified.

Education, on the other hand, asks the question: "What sort of person should you become?". And that makes it an ongoing enterprise. The purpose of education is to enable a person to fulfil their potential, to help them become the very best they are capable of. The etymology of the word 'education' emphasises this forgotten truth — the Latin word 'educare' means to lead out or to draw out potential to fruition. That is why education must focus on the development of a virtuous character, informed judgment, and a humane worldview.

Albert Einstein once said that the modern age was characterised by a perfection of means and a confusion of ends.

Unfortunately, what passes for education today rests on an incomplete understanding of what constitutes knowledge. The ancients recognised that knowledge is of three kinds: knowing *that* (facts), knowing *how* (technique) and knowing *what* (judgment)*. The first two are knowledge of means, while the last is knowledge of ends, involving the consideration of truth and purpose, and judgments about right and wrong. Our age concentrates on the first two to the detriment of the last and most important — the 'ends' of good judgment. Knowing what to think, feel, or do in any given set of circumstances requires understanding of ourselves and our place in the world in relation to others, and a commitment to doing what we believe to be right. It enables us to answer questions such as "What should I do about this disruptive member of my team?", "What should I think of this blatant deceit on the part of my client?", and "What should my feelings be in relation to the heart attack suffered by my rival?". Leadership is about people, not processes.

It does enormous harm in our workplaces, and our society in general, to have people in positions of responsibility who believe they can and must deal with others according to mechanical, formulaic sets of guidelines garnered from some training programme or the latest management best-seller. Training can only produce what it sets out to produce, namely functionaries who are there simply to ensure that the system operates smoothly. Training, furthermore, works on the principle that

* I am indebted to Roger Scruton for this insight

the desired abilities can easily be replicated, so that replacing managers never presents a problem because the vacant slot can be filled by another clone. This commitment to management by formula not only ignores the complexities of individual people and the intricate dynamics of human relationships, it also inhibits the one thing leaders have to do every moment of every day — think for themselves.

Education, by contrast, focuses on individuals, their ideas, and their cultures, ensuring a rich reservoir of knowledge and experience that enables a leader to comprehend, at the very least, just how difficult it is to understand people. And education is only what it claims to be if it inspires and equips a person to think for themselves.

THE EVIDENCE SPEAKS FOR ITSELF

My case files, like history itself, are replete with stories about highly skilled and intelligent people who fell tragically short when measured against the definition of leadership proposed in this book. Character, judgment, and worldview are revealed in all our behaviours and interactions with other people, providing points of comparison between individuals caught up in the widely different circumstances of human experience.

Victor Frankl's *Man's Search for Meaning* is a personal account of someone who survived the Nazi death camps. The reflections of this Jewish psychiatrist on his first-hand experience includes a chilling passage about how prisoners who were given certain duties by their Nazi tormentors often turned out to be more cruel to their own people than their bestial captors. Frankl recounts:

'The more "prominent" prisoners, the Capos*, the cooks, the storekeepers and the camp policemen, did not, as a rule, feel degraded at all, like the majority of prisoners, but on the contrary — promoted! Some even developed miniature delusions of grandeur. The mental attitude of the envious and grumbling majority toward this favoured minority found expression in several ways, sometimes in jokes. For instance, I heard one prisoner talk to another about a Capo, saying, "Imagine, I knew that man when he was only the president of a large bank. Isn't it fortunate that he has risen so far in the world?"'

This account tallies with my own experience as a rifleman during the Rhodesian War in the 1970s. I was in a reserve holding unit consisting of professional men, such as teachers, lawyers, and accountants, as well as

* Prisoners assigned to help the guards

businessmen from strategic industries that could not afford to lose their operatives for the longer spells required in the active battalions. Early in the war we were used to protect surveyors and road construction gangs in the war zones and to enforce the curfew. It came as a shock, as well as a warning about human nature, to hear some of these well-qualified, supposedly civilised men talk enthusiastically about "pulling" a curfew violator — man, woman, or child. I understand now that they had multiple professional skills, but very little of the humanity a proper education would have given them.

The point is that they, like the Capos described by Frankl, no longer thought for themselves. Their minds, placed under enormous stress by fear and the survival instinct, submitted to the uninformed racist mantras that had distorted their worldviews over many years, making them behave in ways that would have horrified their families.

It would be a mistake to believe that these examples are irrelevant to, or even somewhat removed from, workplaces of our post-modern world. 'Heartless' would be an apt description of the greed and corruption in government and corporate circles that have resulted in the global financial crisis currently wreaking havoc in the lives of individuals and families round the world. And the callous disregard (often spilling over into active malevolence) that I witness constantly for the well-being of people in the workplace indicates a similarly heartless attitude. When you see workers' lives being destroyed without compunction, it is reasonable to imagine the perpetrators doing far worse in more desperate circumstances. It simply becomes a matter of scale.

A long-time client and close acquaintance of mine runs a very successful retail store that sells some of the world's leading brands in its category. He became embroiled in lengthy and expensive litigation with a prestigious international company when one of his customers detected flaws in their products. For several years my friend was given the run-around by the representatives of the multinational brand. Convinced that he was in the right, he persisted in his quest for a resolution to the dispute, and finally met with some of the top corporate brass at the company's regional headquarters. There, after several hours of further debate, the regional general manager again examined the suspect merchandise, and said that he could see what the client was complaining about, but that he would never acknowledge it.

When my friend then raised the question of who was responsible for carrying the financial burden created by the defective merchandise and the subsequent legal wrangling, the general manager gave the floor to his legal counsel. This champion of the rule of law told my friend that it did not matter who was right or wrong about the correctness of the product supplied — the simple reality was that the company would hold my friend responsible for payment, that the company had the financial resources to ensure that the issue would take many years to come to court, and that by then my friend's little business would have been destroyed.

In terms of character, judgment and a humane worldview, these people were severely deficient, and one can only presume that they promote similar attitudes to the members of their workforce. They were obviously not thinking for themselves; their minds were rigidly governed by the politics of power and a slavish devotion to making money. Theirs is a clear case of skilful people being misleaders rather than leaders. No amount of further skills-training could improve their leadership abilities.

The damage such people do extends further than their own milieu. That kind of cynical, deceitful, and bullying behaviour saps the morale and weakens the resolve of a responsible democratic society. It is greatly concerning that people who harbour such attitudes are involved in the everyday operation of the free market and the global economy, the resolution of geopolitical conflict, and the allegedly responsible stewardship of the environment, among many other life-and-death issues.

Such men are as dangerous to democracy as were Hitler and his henchmen. The Jewish philosopher Hannah Arendt, writing about Adolf Eichmann, the Nazi mass-murderer, said: *"the longer one listened to him, the more obvious it became that his inability to speak [without clichés] was closely connected with an inability to think, namely, to think from the standpoint of somebody else."*

Eichmann had slipped into the role of functionary, his undeveloped human sensibilities providing easily malleable material for the Nazi ideologues. He openly admitted that he had never been a reader of books. This, added to the fact that his knowledge of history would have been badly misshapen by propaganda, makes it easy to understand why his worldview was that of the skilled functionary rather than the educated human being.

When I have people break down emotionally in discussions with me because of the intimidation and lack of respect they endure in the workplace, and see managers who close their minds to the suffering of people in their teams — people who are overworked, stressed, demotivated, and demoralised — it is an emphatic reminder that indifference to the pain of others is as cruel as actively causing the pain. Eichmann is a warning not just about people in positions of power over millions, but about any human being who has influence over the lives of others. The scale of their evil merely reflects the scope of the opportunity available to the perpetrator.

Our post-modern society is intellectually enslaved by the sound-bite, the slogan, and political correctness, which are conveyed through manipulative media where misleadership is rife, This, together with a firm belief in the efficacy of skills-training and a quick-fix mentality (even in personal relationships, where they are never appropriate) actively inhibits the most human quality of all — thinking for ourselves. Our society is consequently both structurally and emotionally incompetent to produce leaders. The only hope at present is in the mavericks who refuse to be constrained by ideology, technology, and bogus psychology, and who vigorously pursue their own education.

But more on educating oneself in chapter 6.

THE MOST APPROPRIATE MODELS FOR LEADERSHIP

The causal chain that links leadership at seemingly mundane levels with leadership on more elevated planes should never be underestimated. To believe that a society of broken homes and dishonest relationships can ever be effective at promoting international harmony is brazen self-deception. To assume that bored, frustrated, and ill-disciplined schoolchildren will miraculously turn into model citizens is to abdicate responsibility in the face of the rising tide of social pathology. To pretend that dysfunctional communities are isolated phenomena that have nothing to do with the rest of society is to live in a world of make-believe. To imagine that unhappy people in a malicious corporate culture will somehow deliver on advertising promises of superior customer service is professional negligence and incompetence. How dismal is our failure to think for ourselves when we refuse to contemplate the screaming contradictions in our lives.

As noted earlier, it is of profound significance for the promotion of genuine leadership that the etymology of the words 'educate' and 'lead' are intimately entwined. Teachers, like parents, are invested with the responsibility to lead young people from potential to fruition, helping them understand the possibilities of their lives and giving them direction and encouragement. This closely mirrors the responsibilities of leaders; indeed, responsible parenting and teaching provide the most appropriate models for leadership because they are essentially about inspiring others to be the best that they can be. But leaders can only do this for others if they themselves are educated and want to help others. Only then can they inspire and enable other people to move to a better place by analysing the current situation, postulating a preferable alternative, and proposing practical steps to achieve the goal — to think for themselves. **And the inclination and ability to think for oneself can only be derived from a proper education.** Our society has forgotten that simple truth — that is what has gone wrong!

Leaders and Misleaders

CHAPTER 3
LEADING LIKE YOU MEAN IT

"Character cannot be developed in ease and quiet. Only through experience of trial and suffering can the soul be strengthened, vision cleared, ambition inspired, and success achieved." Helen Keller

LIFE IS NOT EASY

Life is hard. That is the opening salvo of M. Scott Peck's best-seller *The Road Less Travelled*, a book I have bought six times and given away six times, so convinced am I of the healing potential of its wisdom. Of course, Peck's initial verbal jolt should not come as a shock to anyone, given the facts of history as well as the personal experience of individual lives. But his intention was to grab the reader by the collar and shake him with a stark statement of reality, knowing that most people in our society, being largely ignorant of history and the great literature of humanity, believe that life is meant to be easy, and that suffering and struggle are evil anomalies, which governments, with the aid of science, will soon eliminate.

Nobody is indifferent to their own personal suffering, and anyone who is merely philosophical about the suffering of others has lost a measure of their own humanity. However, we live in a constantly evolving cosmos in which change is the dominant reality, and suffering is an inescapable concomitant of change for self-conscious beings. The experiences of pain, stress, failure, and grief that accompany all personal and corporate growth prompt thinking creatures to ask why this should be, and where there is an absence of satisfactory answers the result is the mental anguish we call suffering. The implications for leaders are obvious because leadership is by definition an agent for change.

THE COST OF GREATNESS

Among all the kings and queens of England, only one has ever earned the cognomen 'the Great'. The Saxon King of Wessex in the ninth century, known to history as Alfred the Great, achieved this distinction in a reign when strife and suffering were a frequent reality. When he ascended the throne in 871 on the death of his older brother, the Viking threat that hung over most of Europe was at its peak, and many parts of the British Isles had experienced the violence, burning, and looting of the Norse raiders.

Two large Viking armies were loose in Wessex at the time, the economy was in tatters, literacy and learning seemed to be on the verge of extinction, and the morale of his people was at a low ebb. To compound his problems, he was struck by a long-term, mysterious illness on his wedding day, and he had to contend with the royal claims of his two nephews. Inconclusive engagements with the Danes over the next few years led Alfred to try and buy security for his kingdom, making a large payment of tribute to the invaders. They did not keep their side of the bargain.

Further defeat at the hands of the Vikings in 878 drove him to seek refuge in the marshes, and for a few months he was obliged to campaign as a guerrilla commander. Through all the hardship and uncertainty, Alfred's courage and perseverance kept the spirit of resistance alive, and his fame and popularity remained strong, enabling him in that same year to amass a significant army at Ethandun, modern day Eddington, where he inflicted a major defeat on the Danes. His attitude in victory was far-sighted — accepting that there was little possibility of driving the enemy from the shores of England, he made peace with their leader, Guthrum, and persuaded him and his followers to accept Christian baptism.

Alfred's determined efforts restored the confidence of the people of Wessex, and led to a widespread recognition in the other Anglo-Saxon kingdoms and in Wales that unity under the kind of rule forged by his dedicated leadership was an ideal worth striving for. He recaptured London from the Danes in 886 and when a renewed threat to his kingdom arose in 892 he and his sons proved well-equipped to disperse it, but at no stage in his twenty-eight year reign was he without serious challenges to the survival of Anglo-Saxon culture and community.

In addition to his military acumen, Alfred was alert to the dangers of social and economic backwardness. He used the periods of relative peace to rebuild the economic life of the nation — a task requiring faith in the future — doing so by constructing fortified towns in strategic places throughout the country, and by reorganising the national militia to ensure he could always meet future threats quickly and efficiently. He also laboured tirelessly to restore religion and learning in Wessex, both of which had declined dramatically in Europe, leaving the light of civilisation flickering precariously. He attracted great scholars from abroad, instigating a cultural renaissance in Wessex to which he further contributed by his own translations of classic texts. His attitude is made plain in the preface he wrote to his translation of Pope Gregory's *Pastoral Care*:

'When I reflected on all this, I wondered exceedingly why the good, wise men who were formerly found throughout England and had thoroughly studied all those books, did not wish to translate any part of them into their own language. But I immediately answered myself and said: 'They did not think that men would ever become so careless and that learning would decay like this; they refrained from doing it through this resolve, namely they wished that the more languages we knew, the greater would be the wisdom in this land.' Then I recalled how the Law was first composed in the Hebrew language, and thereafter, when the Greeks learned it, they translated it all into their own language, and all the other books as well. And so too the Romans, after they had mastered them, translated them all through learned interpreters into their own language... Therefore it seems better to me — if it seems so to you — that we too should turn into the language that we can all understand certain books which are the most necessary for all men to know...'

Alfred's reign was a struggle from beginning to end. Constant vigilance and innovative change were essential to preserve the traditions on which Anglo-Saxon liberty was built. There was no guarantee of success, and he must have died wondering whether his heirs would consolidate and extend the gains that had been made. But there was never any question about the integrity of Alfred's response to the challenges of wearing the crown. He always meant to lead, and he always led like he meant it.

THE ORIGINS OF LEADING LIKE YOU MEAN IT

The first seminar I put together on effective leadership nearly ten years ago was deliberately written without reference to well-known books on business leadership and management. The measure of confidence I felt in my own ability to help people make themselves better leaders was based on long personal experience in education, sport, the army, and a broad swathe of business categories, as well as a fairly wide knowledge of history, philosophy and politics. But I was further inspired by a deep scepticism about the efficacy of management texts and leadership workshops, which appeared to make little difference in the diverse workplaces I was familiar with, and by a justifiable suspicion of the personality tests and the leadership-styles approach common to many training programmes. When I subsequently made a study of much of the current literature available on leadership, I was grateful for the impulse which had persuaded me to build my own programme from scratch.

Looking back at the notes for that initial seminar, I am struck by how closely I have adhered to the basic principles despite the considerable development of content over the years. The original seminar was written on four main pillars: the meaning of leadership; an understanding of human nature; human creativity and the dynamics of strategy; and the building of sound personal relationships from the one-to-one level through to the more complex realities of teams, organisations, and communities. Most important of all, from the very beginning I have worked on the conviction that leadership is not just a set of skills, but primarily a state of mind to be cultivated on a daily basis. Hence the programme's title — *Leading Like You Mean It*.

AN OUTSTANDING EXAMPLE

A leader who embodied leading like you mean it was Abraham Lincoln. In her Pulitzer Prize-winning book, *Team of Rivals*, Doris Kearns Goodwin relates how some forty years after Lincoln's assassination, Leo Tolstoy was asked by villagers in a remote region of the Caucasus to tell them stories of the great men of history. Tolstoy obliged and spoke of the exploits of Alexander, Caesar, Frederick the Great, and Napoleon, but the person the villagers really wanted to hear about was Lincoln. Goodwin quotes the reflections of the great Russian novelist on this event:

"This little incident proves how largely the name of Lincoln is worshipped throughout the world and how legendary his personality has become. Now, why was Lincoln so great that he overshadows all other national heroes? He really was not a great general like Napoleon or Washington; he was not such a skilful statesman as Gladstone or Frederick the Great;

but his supremacy expresses itself altogether in his peculiar moral power and in the greatness of his character."

Lincoln continues to inspire people all around the world because of his convictions, his firm resolve in the face of repeated misfortune and provocation, and his profound compassion and generosity of spirit for all people, even his enemies. Goodwin continues:

"An indomitable sense of purpose had sustained him through the disintegration of the Union and through the darkest months of the war, when he was called on again and again to rally his disheartened countrymen, soothe the animosity of his generals, and mediate among members of his often contentious administration…With his death, Abraham Lincoln had come to seem the embodiment of his own words — "With malice toward none; with charity for all"— voiced in his second Inaugural to lay out the visionary pathway to a reconstructed union."

According to the definition of leadership proposed in this book *(Leadership inspires people to be the best they can be in mutual pursuit of a better life for all),* Lincoln provides a compelling example of what leading like you mean it involves. A self-educated man, with multiple failures and disappointments in his life plus the heartbreak of debilitating family tragedy, he steadfastly steered the damaged ship of state through a savage storm, deploying a surly and uncooperative crew to meet the challenge of their mutinous compatriots. Leadership is never easy; for Lincoln, it was a living hell. Yet he persevered and saved the United States by removing the terrible institution that contradicted her commitment to freedom — slavery.

THE TROUBLE WITH LEADING LIKE YOU MEAN IT

Most people in positions of authority today do not lead like they mean it because even if they had a proper understanding of what leadership meant, they would not choose to accept the hardship that inevitably comes with the job. It is one of the sad realities of life that while all are naturally equipped to be leaders in some way, few want the responsibilities. The great majority who do attain leadership positions are motivated more by the perks, the prestige, and the power, than any sincere interest in improving the lives of the people they have been appointed to lead. They start from a position of self-interest, which almost inevitably influences them to be misleaders rather than leaders.

Poor leadership arises less from a failure of the intellect than a failure of the will.

Those who doubt that all human beings have the natural ability to be leaders should try answering the question: "What is the first thing all human beings have to learn?". While a host of plausible responses could be framed, the unexpected yet cogent answer is "To lead" — in the sense of self-leadership through the exercise of the free will that makes us human. As their parents start the process of socialising them, children learn to exercise their free will and make choices. They may make wrong choices, but that is part of the long journey of self-development, and by learning to make the right choices they absorb the lessons of self-leadership, without which they will never be effective in building satisfying relationships with other people or in negotiating the challenges of life successfully.

The self-leadership they need to learn in the course of their socialisation is in essence attitude training and the development of character. It is affirming to note that the required key attitudes mirror those seen as central for effective leadership: respect, aspiration, confidence, discernment, courage, fairness, and self-control. Every one of us struggles to develop and maintain these vital attitudes because they entail self-discipline and self-sacrifice, qualities that are demanding, particularly in an age of rampant individualism.

Children who fail to learn the lessons of self-leadership become adults who are unlikely to become effective leaders themselves — as parents, as teachers, or in the workplace. They fail to grow emotionally, and often intellectually, and may become social misfits who struggle in relationships at home and in the workplace and community. Even good schooling will struggle to repair the damage done by a lack of devotion to the task of proper socialisation in the early years of a child's life. This is how parental failure contributes to the virulent social pathology that afflicts Western societies today and to the lack of leadership that is essential to finding a better way forward. Leading like you mean it is hard, and consequently is the road less travelled, while the freeway of misleadership is choked with traffic.

LEADERSHIP DEMANDS CHANGE

One of my methods of sparking debate in workshop sessions is to expose participants to this quotation from John Kotter, from his book,

A Force for Change:

"Leaders produce change. That is their primary function."

The logic of the assertion unsettles people who are already uncertain about their own performance as leaders, and though many nod their heads ruefully, others take refuge in silent denial while a few launch into a heated confrontation. One common (and valid) objection is that change is not necessarily progress. However, we should also acknowledge that progress would be impossible without change. Kotter deliberately employed shock tactics, and it seems to me that he was justified, given the prevalence of leadership inertia in business.

That inertia, I believe, is often a case of the possum caught in the headlights — leaders frozen by uncertainty and fear of failure. It may also be due to resistance to change. All organisations experience the ongoing tension between the need for efficient, productive routine and the never-ending imperative to drive change. Whenever an efficient, productive routine is achieved with everything running smoothly and the desired results being generated, the very human temptation is to oppose any change. Clichés such as "Don't make waves!", "Don't try to fix what isn't broken!" or "We're doing fine as we are!" are heard.

But everything is always changing, and to try to stand still is inevitably to fall behind. Markets change, competitors change, technology changes, and personnel changes. Change is a feature in all areas of life. No matter how good things are today, the world is constantly changing, challenging us to think about and plan for the things that might eventuate tomorrow. It was the philosopher of science, Stanley Jaki, who said in a Baccalaureate address given at Drew University in 1998:

"Change means future. There is no future unless there is change."

And leadership, by definition, means changing things with the intention of making them better. Change is a fundamental reality of our lives. We start with potential and aim at perfection, then drive the change necessary to achieve that perfection. The fulfilment or the integrity we seek demands that we go through many changes to reach our goal — it is fundamental to effective leadership to drive positive change.

Recognising the lie behind work overload in leaders

The single most common lament I hear from business managers is that they have insufficient time to meet the demands of their management and operational responsibilities. For many managers the nightmare of the 24/7 world of total work is a stark reality, with cell-phones, e-mail, the internet, and intranets placing increasing pressure on them. In consequence, the needs of the people they are required to lead may well lose priority, as may their domestic relationships.

One can only feel sympathy for these mostly well-meaning people as they wrestle with the Medusa-like monster that post-modern business and social life has become. The first step in helping these managers is to enable them to recognise the lie at the heart of their situation. To work excessive hours under severe stress for a protracted, often open-ended period is inimical to one's psychological and physical health. The unmanaged stress, frequently attended by eating and sleeping disorders, undermines personal efficiency, eroding self-confidence and self-esteem, and it can also have a negative impact on the immune system, leading to physical illness. Over-working steals the time needed to build and maintain important personal relationships, and the dysfunction created here exacerbates the stress, often resulting in mental and emotional disorders.

These facts contradict the spurious belief that working longer hours is the way to achieve success. If a business can only turn a profit by running its people into the ground, then it deserves to go bust, and the sooner the better.

Human beings have finite capacities and definite needs; to ignore this is to court disaster. I have witnessed it equally among schoolchildren, adult workers, salespeople, and scientists. Just as free people are more productive than slaves, so most people perform much more efficiently when they have well-rounded lives and well-adjusted minds. Clearly, eight hours a day from an energetic and enthusiastic person is preferable to ten hours from a demoralised and demotivated functionary.

Programmed functionaries must still make the time to deal with a whole raft of people issues that arise from their lack of leadership, not to mention under-performance issues and consequent customer complaints, loss of productivity and profitability, and the expensive and time-consuming activities that characterise the revolving-door phenomenon of the post-modern workplace. A pseudo-leader, who is too busy to lead, actually creates huge amounts of unnecessary and unprofitable work for himself and the business. He becomes his own worst enemy.

Real leadership can make an immediate difference. Having recognised the lie behind the total world of work, the leader must now start to lead like he means it.

GETTING OUT OF THE OPERATIONAL BOX

As Einstein recognised, it is lunacy to keep doing the same things and expect different results. Change is required. A genuine leader, in circumstances that undermine people's efforts to perform at their best, would immediately analyse the problem and drive the changes needed to create a happier and more productive workplace. How would he go about doing that?

Typically, most people when placed in a position of leadership tend to view their position in terms of their own operational and administrative responsibilities, together with the role of supervising the operational performance of a group of other people (see Figure 3.1).

HOW DO YOU THINK OF YOUR ROLE AS LEADER?

YOU OWN JOB PLUS SUPERVISING OTHERS

Figure 3.1

They set out with a managerial attitude, focusing on systems and procedures, and the need 'to get things done'. The idea that they will need to make time available to deal with 'people issues' floats around in the back of their mind, undefined and underestimated, and when the inevitable demands are made on their time, these are considered intrusions and a nuisance. This managerial attitude — expecting the system to work like a well-designed machine, with each functionary carrying out their prescribed tasks — is so far removed from the realities of life that its persistence in the workplace is dismaying.

It is clear that this person-in-charge is going to be hard pressed to find the time to do all that is required. The temptation to devote most of his time to his own operational responsibilities is inevitable and is what most beleaguered managers retreat to when the pressure becomes too intense. They do, however, find few answers to their problems; the uncoordinated and uninspired people they are required to lead inexorably lose whatever harmony may have existed previously, and the people issues, from the trivial to the serious, become an avalanche. Unless the person-in-charge changes their attitude and starts again, the pressures simply worsen.

Leading like you mean it requires an attitude of leadership, rather than a managerial attitude, right from the start. It demands an immediate appraisal of the current situation, measuring existing resources against prevailing goals and tasks, and an organisational vision. No such appraisal can be made from within the confines of the leader's operational box; rather, it entails the leader taking up a position from where he can view the operation as a whole, and then drawing his conclusions about aspirations and viability. Escaping the operational box takes him into the leadership sphere (see Figure 3.2), where he needs to be in order to craft for his team a new vision — one that includes the strategic alignment of all concerned — and to ensure that the reorganisation gives everyone the opportunity to perform at their best.

Leaders need to spend most of their time outside the cloistered atmosphere of the operational box, even if it means delegating much of their own operational workload to others. The leadership sphere is where a leader must be in order to monitor performance and progress, and to engage in activities such as strategy, coaching, resourcing, succession planning, delegation, managing relationships, and dealing with cases of internal and external conflict, which left alone, quickly erode the effectiveness of any organisation. Moreover, the sphere is where a leader can engage in the most important activity of all — reflection, or thinking for himself. In my experience of leadership, this is where most would-be leaders fail; by refusing to get out of the operational box and into the leadership sphere, they make it impossible for themselves to lead like they mean it.

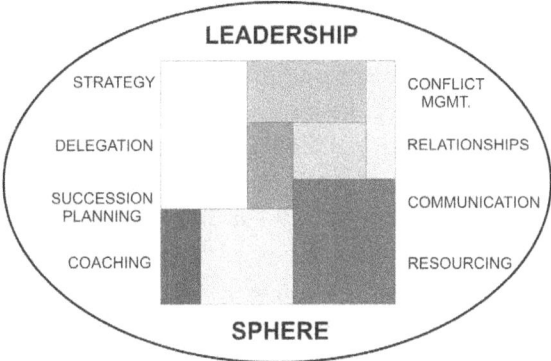

Figure 3.2

These first crucial steps — confronting the lie about leadership workloads and getting out of the operational box into the leadership sphere — often transform struggling persons-in-charge into confident and effective leaders overnight, suggesting that many people do have leadership skills, but few lead like they mean it.

The examples are legion. A senior scientist who was close to a nervous breakdown was inspired by the leading like you mean it ethos to take those first steps, and so enthusiastic was the response from his colleagues that he re-energised and refocused the team, while also easing the pressure for himself. An ambitious and hard-working call-centre manager experienced the same rapid turnaround in the morale and performance of the marketing representatives in her team when she started *inspiring people* instead of *drilling functionaries*. A franchisee in the automotive trade whose business was going nowhere (although he was working himself to the bone), chose in desperation to review his operation and reflected on all the activities he could delegate. In doing so he glimpsed a new vision for his business and now has three retail outlets, all flourishing under his dedicated leadership.

I have seen this happen often enough to be fully satisfied in my own mind that leading like you mean it works.

One of the greatest creative business minds of the past century, Walt Disney, provided a fine example of achieving remarkable results through leadership rather than management. He once likened his approach to leadership to "gathering pollen and stimulating everyone".

Disney was as good as his word, delegating the development of cartoon characters and the animation cells required for his feature films to the many talented people he employed, even though his love of cartooning had provided the inspiration for his career. The basic ideas were his, and the integrity of the Disney style still impresses today, but he had a much larger vision, and to pursue that he surrounded himself with people of ability and gave them the freedom to make their own contribution. Significantly, Disney's stated purpose, as discussed in *Built to Last* by James Collns and Jerry Porras, was not "To make brilliant cartoons" or "To make massive profits", but "To make people happy".

THE TASKS OF LEADERSHIP — CONFRONTING THE STORM

Examining the activities within the leadership sphere, it becomes possible to specify the actual responsibilities of leadership, the tasks that a leader should be engaged in on a daily basis. This is important because it helps the leader to stay focused on his priorities. Once I had reached my own conclusions about leadership, I sought out what contemporary management gurus had to say on the subject. Some of these authorities are all well worth reading. Their prescriptions can be summarised thus:

- John Adair, who wrote *Effective Leadership* (1983) and whose military and academic background equips him to provide some insightful thinking on leadership, believes that the central tasks of leadership are planning, initiating, controlling, supporting, informing, and evaluating.

- Peter Drucker, author of *Management: Tasks, Responsibilities, Practices* (1974), is perhaps the most famous of modern thinkers on leadership, and he saw the key activities for a leader as being

the setting of objectives, organisation, motivation, measurement, and developing people.
- John Kotter, who has already provided some valuable perspectives for this discourse on leadership, wrote in *A Force for Change* (1990) that the prime responsibilities of a leader were vision (including strategy), the alignment of people, and motivation.
- Warren Bennis, author of *Leaders: the Strategies for Taking Charge* (1985) and a strong advocate for less hierarchical and more democratic workplaces, famously stated that the essential abilities of leadership are managing attention, managing meaning, managing trust, and managing self.
- Henry Mintzberg, who wrote *The Nature of Managerial Work* (1973), which is based on an in-depth study of business managers that yielded a wealth of unexpected information, concluded that leaders must be engaged in managing relationships and team-building, monitoring and disseminating information, providing enterprise, trouble-shooting, allocating resources, and negotiating.

Nothing these leaders said about business development conflicted with the conclusions I had reached about the essential daily activities of someone who leads like they meant it. I lay these conclusions out below not in order of priority, but to create a useful mnemonic — a mnemonic suggested by the words of the ancient Roman writer, Publilius Syrus:

"Anyone can hold the helm when the sea is calm."

Since the evidence suggests that life is mostly stormy with brief patches of calm weather, I propose that a helmsman — a leader — is needed at all times. And so, my mnemonic device to trigger the tasks of leadership in the minds of leaders is **STORM**:

- **Strategy** — this includes understanding the potential at the leader's disposal in the context of the marketplace; developing the vision; establishing the means by which it will be achieved; and constantly reassessing progress and further possibilities.
- **Team-building** — this activity should extend beyond the individual and group dynamics of the team itself to cover all the relationships in the entire value chain of the organisation, i.e. the multitude of relationships with everyone required to add value in any way to the work of the organisation. In this sense, corporate

culture, branding and customer service, for example, become essential parts of the leader's team-building responsibilities.

- **Organisation** — this task should flow logically from Strategy, and is perhaps best described in the wise words of A. A. Milne, who said:
Organising is what you do before you do something, so that when you do it, it's not all mixed-up.

    In business, it can be thought of simply as making sure things happen on brief, on budget and on time. Organisation involves operational dynamics relating to resourcing, systems and procedures, time management, knowledge management, accounting and administration; and it provides a host of opportunities for delegation, the empowerment of people, and the development of incipient leaders.

- **Reflection** — as has already been suggested, this is the most important task a leader has to perform. Thinking for oneself is an essential quality of leadership and it is significantly the first casualty when a leader becomes trapped in the operational box. In a society saturated with noise and intrusions, where people are unsettled by being alone with their own thoughts, this requirement presents a serious challenge for most of us. But leaders who do not take time daily to think about their people and their business simply fail to equip themselves to understand the challenges and to drive the necessary changes. They should at the very least make sure that their competitors do not think about their business more than they do themselves.

- **Making decisions** — this responsibility perches on a leader's shoulders every moment of every day and cannot be shirked. Fear of failure is probably the single biggest reason for people being reluctant to making decisions, but we should remember the saying that good judgment comes from experience and experience comes from bad judgment. Nathan Myhrvold of Microsoft probably expressed the truth about decision-making best when he said that most decisions are inevitably a leap of faith, resting more on intuition than reasoned argument.

    Leaders may consult, consider and confirm all they like, but they must still reach a conclusion for themselves, and the more expeditiously they make that decision, the better for their business and all concerned. In a very real and sobering sense, making no decision is a decision to let someone else lead.

The demands for leadership are those of STORM — and these requirements will be dealt with more fully in the chapters ahead.

How can we help people to lead like they mean it?

While initial responses to the *Leading Like You Mean It* programme are overwhelmingly positive and enthusiastic, I am the first to acknowledge that in addition to the success stories, there have also been many people who, sometimes predictably, have failed to drive the necessary changes in any kind of sustained effort. This is not unexpected, because those changes are challenging and it is all too easy to slip back into deeply ingrained habits, into cynicism in the face of repeated frustrations, or into the fatalistic drift of indifference to which everyone is susceptible. But where there is a sincere desire to be an effective leader, the person concerned can be inspired and enabled to make something better for the enterprise they head and the people they lead. As has been emphasised, at the very heart of the matter, leadership comes down to a personal act of will.

The following qualities, which will be examined in later chapters, must be nurtured so as to help people lead like they mean it.

- **Personal integrity** — genuine leadership can only be built on this.
- **Daily reflection** — leaders must think for themselves.
- **Ongoing education** — understanding the world and their part in it.
- **Respect for human potential** — getting the best out of themselves and others.
- **Trust and character** — understanding attitudes and emotional intelligence.
- **Creativity and strategy** — leadership means finding a better way.
- **Empathy and compassion** — leadership is about people, people, people.

- **Communication and motivation** — leaders seek fulfilment for all.
- **Confidence** — where there is no hope, there is no leadership.

In short, aspirant leaders first need to be inspired to become more complete people, knowing that that is the only way they will become effective leaders.

CHAPTER 4
THE POWER OF INTEGRITY

"A man is only as good as what he loves." Saul Bellow

A LESSON IN PERVERSITY

In *A History of the American People* Paul Johnson provides an eye-opening account of the clash, during the 1820s presidency of James Monroe, between the Federal Government and the Native American peoples they were determined to shift beyond the Mississippi. Johnson demonstrates that the old popular image of industrialised Western civilisation confronting tribes of primitive hunter-gatherers is misleading, particularly in the case of the 'Five Civilised Tribes' — the Creeks, Cherokees, Choctaws, Chickasaws, and Seminoles. It is worth quoting Johnson at some length:

"Calhoun, Secretary of War, argued that 'the great difficulty' was not savagery but precisely 'the progress of the Cherokees in civilisation.' He said there were 15,000 in Georgia, increasing just as fast as the whites. They were 'all cultivators, with a representative government, judicial courts, Lancaster schools, and permanent property'. Their 'principle chiefs,' he added, 'write their own State Papers and reason as logically as most white diplomatists.' What Calhoun said was true. The Cherokees were advancing and adopting white forms of social and political organisation. Their national council went back to 1792, their written legal code to 1808. In 1817 they formed a Republic, with a senate of thirteen elected for two-year terms, the rest of the council forming the lower house. In 1820 they divided their territory into eight congressional districts, each mapped and provided with police, courts, and powers to raise taxes, pay salaries, and collect debts. In 1826 a Cherokee spokesman gave a public lecture in Philadelphia, describing the system. The next year a national convention drew up a written constitution, based on America's, giving

the vote to 'all free male citizens' over eighteen, except those of African descent'."

It was the successful establishment of a homogenous and independent Native American republic, constitutionally beyond the control of the United States, that worried the Federal Government and most whites. The destruction of these nascent democracies, and the shameful treatment of the Native American peoples in the process, was an egregious contradiction of the young American nation's professed Christian and constitutional principles. Similarly, the sweeping aside of women's and African Americans' human rights contradicted the liberal socio-political system of both the whites and Native Americans. And we still see the same problems today in many parts of the world, even with the benefit of hindsight and the ugly experiences of twentieth century history fresh in our minds. Integrity is an elusive goal.

The persistent failure of Western civilisation to live up to the humane standards set by Christian teaching and the spirit of democracy in no way undermines the validity of those standards. While it provides evidence of the perversity of humankind, it also gives a clear indication of the possibilities we fall short of. The call to love thy neighbour has always been a cornerstone philosophical justification for the principles of equal human dignity, freedom, justice, and solidarity for all people. I would argue that any rejection of these principles renders the concept of personal, corporate, or national integrity meaningless. (I am here defending the principles rather than Christianity per se or any particular democratic model.)

FORGOTTEN TRUTHS

The examples of leadership and misleadership presented so far have already heralded the central message of this chapter — leadership can only be built on integrity and misleadership fosters disintegration: people fall apart, organisations fall apart, communities and nations fall apart as a result of misleadership. Ultimately, even apparently indestructible social and political structures fall apart, as did the USSR in 1989.

History is replete with illustrations of leadership and misleadership. The Roman republican hero Cincinnatus has already been mentioned. Regrettably this man, whose personal integrity provided an inspirational role model to the Western world for over two thousand years, is almost unknown today, even to highly qualified people. I have yet to meet a single participant in my leadership programmes who has heard of his deeds.

Around 450 BC, Cincinnatus, a Roman citizen, was ploughing the field on his small farm, when he was approached by a mission from the Senate. The civic authorities believed he was the best soldier and leader to save the infant republic from the depredations of a neighbouring army. He was appointed Dictator for the duration of the war and met with such success that when his victorious army returned to Rome, the populace wished to make him their king. However, Cincinnatus valued the Roman republic's ideals more than self-aggrandisement. He returned to his family farm and the ploughing he had left unfinished. It is sad that this edifying example of republican virtue has been forgotten.

SELF-CONTRADICTION AND FATAL INCONSISTENCIES

Plato observed in *Republic* that:

"What is honoured in a country will be cultivated there."

This applies equally to communities, businesses, schools, families, and even individuals. What is honoured in a community will be cultivated there. What is honoured in a business will be cultivated there. What I honour in my life, I will cultivate in my life. But what happens when conflicting ideals are honoured?

One of the enduring controversies about the French Revolution centres on the reasons behind the bloody Jacobin 'Reign of Terror' in Paris and other French cities, and the massacres of men, women and children in the Vendee region, all perpetrated by a political party dominated by a man known as 'The Incorruptible'. Robespierre was an articulate advocate of human rights and democracy, yet also the architect of the atrocities that defined and ultimately destroyed the Jacobins and the Revolution, and cost him his life. The contradiction could not be sustained because the ideal of a democratic France was not credible while those in power used terror as a political weapon. The question raised by this contradiction was what the Jacobins stood for — human rights or power at any price. J. M. Thompson in his book *The French Revolution* succinctly described the Jacobin descent into misleadership:

Soon signs were not wanting that the Jacobins were falling into the most dangerous snare of dictatorship. They were beginning to despise the people; to lecture them instead of consulting them, to force them instead of persuading them, to keep them excited by trifles instead of exercised by responsibility, to feed them on fables instead of telling them the truth.

History records similar folly in politics, society and the lives of men and women. Inconsistency and self-contradiction underlie all the tragedies of misleadership, from Albania to Zimbabwe, from Attila to Zhivkov. The first four decades of my life were dominated by the inevitable personal, communal and societal conflicts that arose from the inconsistencies on which Rhodesia and South Africa were founded. Looking back it seems astonishing that most white people complacently ignored or speciously explained away the blatant contradiction — a commitment to democracy and freedom incongruously shackled to the legislated degradation of the greater part of the population — by using ideological justification. That contradiction meant that Rhodesia and South Africa lacked a clear vision of the future, and the people in charge lacked the integrity on which to build the leadership that might have altered the course of history. Similar tragedies in countries such as Nigeria, Iraq and Serbia also reveal the absence of the integrity on which meaningful leadership might have been established, and it is an everpresent challenge to all countries, as the current experience of America, China, Britain, the European nations, and many others attests.

THE LIVES OF INDIVIDUALS

The same pattern can be seen in the lives of individuals. A client of one of the agencies I worked for provides a dramatic example. Tony was a talented young marketing professional who by virtue of a sincere interest in people and their potential, and a willingness to make the needs of others his own, rose to the position of marketing director with a multinational corporation. His leadership brought the best out in people, and clients and colleagues were receptive to his enthusiasm and openness. Tony was expected to continue his rise in the marketing world, but his appointment to the position of regional marketing director was accompanied by some undesirable changes.

Although he continued to excel at motivating people throughout the regional offices, and enjoyed being the catalyst for some excellent results, he quickly learned that he had a political role to play: following directives from above was usually the easier and safer option. Then a new global CEO established a policy whereby profit took precedence over creating effective marketing campaigns. He backed this with some corporate 'ten commandments' that essentially instructed people to shape up or ship out. Tony chose to protect his position and his lifestyle by transforming his role from head coach to corporate hatchet man. By then, of course, his lifestyle had drifted into the exhilarating but risk-filled activities of a jet-setting high-flier.

One of his new acquaintances had recently made a fortune by setting up an international call-girl web-site and Tony eagerly took up an offer to become a partner. Colleagues who had witnessed the depressing transformation of the previous few years were shocked that Tony seemed perfectly comfortable with the new direction his life was taking and by his indifference to the impact on the lives of other people that his activities were having — his children, his colleagues in offices across the region who looked to him for guidance and inspiration, the clients who trusted his judgment in marketing their brands, and the women lured into prostitution by the cold and lucrative efficiency of the on-line service.

Tony's story is a record of the drift from inspirational leadership to the cynical exploitation of others in pursuit of self-aggrandisement and the manipulation of people in order to accumulate money and power. While he still likes to portray himself as a person who cares — for his family, for his colleagues, and for his clients — his activities are a flat contradiction of that claim, and his choices are no longer determined by what is best for others but rather by what works for him. His personal integrity has been rapidly eroded and it is no longer possible for anyone to take him at his word. He has, quite simply, become a misleader.

Albert Camus told us that integrity has no need of rules, echoing St. Augustine's words, "Love, and do what you will". A progressive loss of integrity creates the need for more rules and regulation. Where human beings can no longer be united in trust, they have to be bound by laws; community is replaced by contract. The stifling growth of compliance in business goes hand in hand with the loss of mutual trust that arises as a result of people not doing what is right for all, but rather what works for their own selfish desires. The disturbing dearth of leaders in our world is inextricably tied to the erosion of integrity in our society as a whole.

The financial and economic disasters in the early years of the twenty-first century have been erroneously labelled by politicians and partisan media interests as a philosophical and a systemic failure, when it is in fact the result of moral collapse. Blaming big business or government is simplistic and wrong-headed when there was clear culpability among individual businessmen, politicians and bureaucrats, and also among ordinary citizens who had succumbed to the temptation to live beyond their means. Fortunately, many more businessmen, politicians, bureaucrats and ordinary citizens shunned the temptation, choosing to live according to the principles on which the most open, compassionate, and prosperous civilisation the world has ever known has been built. To blame all for the sins of the few and to say that tighter controls are the only solution is to suggest that we all lack integrity.

What is integrity?

What is integrity? And why is it so important? From the prime minister to the prison inmate, we all like to believe we have it. Indeed, to question someone's integrity is a terrible insult, and yet most of us quite readily question the integrity of others.

If you ask someone to define integrity, the common answer is 'honesty' or 'trustworthiness' — being as good as your word. But this understanding needs to be given a little more substance. A standard dictionary definition is that: *integrity means the quality or state of being complete.* It is wholeness, perfect condition, or soundness. When something falls apart, it is said to disintegrate; if it is put together again, but incorrectly so that the parts do not work in unison or in harmony, it is said to lack structural integrity. When the different parts of an organisation work in contradictory or inconsistent ways in pursuit of conflicting goals, the organisation demonstrates a lack of strategic alignment or integrity.

In the 1960s, young people often used the phrase: "getting my head together". What they meant was getting the confusion out of their lives and achieving inner harmony — in effect, integrity. Actually, this was part of a wider social phenomenon which had been developing in the Western world for a few centuries — the personal quest for authenticity. People came to believe that their purpose in life was to achieve the personal wholeness or authenticity exclusive to them as individuals. Apart from the inevitable self-centeredness, and even narcissistic tendencies that accompanied this development, especially when it morphed into the self-esteem movement promoted by influential psychologists, such as

Carl Rogers, Rollo May and Abraham Maslow, there was merit in the idea: each of us is undoubtedly challenged to face life as a journey of self-discovery and to understand the part we are called to play.

The idea was not original, and the view of life as a quest for completeness can be found in many ancient books. Fifteen hundred years ago, the great Roman thinker Boethius in *The Consolation of Philosophy* defined eternity in terms of completeness: '*Perfect possession all at the same time of endless life*'.

In other words, completeness, wholeness or integrity is possessing the fullness of life — past, present, and future — all at once: being everything you were intended to be.

Every human being wants fulfilment, or to be complete. Consciously or sub-consciously, it is our prime goal in life. We have in our minds, however clear or murky, a vision of what we want to be, or what we feel we ought to be. Everything in our lives either works towards that vision or works against it. Whether we move steadily towards total fulfilment depends on the choices we make about our attitudes and education, our health and fitness, our relationships, our careers and our communities — everything, in fact, affects our efforts to achieve that completeness. Hence the practicality of thinking of integrity as consistency, reliability, or being as good as one's word.

Those things that are consistent with our vision will help us grow towards completeness. Conversely, those things that are inconsistent with our vision will undermine our quest for completeness. Inconsistencies are the internal contradictions that frustrate our efforts to grow. They divide us from within, making it impossible for us to function in a reliable manner and for anyone else to know where we really stand. They damage trust and have a deleterious effect on relationships. That is why integrity or completeness as fulfilled human beings demands the progressive elimination of such contradictions.

A good way to view personal integrity is to think of your life as a jigsaw. You begin with all the component parts and the potential to achieve the promised fulfilment of the complete picture shown on the cover of the box. But the hundreds of jigsaw pieces are in chaos, and finding the correct ones to complete the different parts of the picture can take a lot of thought, effort, trial and error. It involves a process of becoming familiar with the shape, the picture content and the colouring of all the pieces, comparing them with aspects of the complete image on the cover and organising them into probable areas of application.

Mistakes are inevitable — often pieces appear to fit a particular part of the puzzle, but do not. Alignment must be perfect, and each piece makes its proper contribution to the picture, thereby bringing closer the final achievement of the overall integrity of the completed picture. Completing the jigsaw demands confidence, commitment, patience, perseverance, and creativity — the very virtues associated with people of integrity.

This process, then, is the means we must employ to achieve personal integrity. And complete integrity is, in the final analysis, the fulfilment we all seek.

ORGANISATIONAL INTEGRITY

This understanding of personal integrity also applies to groups and organisations. But in the case of institutions, integrity may be more formally defined as the strategic alignment of all the elements involved in pursuing the purpose of the organisation, as well as the cultural consensus that enables people to work productively together. Genuine integrity will see all concerned working in harmony to overcome disagreements and to achieve the common goal. Organisational and cultural integrity is an obvious measure for the quality of leadership in any business.

A few years ago I facilitated a management forum for a large, new commercial property corporation. The prospects for rapid growth and market leadership were excellent because of the combined expertise and experience of the people concerned, as well as the network of powerful contacts created by the merger. However, during preparations for the management forum, I discovered that all was not well. Among other concerns, one well-placed insider spoke about directors in one of the merger companies bleeding it by claiming all sorts of unwarranted personal expenses.

The core problem, however, was a power struggle between the CEO, who was determined to integrate the various divisions into an unbeatable market-leader, and the Chairman of the Board, who had formerly headed one of the merger entities and who wanted all his old perks as well as the benefits of being part of the new conglomerate. The CEO stood for dynamic change with all the inevitable risks, while the

Chairman wanted his former business to continue as before, but now with the security of being part of a bigger, stronger enterprise.

Factions gathered around the two men, making for a difficult and often belligerent management forum, but by the end of two intense days it seemed as if progress had been made. I felt uneasy about one of the Chairman's closest allies because of the patently selfish sentiments he had expressed to me privately, but I believed that the Chairman himself would in future support the CEO. My hopes were reinforced a few weeks later when I joined the two men in an informal consultation about the future direction of the corporation. The Chairman indicated that he shared the vision and would work with the CEO to realise it. Sadly, this proved not to be the case.

Two years later, the corporation had demonstrated that its potential as an industry blockbuster had been no mirage: it had grown impressively, producing excellent rewards for its shareholders. What was remarkable was that the CEO and his supporters had been able to achieve this despite the destructive tactics of the Chairman and his, by then dwindling, band of malcontents. Tellingly, the man I had harboured concerns about was trumpeting his disdain for the corporate vision and the interests of stakeholders, and boasting that he was there purely to promote his own self-interest. The Chairman had become increasingly embittered by the success of the CEO and his programme, even though his own financial fortunes had been boosted significantly by the corporate performance.

These two men had made the development of a positive and congenial culture impossible, poisoning the atmosphere and creating obstacles while others had laboured long and hard to produce the results that were achieved. It was all but impossible for the corporation to rid itself of them. Eventually the other shareholders were driven to agree that buying them out would ultimately be less expensive than allowing them to continue their acts of sabotage.

There is something radically wrong when a person is enriched by the very system he sought to undermine. Sadly, it is a fact of life in a society where words like 'honour' and 'virtue' sound like quaint echoes from a forgotten past.

In another example, a notorious incompetent who had risen to a senior management position with one of Australasia's best-known companies was finally squeezed out by means of a very substantial redundancy package. He promptly secured a management position with a multinational giant, and six months later scored an equally liberal redundancy payout when his new employers learnt that he had nothing to offer but politically correct plausibility. One hopes it prompted senior management to ask some questions regarding the HR department's perspicacity and the analytical efficacy of their personality tests.

Organisational integrity, requiring as it does the *personal* integrity of so many people, depends largely on a corporate culture built on personal trustworthiness.

INTEGRITY AND PERSONAL GROWTH

It is important to remember that nobody ever reaches complete integrity in this life. In the final analysis, integrity is perfection, and we are all imperfect human beings. Our lives are about growing towards the wholeness we are called to in community, in other words about progressively trying to achieve complete integrity — it is a journey, one on which wrong turns are an ever-present possibility. And it requires each individual to ponder the questions that Immanuel Kant suggested all human beings inevitably have to confront sooner of later : "Who am I?", "What ought I to do?", and "What may I hope?".

Thereafter, we have to make sovereign choices about our lives — choices no one else can make for us and which should, logically, be based on the answers we give to those questions. Kant's questions may be paraphrased as just two questions: "What is this life all about?" and "What part must I play?" These are hard questions to answer, but the alternative is to drift through life, being directed by whatever circumstances assail us. Often the people who do answer them most decisively are adherents of traditional religions, contemporary cults, or a prevailing ideology. Ideologies, we should emphasise, are closed systems of thought, which at some point or other shut out reasoned inquiry and discourse, as did Communism, Nazism and, more recently, deconstructionism and political correctness in the post-modern Western world.

All human beings are in some way or another religious, even if it is not of a spiritual nature. We derive our word 'religion' from the Latin word 'religere', which means 'to tie or bind back'; religion is, in effect, binding oneself to some first principle or other. Whether that first principle be God, the cosmos, nature, science, humanity, human reason, the state, the nation, the community, one's ancestors, one's culture, the family, or merely oneself, we all hold on to it as the most important commitment in our lives, even though we may only think about it in times of crisis. J. M. Barrie, the creator of *Peter Pan*, concluded that our religion is whatever we are most interested in.

Our religion, whatever it may be, is the foundation of our worldview — how we see the world and life itself — or the broad personal understanding that shapes the answers we construct to the questions posed by Kant. All our attitudes in life — to ourselves, to other people and to the world around us — spring from our worldview, and our attitudes shape our behaviour and the way we conduct our lives. Inevitably, the wholeness, fulfilment, or integrity that we seek will be largely determined by our worldview.

Fritz Haber is remembered as one of the great scientists of the early twentieth century, and a worthy recipient of the Nobel Prize for chemistry in 1918, though that achievement was not without terrible irony. This brilliant mind from a culturally rich society was also the evil genius behind chemical warfare, which was conducted for the first time during World War I. Haber himself personally supervised the use of these weapons by the German forces.

His wife, Clara, who also held a doctorate in chemistry, was deeply disturbed by her husband's war-time activities and the apparent satisfaction he derived from them, and killed herself with his service pistol. Haber left for the Eastern Front on the morning of her death. It would be an interesting exercise to try to define the worldview of Fritz Haber, and to observe the curious blend of barbarism and civilisation that so often arises in the mind of a single individual.

INTEGRITY AND YOUR WORLDVIEW

Which of the many widely differing worldviews in our crowded world can provide fertile soil in which people of integrity may be cultivated? It depends on their meeting certain criteria — criteria based on what we know about human nature across cultures. I suggest that a truly human worldview:

- Respects the dignity of every individual human being. This is the basis of all the human rights we Westerners so casually take for granted and is the only meaningful foundation on which all human relationships can be built — in friendships, families, communities, workplaces, organisations, nations, and international cooperation and support.

- Demands respect for the power of human reason, whatever its limits and fallibility. We can only build a better world for all people through reasoned discourse about the things that separate us from others. Human reason is the bridge that allows the development of community and the possibility that the human ideals of justice and peace can become realities in the lives of all. It goes without saying that the purpose of human reason is to know the truth.

- Acknowledges that every human being is gifted with a unique potential, the actuality of which becomes the goal of life. The potential of each individual should be nurtured and developed in childhood to encourage and enable him to pursue its proper fruition in adulthood, within the context of community. As explained earlier, this principle supports the entire ethos of true education; it also underlies the significance of meaningful work. The Spanish writer Jose Ortega y Gasset, in *The Revolt of the Masses*, provided food for thought in this regard when he wrote:

  'An unemployed existence is a worse negation of life than death itself. Because to live fully means to have something definite to do — a mission to fulfil — and in the measure in which we avoid setting our life to something, we make it empty. Human life, by its very nature, has to be dedicated to something.'

- Affirms the personal freedom which is essential for self-fulfilment in each and every individual human being. However, freedom must be properly understood as 'cosmic freedom' — freedom to fulfil our potential within the context of the cosmic order and the freedom to choose those things we know to be good for ourselves, for other people, and for the world around us. Unfortunately, in modern Western society, many people have come to believe in 'chaotic freedom'; that is, the freedom to choose to do what we like. Cosmic freedom affirms that we have a natural orientation towards choosing to do the right thing — an orientation that simply needs to be properly informed and developed. Chaotic freedom on the other hand says that human cooperation and community are only possible through external control — through law and regulation. The difference in approach is between personal responsibility and imposed authority. This philosophical argument has raged for around 700 years, but the evidence of

history strongly suggests that a truly human worldview would need to stand on the principle of cosmic freedom.
- Includes an unshakeable commitment to a scientifically-informed stewardship of the environment fully respectful of both the needs of humanity and the natural world. The world is the common home of countless species, including humans, and should be treated with respect and appreciation by all people who take their human rationality and human responsibility seriously.

These criteria furnish a sound foundation for shaping a coherent worldview and provide a set of principles for assessing our own worldview. And it is the responsibility of each one of us to do the assessment for ourselves, because that is the first requirement of personal integrity. The words of John Stuart Mill, in *On Bentham and Coleridge* are worth remembering:

"There can be no philosophy where fear of consequences is greater than love of truth."

INTEGRITY IS TRANSCULTURAL

That these principles are transcultural and applicable to all human beings is clear from the careers of any number of great leaders from non-Western cultures; for example, Confucius, Aung San Suu Kyi, Mandela, and Gandhi. The courtroom defence put up by Gandhi in 1922, when the British charged him with treason, is an eloquent endorsement of the foundations of civilised standards:

"Non-violence implies voluntary submission to the penalty for non-co-operation with evil. I am here, therefore, to invite and submit cheerfully to the highest penalty that can be inflicted upon me for what in law is a deliberate crime, and what appears to me to be the highest duty of a citizen. The only course open to you, the Judge and the assessors, is either to resign your posts and thus dissociate yourselves from evil, if you feel that the law you are called upon to administer is an evil, and that in reality I am innocent, or to inflict on me the severest penalty, if you believe that the system and the law you are assisting to administer are good for the people of this country, and that my activity is, therefore, injurious to the common weal."

Gandhi, like all great leaders, knew that in the final analysis civilised standards come down to a simple commitment to truth. What he was appealing for from the British judiciary was integrity, adherence to the principles on which the British Constitution and the Common Law were constructed, because he knew that would guarantee him justice. He could confidently point out the utter inconsistency of the British position, knowing that even if he lost the trial, he would win the argument. Exposing a lack of integrity in an opponent issues a reverberating challenge to their moral authority, which rings true in the ears of any civilised culture. Wherever people are afraid to support such a challenge, we can be sure that misleadership has resorted to intimidation and violence.

Alexander Solzhenitsyn in his Nobel acceptance speech laid bare the necessary link between violence and untruth, the enemies of integrity, underlining the abyss that divides leadership from misleadership:

'Let us not forget that violence does not and cannot flourish by itself; it is inevitably intertwined with lying. Between them there is the closest, the most profound and natural bond: nothing screens violence except lies, and the only way lies can hold out is by violence. Whoever has once announced violence as his method must inexorably choose lying as his principle.'

These realities have confronted human beings since the birth of civilisation, and while the overall record of achievement is less than encouraging, there are many beacons of hope. In great literature from Confucius to Camus, in great lives from Socrates to Simone Weil, and in great socio-political advances from Athenian democracy to the American Constitution, we see the fruits of leadership built on integrity— as it can only be. Inevitably, imperfections remain because all the pieces of the jigsaw are not yet in place, but instead of giving in to the cynicism that says human fulfilment is an impossible dream, the beacons of hope remind us that we are called to pursue the ideals of the good life.

In a world lacking inspirational leadership, the challenge is clearly moral rather than intellectual. Integrity, the essential requirement for leadership, is what is missing. Even as I write these words, the British government is being rocked by a corruption scandal that discredits the democracy that once set the standard. And the problem is universal.

Governments in the Western world, working through notoriously ideological and demonstrably inadequate education systems, together with the ratings-hungry media, have for too long promoted an insidious materialism and individualism. This worldview seeks fulfilment in profligate consumerism, a promiscuity that destroys trust and relationships, a licence that spawns all manner of addictions, and a nihilism that breeds the anti-social pathologies commonplace in our tragi-comic society. The same governments then brazenly present themselves as the champions of the lonely, the addicted, and the socially maladjusted — the alleged victims of a heartless consumer society. The contradictions ring out only to be drowned in the blare and bustle of our brave new world.

Little wonder that integrity is at a premium and leadership is lacking. Except in the hearts of men and women who still believe in personal virtue and for whom integrity is the goal. These are the leaders of the future, giving us hope against the predatory machinations of the misleaders. In choosing to help forge a new world, they encourage the rest of us to at least ponder the lines of the poet, John Dryden, from *Translations from Persius* in *The works of John Dryden: in verse and prose, with a life, Volume 1*:

'Hast thou not, yet, propos'd some certain end
To which thy life, thy every act may tend?'

Leaders and Misleaders

CHAPTER 5
Thinking for Yourself

"Party loyalty is a dead end. It's a lethal form of laziness. Issues matter. Character matters. Acting on principle matters. The sound-bite and the slogan do not matter. They belong to a vocabulary of the herd, and human beings deserve better. Real freedom demands an ability to think, and a great deal of modern life seems deliberately designed to discourage that."
Charles, Archbishop Chaput of Denver

THE NEED TO THINK

Leading like you mean it and defining reality are impossible tasks for any aspiring leader who does not think deeply about people, society, work, and life generally, because in the first place you have to know precisely what you mean, and in the second you need to understand the reality before you can define it. Yet I meet great resistance or indifference from those hoping to improve their leadership ability when I recommend setting aside at least ten minutes every day to reflect on the issues confronting them as leaders. I recommend just ten minutes because I know that once they engage in some quality thinking, they will extend the period, recognising its benefits and the fact that it actually saves time in every other area.

Apart from the fact that in the post-modern workplace sitting alone and thinking has come to be associated with goofing off, why do would-be leaders, and in fact most people both today and in the past, prefer to avoid serious thinking about the issues that concern them? Ancient wisdom and modern psychology agree that human nature is a big part of the problem. In the last century it led to a myopia that threatened the survival of civilisation itself.

During the 1930s, with Hitler in power in Germany, Stalin in Russia, and Mussolini in Italy, and the world rushing towards disaster, one of the most reviled men in Britain was Winston Churchill. Even his own party seemed embarrassed by his lonely campaign for Britain to re-arm herself in the face of escalating savagery and aggression on the European continent. While British and European intellectuals, almost en masse, accepted the hollow promises of totalitarian ideology, Churchill agonised over the decline of the deeply-flawed democracies and the preservation of the social and political liberties won over many centuries. It would have been easier to go along with the opinions of the day — after all, Churchill was close to retirement age — but he chose instead to think through the issues for himself. And we should all be grateful that he did. In *Reflections on a Ravaged Century*, Robert Conquest underscores the difference between Churchill and those who were seduced by ideologies that promised a brave new world:

'If Churchill was not deceived as to Hitler, this was not a matter of intelligence, but rather a knowledge of history, and of evil. Chamberlain could not conceive of anyone whose attitudes were not more or less within the limits of those prevalent in the (English) Midlands.'

Unfortunately, the lessons have not been learned.

AMNESIA ABOUT MYOPIA

In the early and middle decades of the last century, prominent scholars and writers such as Christopher Dawson, Romano Guardini, Hilaire Belloc, Simone Weil, George Orwell, T. S. Eliot, Aldous Huxley, and Albert Camus provided articulate and prescient evaluations of the ills of Western civilisation, which pointed towards many of today's societal woes. These writers are still well-worth reading for anyone wanting to develop an understanding of our myopia and the amnesia that has made things worse. The aversion to thinking about significant issues that will sooner or later have a major impact on community, business, or our world, is as curious a tendency in rational human beings as is our obsession with celebrity.

The all-too-common refusal among people to define reality for themselves was brought home to me during the Rhodesian terrorist war of the 1970s, which led to the establishment of Zimbabwe. I saw active service in both the army and the police, and found myself in a rather invidious position as an outspoken opponent of government policy. To be sure, I was even more vehemently opposed to the communist-trained thugs who inflicted atrocities on their own people, the very ones who were supposed to be "liberated" by the armed struggle. However, it seemed obvious that there were alternative, valid, humane, and more constructive approaches than either the perpetuation of white overlordship or the establishment of an African-style Stalinism. Unfortunately, for most white Rhodesians there were no other options and it was a simple black and white issue (the pun is entirely appropriate).

While the responsibility for the tragic mess must be borne by all parties to the conflict, this unthinking stance on the part of white Rhodesians, and the most popular white politicians in particular, made no sense from any angle, moral or practical. The possibility of a resolution based on white supremacy was simply not there. Many justified their stance by posing as the defenders of democracy against predatory communism, but they were as enslaved by racist ideology as the African demagogues were in thrall to Marxist-Leninist ideology. And if there is any definition of ideology that leaders need to keep constantly in mind, it is this: ideology is any system of ideas that tries to stop people thinking for themselves.

It was a terrible loss for not just Africa, but the whole world, that the white Rhodesians, hard-working, resolute, inventive, and sincerely committed to the principles of parliamentary democracy, the rule of law, free enterprise, and a compassionate civil society, should have had the tragic blind spot of racism. What was achieved economically and militarily in Rhodesia during the 1970s in the face of a war on three fronts as well as international sanctions is an object lesson for the soft, hedonistic societies of the post-modern West. Even Julius Nyerere felt obliged in his keynote speech at the independence celebrations in Zimbabwe, to acknowledge the economic miracle that was being bequeathed to the new nation. It was easy to be proud of being a Rhodesian; yet the contradiction that needed to be resolved was never properly thought through.

Another illustration of erroneous thinking is shown in the West's maintenance of the fiction that Robert Mugabe's elevation to power was constitutional, when in fact terror was always his instrument of choice. Violence and intimidation were the most telling factors in the elections that installed him as president. The tragedy of Zimbabwe was as predictable in 1980 as was the coming of World War II in the wake of the weak attitude of the democracies to totalitarian aggression. As rational human beings, we can read the signs and we are foolish if we fail to heed them. The fact that we are often guilty of error and omission in our thinking is no excuse for failing to use our greatest asset.

The examples of a failure to think clearly when confronted by radical challenges proliferate in business, just as in politics. The disasters that swamped the world of advertising in the 1980s and 1990s grew out of a widespread refusal to curb the culture of excess that afflicted the industry, and short-sightedness over the implications of the new information technology. An industry dedicated to the task of helping clients define a clear vision and think strategically about how to achieve it failed to do so for itself, resulting in many entirely avoidable casualties.

On more than one occasion in my own career, I encountered the obscurantism that smothered anything that smacked of new thinking. As an experienced copywriter with an artistic bent, I had learned a great deal about art direction while working with many outstanding art directors. The advent of computers offered the opportunity to both write copy and art direct on my own, just as some art directors wrote their own copy. When I volunteered to increase my own workload and productivity by taking responsibility for at least some of the art direction, my CEO refused point blank to allow me to do so. It was his loss — I was already doing such work on a freelance basis from home, laying the foundations for my own business.

WHAT IMPEDES PEOPLE IN THINKING FOR THEMSELVES?

The disinclination to think seriously about the issues of life has always been part of the human condition. But why is it seemingly at crisis proportions in our scientifically advanced civilisation? More money is now spent on schooling than at any time in history, and in this 'age of information', there are vast resources available to help us find answers to our most pressing questions. Alas, information is not knowledge, and knowledge is not wisdom. And the last requires deep and diligent thinking.

Many excellent books have been written on the decline of intellect in the post-modern West, but the imperative for leaders to be active thinkers in all areas of their lives obliges me to list the ten most insidious obstacles to rational thinking, with a brief explanation of each.

The post-modern mindset is the late twentieth century reaction against modernism, following the disillusionment brought about by the wars, the destruction, and the general inhumanity of the past one hundred years. Modernism, which grew out of the eighteenth century Enlightenment, proclaims that human beings are able to know everything about humanity and the cosmos, and to solve all problems through the use of science and through our ability to reason inductively and deductively. The post-modern mindset rejects this claim out of hand, and thinkers like Foucault, Derrida, and Rorty have persuaded millions, particularly in the West, that there is no such thing as objective truth. Tradition, rationalism, science, history, and classic literature and art are seen as lies upholding the power of the capitalists, though what these writers mean by 'lies' when they refute the notion of 'truth' is mystifying. They deny the possibility of rational debate and assert that the only the meaning in the world is that constructed by each of us as individuals.

You can see both modern and post-modern thinking in all areas of our lives. Modern art was about breaking free from the grip of tradition and authority, and shaking society with new ways of seeing things; post-modern art questions what art itself is, producing oddities like Manzoni's cans of his own excrement, or an unmade bed adorned with a dirty pair of knickers. Modern architecture decreed that form follows function and gave us featureless tenement buildings and high-rise slabs of concrete and glass; post-modern architecture challenges the very idea of what we expect a building to look like. The modern novel uses narrative and character to challenge orthodoxy and cultural complacency; the post-modern novel uses different layers, consciously mixing fact and fiction, to invite the reader to make his or her own truth. Modern television sitcoms often laughed at the traditional roles of men and women; a post-modern sitcom is loose and layered, and filled with the irony and self-doubt that permits shows about nothing, as in *Seinfeld, Extras,* and *Flight of the Conchords*. Modern movies used realism, style and the storyline to make a statement about the human condition; post-modern movies remove the constraints of narrative, style and genre, tapping into eclecticism, nostalgia, revulsion, and our uncertainty about the meaning of life. If you are sitting in a cinema and do not know whether to laugh, to cry, or to throw up, chances are you are watching a post-modern feature film.

While modernism is over-confident about our ability to control our destiny, post-modernism is mired in cynicism. Modernism is optimistic, brashly saying we can know it all; post-modernism is pessimistic and questions our ability to know anything. Both can get in the way of thinking for oneself.

Relativism is a prime feature of the post-modern mindset. The claim that there is no such thing as objective truth is an obstacle to serious thinking. Contrary to the claims of its academic proponents, it has been around for thousands of years. One of the most celebrated confrontations between relativism and truth occurred in ancient Athens when, according to Plato, Socrates set out to expose the dishonesty of the Sophists.

Socrates was committed to seeking the truth, even when it remained elusive, through the painstaking cut and thrust of the Socratic dialogue. The Sophists by contrast used clever arguments and rhetorical tricks to deceive others into accepting their self-serving opinions, as do many lawyers and politicians today, for whom winning is more important than truth. Josef Pieper in his essay *Abuse of Language — Abuse of Power* draws attention to this abuse of the truth:

Public discourse, the moment it becomes basically neutralised with regard to a strict standard of truth, stands by its nature ready to serve as an instrument in the hands of any ruler to pursue all kinds of power schemes…Serving the tyranny, the corruption and abuse of language becomes better known as propaganda…Yet propaganda in this sense by no means flows only from the official power structure of a dictatorship. It can be found wherever a powerful organisation, an ideological clique, a special interest, or a pressure group uses the word as their "weapon". And a threat, of course, can mean many things besides political persecution, especially all the forms and levels of defamation, or public ridicule, or reducing someone to a non-person — all of which are accomplished by means of the word, even the word not spoken…

Due to the post-modern age's commitment to cultural relativism it is considered scandalous and even criminal to question different cultural values. This inevitably leads to equivocation and, even bald-faced mendacity. It would make a nonsense of this book and of all books that sought to make a statement about the human condition, if we embraced the relativist claim that all cultures are of equal value. If relativists believe in human rights, then they are affirming the equal dignity of all human beings and acknowledging that every human being is an end in himself or herself and should never be used as the means to someone else's ends. This standpoint plainly condemns cultural perversities that do serious harm to people, such as apartheid, slavery, the subjugation of women, religious intolerance, and ethnic cleansing, amongst others. If we adhere to the principle of human dignity, there are moral imperatives we must take as absolute; if we deny the principle, or try to exclude certain individuals or groups, then we concede that might is right, thereby opening a Pandora's box of anarchy and mayhem.

Keith Windschuttle, in an essay entitled: *The Perverse Anti-Westernism of the Cultural Elite,* quotes Sir Charles Napier, the British Commander-in-Chief in India from 1849 to 1851, who challenged the cultural relativism of a group of Hindu leaders over the practice of sati:

'You say that it is your custom to burn widows. Very well. We also have a custom: when men burn a woman alive, we tie a rope around their necks and we hang them. Build your funeral pyre; beside it, my carpenters will build a gallows. You may follow your custom. And then we will follow ours.'

If we are not capable of knowing the truth, or worse, if there is no such thing as truth, then thinking is a pointless task, other than to scheme nihilistically how we might get our own way. The levels of cynicism in the post-modern workplace are intimately related to the unthinking relativism that leaves people adrift without an anchor, living lives without any clear meaning or purpose, and easy prey for misleaders.

If we do not believe in truth, then the possibility of answering Kant's three questions is jettisoned, and we are left with the existential conundrum that pushes people into nihilism.

The demise of education has accompanied the development of the post-modern mindset and will be examined in the next chapter, but it must still be listed here as one of the obstacles to independent rational thought. John Taylor Gatto, a highly-acclaimed teacher and radical advocate for educational reform in the United States, can sometimes sound like a conspiracy theorist, but nonetheless makes a historically valid point with serious implications for democracy and leadership at all levels of society. It is taken from his book, *Dumbing Us Down*:

'Schools are a great mechanism to condition the on-rushing generations to accept total management, to impose a kind of lifelong childishness on most of us in the interests of scientific management. Efficient management requires incomplete people to manage because whole people, or those who aspire to wholeness, reject extended tutelage.'

Gatto's devotion to young people over many decades compels us to weigh carefully the description he gives of his pupils: indifferent to the adult world; handicapped by a short attention span and a lack of curiosity; without a meaningful sense of the future or the past that created the world they inhabit; cruel and bereft of compassion; uncomfortable with intimacy; materialistic; dependent, passive, and timid. Schools in the Western world have, for various reasons, abandoned the prime goal of education — to inspire and equip people to think for themselves.

Political correctness is a feature of post-modern society and a favourite tool of ideology, building on the ruins of education to try and stifle independent thought altogether. It is the attempt by government, academia, the media and other interested parties to control the way we think by making it taboo to express certain ideas. Restricting freedom of speech sabotages freedom of thought, and the effects can be devastating. In a broadcast to the people of Czechoslovakia in 1990, Vaclav Havel, who became President of the Czech Republic, saw political correctness as fundamental to the nightmare from which his country was just emerging:

"The worst thing is that we live in a contaminated moral environment. We fell morally ill because we became used to saying something different from what we thought. We learned not to believe in anything, to ignore one another, to care only about ourselves."

Genuine freedom of speech demands courage and confidence, but if people are encouraged to think for themselves and express themselves openly, bad ideas can be shown up for what they are. Racism, for example, is a misguided and malignant attitude, but the most effective way to defeat it is by allowing racists to debate their views in the open. It takes very little to dismantle their arguments by means of rational discourse. Unfortunately, overcoming their emotional objections will inevitably be a much more difficult task.

Both sides in the debate about anthropogenic global warming have discredited their own standpoint by deploying fallacious reasoning and resorting to mud-slinging, but the worst tactic has been to try and stifle debate — arguments are not won by forcing your opponent to remain silent. And when both sides of a supposedly scientific argument take on manifestly ideological overtones, the truth remains an elusive target. Little wonder, then, that many ordinary people worldwide have given up trying to decide which side is right; others, however, have been convinced by Al Gore's arguments in *An Inconvenient Truth*, while still others are equally sure that US Senator Inhofe is right in attacking the theory of global warming. Rational debate is required in order to make progress in our understanding.

Political correctness is inimical to democracy and personal freedom: democracy cannot survive the death of independent thinking among the population at large, and its current fragility is proof of that reality. The objective of thought is truth; the objective of political correctness is control. Thinking is for leaders; political correctness is for misleaders.

The media mushroom is proving to be as destructive of mental well-being as the nuclear variety is of physical well-being. Quality thinking demands peace and quiet, but we now live in a world of incessant noise. The farrago of advertising, info-tainment, and 'reality' shows that assaults our senses 24/7 makes thinking an impossibility for all except the resolute few who proactively limit the influence of television, radio and the internet in their lives, in order to draw intellectual sustenance from good books, cultured conversation, quiet contemplation, and rational reflection.

The post-modern media is not motivated by the public good, but by commercial gain and some or other political agenda. Nonetheless, and even though their messages are repeatedly shown to be untrustworthy, the majority of people still regard information received through the media as authoritative. This explains the proliferation of the urban myths and ideological standpoints that, working in tandem with political correctness, derail any disposition towards serious thinking.

Traditional print media are losing out to electronic media, and the social and psychological implications of this are only beginning to be understood. Just as the advent of writing, and then the invention of printing, slowly suffocated the oral tradition, eroding the capability of human memory in the process, so the seductive charm of television is crushing the printed word, replacing knowledge with information, and undermining thoughtful and articulate debate. In the age of the image and the sound bite, an intellectual shallowness has spread through homes, schools and workplaces, and people are no longer even aware of the rich cultural heritage that is being lost. Neil Postman, in his disturbing book *Amusing Ourselves to Death*, identified the insidious core of television's appeal:

'*Entertainment is the supra-ideology of all discourse on television. No matter what is depicted, or from what point of view, the overarching presumption is that it is there for our amusement and pleasure. That is why even on news shows which provide us daily with fragments of tragedy and barbarism, we are urged by the newscasters to "join them tomorrow".*'

Postman identified television commercials as "the single most voluminous form of public communication", and described the "instant therapy" they provide as specious persuasion that all problems can be solved quickly and easily through science, technology, and technical skills. Postman was writing before the phenomenal rise of the internet, but far from detracting from his thesis; it has merely exacerbated the problem. Consider the entertaining but shallow hours spent on YouTube, Facebook, Twitter, and the like, and the sameness of their worldview and that of television. Family and community are hard-pressed to compete with the media in shaping the way children come to see the world. The former want well-rounded people, while the media want only consumers. The last thing media magnates want you to do is to think.

As long ago as 1952 the German philosopher Josef Pieper, in an essay in the book *Only the Lover Sings*, tried to alert Western civilisation to the dangers of a technology-driven consumer society:

'*At stake here is this: How can man be saved from becoming a totally passive consumer of mass-produced goods and a subservient follower beholden to every slogan the managers may proclaim? The question really is: How can man preserve and safeguard the foundation of his spiritual dimension and an uncorrupted relationship to reality?*'

Pieper's worst fears are being realised in a world of misleaders.

Information overload is a product of the media mushroom. There are many bright, responsible, enterprising people in all areas of the economy who receive every day a deluge of e-mail messages from clients, prospects, suppliers, colleagues, and managers. In addition to attending to this avalanche of information, or requests for such, their work will require them to search widely on the internet for further information, and to peruse quantities of data in other media. Ironically, in their break time, most will visit other websites, and on returning home at night, they will seek refuge in various electronic media before retiring to bed. Exhausted by all this, they will feel no inclination to become absorbed in a book which might inspire them to think about their lives and the lives of others.

It has been said that people today read much more than previous generations. True, they spend their lives snatching bits of information from here, there and everywhere. But skimming information on the internet, focusing occasionally on certain chunks and bites, is not a form of reading designed to expand cultural understanding and to commit knowledge of human possibilities and achievements to long-term memory, thereby promoting self-development. People are not required to retain beyond the deadlines of the current project the information they flit through, if only because it is safely stored away in the global electronic warehouse. This is a far cry from gaining knowledge by reading books, especially classic literature, from cover to cover. Replacing the pursuit of knowledge with a search for information erodes the capacity of people to think deeply.

I was once called in by a large retail venture which had recently paid a marketing consultant $25,000 for a marketing plan. The document, running to some three hundred pages, was very impressive and was filled with everything one needed to know about the business, the market, the competitors, and the opportunities. But it reached no conclusion and provided no clear goal or plan of action. I returned two days later with a vision the managers found inspiring and a strategy to turn it into a reality, all laid out in six PowerPoint slides. Seven years later, the central thrust of this $750 plan was still working effectively, while the $25,000 'plan' was collecting dust on the bottom of the marketing manager's bookshelf, silent testimony that volumes of information is not evidence of deep thinking. I prefer to be guided by the perspicacity of Pascal when he wrote in *Provincial Letters:*

'I apologise for this letter being so long; I did not have time to make it short.'

Specialisation is both cause and consequence of an explosion of knowledge and information. It has long been one of the central sociological trends accompanying the rapid growth of science and technology and also the reform of public schooling to meet the needs of a changing world. Vocational specialisation is required every day in a scientific-technological civilisation, but when it becomes the all-consuming endeavour in people's lives, it constricts their knowledge and understanding of the world around them, diverting them from the free thinking that is fundamental to their fulfilment as human beings and reducing them to functionaries.

This is tragic when it hinders people who are being exploited from questioning the system or challenging the misleaders who benefit from their passivity. It is equally calamitous when it prevents those capable of providing the necessary leadership from thinking about their responsibilities and about more humane possibilities. And there is still another level where specialisation has exacerbated intellectual decline.

We now live in the era of the expert, the consultant and the PhD, of functionaries created to know everything about one thing and little about anything else. Governments, professional firms, commerce, industry, and tertiary institutions are awash with highly-qualified people who may have meagre intellectual resources in fields other than their own, and little inclination for meaningful and necessary dialogue with their peers or the rest of the community. Jacques Barzun in *The House of Intellect* pin-pointed how specialisation has erected a new Tower of Babel:

'That same abundance of information has turned into a barrier between one man and the next. They are mutually incommunicado, because each believes that his subject and his language cannot and should not be understood by the other. This is the vice we weakly deplore as specialisation. It is thought of, once again, as external and compelling, though it comes in fact from within, a tacit denial of Intellect. It is a denial because it rests on the superstition that understanding is identical with professional skill. The universal formula is: "You cannot understand or appreciate my art (science) (trade) unless you yourself practice it".'

At the same time, so great is the esteem in which the expert, like the celebrity, is held in the post-modern world that their opinions on subjects unrelated to their areas of expertise are often used by propagandists to influence an unthinking public. Consider only the leading German scientists who supported Nazism, and the treasonous activities of some western intellectuals in support of the Soviet Union.

In an age of specialisation, no one can be expected to know even a little about everything, and it is inevitable that all people, even the experts, have to turn to others for knowledge in most areas of their lives, trusting the authority and good faith of other experts. Scientists are not politicians, are not doctors, are not lawyers, are not motor mechanics, are not farmers, are not computer technicians. But that is no reason to abandon the one thing that can save us from the perils of specialisation, the very thing that led us to implement specialisation in the first place — thinking for ourselves. And this poses serious questions for education, especially the education of leaders, but we must reserve the answers for the next chapter.

Trust in formula has become an epidemic in the post-modern era. Its popularity grew from the success of the scientific revolution. Formulae are used legitimately and laudably in facilitating mechanical procedures, providing benefits in the hard sciences and technology, but their efficacy in those disciplines has led to a belief that they should be applied to all areas of human endeavour — a conclusion that is neither rational nor scientific, and which has promoted mental laxity. Formula, by definition, removes the need for independent thought, and believing that everything can be dealt with by formula encourages complacency.

The obsession with formula is related to the facile 'problem–solution' approach to the challenges of life with which the post-modern mindset deludes itself. The reality is that there are no 'simple problems' in human society which are susceptible to 'simple solutions'. Human society, like each individual human being, is a complex phenomenon; thus, a rash of graffiti in a city is not a 'problem', but rather a symptom of inter-related dysfunctional relationships and conflicting social visions, just as an individual's heart disease is not a 'problem' to be 'solved' but rather the symptom of genetic predisposition or diabetes, and/or a swathe of misguided lifestyle choices.

We can provide neat and tidy solutions to problems in mathematics, but not to human lives, where there will always be trade-offs, inexplicable contradictions, and unresolved spillage. The problem–solution approach encourages belief in easy answers and the quick fix instead of an acceptance of complexity and the challenges it poses for human community. The latter calls for visionary and creative thinking, informed by a sincere commitment to the dignity and well-being of the people concerned. As Robert Conquest explains in *Reflections on a Ravaged Century*:

'There is no formula that can give us infallible answers to political, social, economic, ecological and other human problems. There is no

simple concept that will answer such questions as how much the state can do (though we have learned that to give it too much power is disastrous), or how far market forces can give positive results (though we have learned that their abolition is disastrous). Nor is there a simple guide to the conduct of foreign policy.'

Nor, it must be added, are there infallible, simple guides for raising a child, building a community, running a business, or any other activity involving human beings. Formulae are wonderful tools in specified areas of applicability. Beyond that they become a device of charlatans, the indolent, and manipulators seeking to stop people thinking for themselves.

Fatalism is a block to rational thought — one that is more prevalent in the Western world than our sophisticated technological civilisation would suggest. Never has so much time and money been expended on schooling, and the remarkable advance of science and technology would seem to justify the tarnished but still tenacious belief that 'man is the measure of all things'. Yet in our allegedly enlightened civilisation, many people believe that all things happen according to an inexorable fate. As a result they are highly pessimistic and consequently resort to escapism in the form of drugs, alcohol, television, movies, the Internet, shopping, and being spectators as opposed to participants in life — all pursuits that discourage real thinking and sabotage any desire to be a complete person.

The persistently low polls in Western democratic elections, the chronic social decay, the gullibility in the face of There-Is-No-Alternative proclamations by politicians, economists and scientists, and the passive acceptance of egregious injustices and inefficiency, are all manifestations of this pervasive fatalism.

I once spoke to a large group of university administrators and academics about ways of building more mutually rewarding relationships in the workplace. It was a most depressing experience. Every attempt on my part to elicit their participation in the workshop unleashed a torrent of cynicism and abuse directed at their senior managers (who were not there to answer the charges levelled against them) and at me, for not having ready-made solutions to their problems. Every suggestion I made had been tried before with no success, it was claimed. After an hour and a half of fruitless discussion, I asked them why they remained in employment that gave them no satisfaction. Their response was that there was no hope of finding alternative employment better than their current conditions.

Christopher Lasch in *The Culture of Narcissism* reflected on the fatalism that is an inevitable part of the post-modern mindset. Noting the increasing difficulty people have in developing a sense of continuity, permanence, or connection in a world of fragile and shallow relationships, and of the transient pleasures of a throw-away consumer society hypnotised by the flickering images of virtual reality, Lasch foresaw the widespread loss of confidence in the face of life's challenges:

'The ethic of self-preservation and psychic survival is rooted, then, not merely in objective conditions of economic warfare, rising rates of crime, and social chaos but in the subjective experience of emptiness and isolation. It reflects the conviction — as much a projection of inner anxieties as a perception of the way things are — that envy and exploitation dominate even the most intimate relations…The ideology of personal growth, superficially optimistic, radiates a profound despair and resignation.'

Victimhood provides a means to escape from the responsibility of thinking for oneself. Over several decades the West has propagated the notion of victimhood by encouraging people to see the challenges of life as calamities inflicted on them by other people or outside agencies, and to turn to the government and the bureaucracy for salvation in their distress. Tax-payer funded advertising presents messages of support for 'victims' who are 'suffering the pain' of alcoholism, divorce, or gambling, and who are promised solutions in tax-payer funded programmes that are free, easy, and full of useful tips — as if simple solutions were possible for the severe and complex social dysfunction and human suffering that have generally been caused by long years of selfish and/or vindictive behaviour, originating in weak, uneducated, and damaging personal choices.

This mendacious trivialising of tragedy misleads millions into believing there is nothing they can do about the disintegration of family and community, and the depressing and destructive social decay, except trust the omniscient and omnipotent state to keep providing free and easy solutions. People in that fatalistic frame of mind are unlikely to think through the issues in order to provide the leadership needed in their families, workplaces, and communities.

There are many intimidating challenges confronting our world. However, to believe that we are the first generation to come up against seemingly insurmountable hazards is to be blind to the lessons of history. The philosopher, Jacques Maritain, once remarked that the world had always been in a hopeless state, and had always muddled through, and had always seemed to be lost, yet had always been saved.

Every generation has its challenges, and every generation has to find its own answers. We can only do so by thinking for ourselves.

Overcoming the Obstacles

As quoted in a New York Times article in April 1999, Albert Einstein once said:

"The most incomprehensible thing of all is the fact that the world is comprehensible."

This truth that the world is comprehensible to human beings through the use of our rational minds indicates that to refrain from using that faculty is to reject the dignity of being human, to shrink from the challenge of answering the riddle of life. Indeed, the human capacity for rational thinking implies a responsibility to use it for the obvious purpose of discerning the truth, and acting in line with it. This involves exercising our free will to make choices that are in accordance with our personal conscience. If we do not think for ourselves, our conscience will be shaped by someone else's propaganda which distorts the facts for their own ends. Freedom of thought is the most basic of all human rights but it demands of us the self-discipline to nurture, build, and use our intellectual capacity to its full extent.

So how do we overcome the ten obstacles discussed above and start thinking for ourselves? Awareness of what inhibits our attempts at serious thinking should help us counter them. Then it becomes a matter of setting aside dedicated time on a daily basis for quiet reflection so as to re-ignite education. Education is the subject of the next chapter, but reflection also needs consideration if it is to be fruitfully pursued. There are many excellent books on logic and on thinking to a purpose, including Anthony Flew's *Thinking about Thinking*, Robert Thouless's *Straight and Crooked Thinking*, Madsen Pirie's *The Book of the Fallacy* and Darrell Huff's *How to lie with Statistics*. These are all short, entertaining texts that help sharpen thinking abilities. More especially, Aristotle's *Rhetoric* is most instructive.

In addition to recommending these books I would also make the following observations about using time constructively in reflecting.

UNDERSTANDING THINKING

We think in order to know or to gain knowledge — that is the purpose of reflection. We think to discover the truth about ourselves and the world around us. Knowledge is truth: there is no such thing as false knowledge, only false information. False information is not knowledge; it is misinformation, or propaganda for misleaders to use. So when we know something, we have the truth of it, even though our knowledge is limited in scope, as St. Thomas Aquinas put it well when he said that human knowledge is at the same time true and not fully sufficient.

There are many degrees of knowledge. I may know that my car is powered by an internal combustion engine without knowing how that piece of technology actually works. In order to understand how my car is powered, I need to expand my knowledge of the composition and operation of the internal combustion engine. Increased knowledge helps to develop understanding, which should be thought of as knowing the cause, the effects, and the meaning of something. Despite the invaluable advances made in neuroscience in recent times, the human act of understanding, like consciousness itself, remains an elusive mystery. As Stanley Jaki, the eminent philosopher of science, amusingly explained in his book *Means to Message – a treatise on truth*:

'To understand understanding in terms of understanding is going round in a circle while understanding the process all the time.'

Nevertheless, we can state that when we understand something, we know it in such a way as to be able to classify it or to make a generalisation about it, possessing in our minds an idea or a concept that we express with a term or a name.

The great neo-Platonist pagan philosopher Plotinus concluded that any form of thinking was an indication of inadequacy or deficiency. He believed that The One (God) transcended all thought and being, while the pure intelligences, or spirits, knew intuitively. Plotinus pointed out that only human beings have to reason their way to knowledge, even though they do know a few basic truths, or axioms, through their rather limited intuition.

Rational thinking involves three distinct mental acts:
1. Understanding concepts or ideas which we express as terms or names.
2. Making judgments about ideas and facts, which we express as propositions or premises.
3. Reasoning about causes, which we express as arguments.

We evaluate terms as either clear or unclear, while propositions are either true or false, and arguments are either valid or invalid. A term is clear if it can be comprehended without any ambiguity. A proposition is said to be true if it is an accurate representation of reality. And an argument is valid if the conclusion is a necessary or unavoidable consequence of the premises or the logical steps from which it is inferred. In any rational dispute, the side which presents clear terms in premises or propositions known to be true and in a validly structured argument that does not resort to fallacious reasoning, has proved its case. It has defined reality and has won the argument, even if the other side has won the audience through emotional appeals, mud-slinging, or deceit.

The process of thinking is still mysterious, notwithstanding the spectacular advance of research into how the brain works. But we know that it starts with you — a conscious self and a unique identity. You are required to relate or make connections between the contents of your experience and emotions to extend your understanding of yourself and external reality. The information we use is provided by our senses and our memory. Our innate mental tools of intuition, imagination, inference, and language help us turn the information into knowledge, which we can then use. The more knowledge we have in our brains, the more connections we will be able to make. So people who read a lot will have an advantage over those who do not, and the older you are, the more knowledge you should have accumulated, and therefore, the better your thinking should be.

Two and a half thousand years ago, Aristotle gave us a straightforward understanding of how we think in order to reach conclusions. He called the process a syllogism and it involves taking two statements, called premises, making the connection between them, and then drawing a conclusion. His most famous example was:

- All men are mortal.
- Socrates was a man.
- Therefore Socrates was mortal.

In the nineteenth century, Lewis Carroll showed that you could make the syllogism much more complicated, improving your thinking power no end and having a lot of fun in the process. Here's a simple example of Carroll's symbolic logic:

- Babies are illogical.
- Nobody is despised who can handle a crocodile.
- Illogical persons are despised.
- Therefore, a baby cannot manage a crocodile.

Here's a slightly more complicated one:

- Promise-breakers are untrustworthy
- Wine-drinkers are very communicative
- A man who keeps his promises is honest
- No teetotallers are pawnbrokers
- One can always trust a very communicative person
- Therefore, no pawnbroker is dishonest

Carroll's examples get a great deal more complicated and even more amusing, but the important thing to keep in mind is that we are all capable of solving these brain teasers, as long as we are prepared to think about them long enough, making all the connections and drawing conclusions. In fact, we unconsciously use this logical method of thinking in our daily lives, but are often put off when it gets too hard, and can be misled by dishonest arguments called fallacies.

TRAPS TO AVOID

There has always been conflict between the defenders of truth and the purveyors of falsehood, between the leaders and the misleaders. The rhetorical device used to distort rational thinking is the fallacy or fallacious reasoning. There are scores of different kinds, but here are some of the more common types of fallacy heard daily in business, the media, politics, and social life in general.

- **Ad hominem** involves attacking your opponent instead of his argument. It comes in two forms — the abusive ad hominem and the circumstantial ad hominem. An example of the first would be: "The member of parliament proposing tax cuts is the same man seen having dinner last week with the Ku Klux Klan". The member's choice of dining companions has nothing to do with the pros and cons of tax cuts. An example of the second type of ad hominem would be: "The Australian Rugby Union has called for a review of scrummaging laws — well they would, wouldn't they?" Even if their motive is suspect, the issue is worth debating regardless of who is proposing further discussion.

- **Petitio principii** or begging the question is a popular way of trying to deceive people. We beg the question whenever we use something we are trying to prove as part of our argument; in other words when we smuggle our conclusion into our premises. An example would be: "We must persist with early childhood sex education because it ensures children grow up with a healthy attitude to sex". Prove it and you may have an argument worth listening to.

- **Loaded words** can influence people powerfully when they are trying to decide which side is right in an argument. The old example is the easiest to remember: "I am firm, he is obstinate, and you are plain pig-headed". You see and hear a lot of this type of thing in the media — it is usually very effective but mostly dishonest and certainly fallacious.

- **Emotional appeals** to our fears, envy, dislikes, prejudices, or pride often blind us to the true merits of an argument. Most big issues — global-warming, tax-cuts, corporate fraud, and so on — are clouded by our emotions being aroused. Images of Chernobyl or Hiroshima are usually enough to give pause to even the most rational supporters of nuclear power.

- **Poisoning the well** is another fallacy used by politicians and talk-back hosts who try to besmirch the reputation of their opponents before they can speak. For example, "Only a simpleton would believe that the country needs to spend more money on the defence forces". Would any simpleton care to step forward and debate the issue? "What sort of monster is going to vote against a bill to protect children from violence?" Would all the monsters in the audience who believe an occasional light smack on the bottom to be appropriate in childrearing raise their hands?

- **Argumentum ad numeram** is an appeal to numbers and is naturally popular in democratic societies. But public sentiment cannot decide matters of fact. The claim that "Everybody knows the Wright brothers were the first people to fly" may mean that everybody is wrong if it can be proved that a medieval monk beat them to it. Democratic opinion can be wrong on matters of morality and good taste, too; for example, if a majority supports racist policies or considers reality TV to be the height of good taste.

Most people are inclined to try and win arguments by any means, so it is important to be aware of these fallacious methods of arguing and to question what other people say. Politicians, the media, and advertisers clearly need to be treated with suspicion, but we also need to monitor ourselves — so pervasive has fallacious reasoning become that most people slip into it quite innocently and have trouble understanding why their arguments are invalid. Misleaders, of course, use fallacies deliberately.

A BETTER WAY

History provides some spectacular examples of a better way for people to use their rational faculties to find answers to the issues that confront them. The Socratic dialogues recorded in the works of Plato, and the scholastic 'disputation' of the Middle Ages offer models for reasoned discourse that is based on disciplined thinking, which ailing post-modern democracies badly need. Medieval universities such as Paris and Bologna helped lay the foundations of the modern world, scientifically and philosophically. Although they were also places of volatile democratic passions, St. Thomas Aquinas and other great teachers were able to inject a standard of reasoned discourse which is embarrassing to our allegedly more enlightened society. Any written or oral dispute was always considered by St. Thomas to be a dialogue or conversation in search of clarity and truth rather than an argument to be won or lost. The first rule was to be open and receptive to the opposing argument. He made listening a virtue, repeating his opponent's argument in more polished and compelling form, so that he often gave the impression that he was in agreement.

Not only did this demonstrate his clear understanding of the opposing argument, it also showed due respect for the dignity of his adversary, without whom the dialogue in search of truth could not proceed with the same potential. Only then did St. Thomas put his own case forward, aiming always to be comprehensive and clear so that there would be no room for misunderstanding on the part of his opponent or the audience. Esoteric jargon had no place in the disputation as practised by St. Thomas. The adoption of the spirit and the guidelines of the disputation by the legislative assemblies in the Western world would benefit democracy no end.

ASKING THE RIGHT QUESTIONS

Using the guidelines proposed above can aid better thinking, and it is important to ask yourself: "What should I be thinking about on a regular basis?" Kant's three questions, mentioned in an earlier chapter, echo the ancient philosophical injunction to 'know thyself', and are always a good starting point. But beyond those existential interrogatives, here are some other essentials:

- Are my close relationships everything I want them to be?
- How can I make them better?
- Am I happy — and if not, why not?
- Am I growing as a person — what progress am I making towards being what I want to be?
- Do I enjoy my work? If not, why not?
- Are my working relationships beneficial for all concerned?
- Am I happy with the way my community is?
- Am I happy with the way the country is being run?
- Am I confident about the future for my family and me?
- What am I doing about the things that worry me most?
- What is the meaning of life?

Leaders in business have a responsibility to be thinking constantly about their staff, customers, community, goals, and performance. These are the types of question they need to think about on a daily basis:

- Are our customers enthusiastic about doing business with us?
- Are they inspired to talk to others about our service?
- What do we bring to this community?
- Are our people inspired to make our vision a reality?
- Do they live up to the commitments they have made in being part of the team?
- Are our people enthusiastic and confident in their work?

- Are they properly trained and equipped?
- Are the workloads too heavy or too light?
- Do people provide and receive constructive feedback on a regular basis?
- Am I getting a lot of innovative thinking from the team?
- Are we as efficient as we need to be? What improvements could we make?
- Where are we profitable and where are we unprofitable?
- Are we closer to realising our vision than we were last week?

The ability to think on a regular basis requires the time to do so. Leading like you mean it is only possible if you devote quality time to thinking about what you do and the difference it makes. Solitude is important, but even sitting in traffic can be a good time to reflect on your life.

Your business, and indeed the whole free enterprise system, just like freedom and democracy themselves, needs people who think for themselves, people capable of self-leadership and therefore the leadership of others. This is hard in a socio-political atmosphere that conditions us to go with the flow, but that is our challenge and the future depends on our response. Thinking produces leaders; conditioning produces misleaders. Frederick Douglass, the great American educator and former slave, said in *A plea for free speech* in 1860:

> *"Liberty is meaningless where the right to utter one's thoughts and opinions has ceased to exist. That, of all rights, is the dread of tyrants. It is the right which they first of all strike down. They know its power. Thrones, dominions, principalities, and powers, founded in injustice and wrong, are sure to tremble, if men are allowed to reason..."*

Leaders and Misleaders

CHAPTER 6
Education and Personal Growth

"All who have meditated on the art of governing mankind have been convinced that the fate of empires depends on the education of youth."
Aristotle

LEADERSHIP, THINKING, AND EDUCATION

I have argued that leading like you mean it demands that people think for themselves, both proactively and retroactively, as a matter of course in all aspects of their lives, and that the necessary freedom of thought is only possible through a proper education — something that has been denied to millions of people throughout history. In its place, propaganda or an imposed intellectual silence have been instituted, so that people have been actively, and even violently, discouraged from thinking for themselves, and thereby prevented from developing their full potential as human beings.

During the Rhodesian War of the 1970s, it became apparent that the armed forces of the white government would not overcome the terrorist insurgency unless the hearts and minds of the black villagers and townspeople could be won over. However, these poor people were assailed by Marxist propaganda and the sadistic intimidation of the terrorists, making their hearts and minds inaccessible to the colonial regime that had failed to educate them as full citizens with equal opportunities. Although white Rhodesia had made a substantial investment in the education of the black population, it had been inadequate, and in any case the content of the humanities curriculum reinforced for Blacks the injustice of their situation.

Nevertheless, I recall one occasion during the war, when I was invited to talk to the Upper Sixth pupils of the largest black secondary school in Bulawayo on the subject 'War and Civilisation'. My audience was well-informed and articulate, and though they received my address with courtesy and interest, the scepticism they harboured in regard to my advocacy of the liberal democratic ideal quickly emerged in the lively discussion that followed. This revealed the effect that Marxist thinking had made on them, but apart from one particularly angry young man, most were still open to the possibility of a constitutional process in the direction of enfranchisement and independence. Naturally, they were suspicious that it might be a smokescreen for continued white domination, but their schooling had equipped them to resist the temptation of the manipulative ideological alternative. These young people recognised that their tribal world had been overtaken by a technological civilisation, and that they now had a part to play in the development of a new world. Their education, albeit limited, had enabled them to make valid judgments.

In my own case, education saved me from the racism that had disfigured my early development. The racial prejudice that burdened me for over thirty years gradually receded, creating a sense of personal freedom for me and enabling me to reflect on education and leadership, and to reach a more complete understanding of their nature. I was educated, or led, out of my deeply ingrained racist attitude by the examples of others and by the growth in my knowledge, which increasingly challenged the perverse worldview that contaminated both my Christian faith and my democratic sentiments.

My most influential teachers were: one of my family's domestic servants in Rhodesia, Webber, whose surname I never knew; Isaac Zulu, the younger brother of Grey Zulu, the Minister of Mines in the Kaunda government in Zambia; several schoolmasters, of whom Ted Hansen and Noel Wright — my history and English teachers — stand out; Harry Fincham, one of the two really fine headmasters I served under in my own teaching career; two colleagues from my days in the advertising industry, Johan Roux and Nkwenkwe Nkomo; and my brother, Johan, who travelled the same road of reproach and redemption. Their constructive influence, in other words their leadership, inspired the radical changes that only I could make. They helped to educate me. They helped me to think for myself and change the whole direction of my life.

Hence my encouragement to aspirant leaders to actively pursue more complete personal growth through ongoing education.

Defining education

There is an age-old dilemma regarding the purpose of education — is it the acquisition of knowledge by a learner, or the development of the learner's character? (For the ideologue it is neither of these, of course — it is for the control of the learner's mind for the ends of the state, the party, or the cause — for misleadership.)

It was proposed earlier that a genuine education provides four of the qualities essential for leadership — knowledge, strength of character, sound judgment, and a humane worldview, all of which are dependent on a person developing positive and constructive attitudes, which in turn requires a predisposition to think purposefully about the issues of life. It was also proposed that education, in the sense of ongoing personal development, is an essential quality of effective leadership, and so must aim at the most comprehensive understanding of humanity and the world. Josef Pieper, in *Leisure, the basis of culture*, explained that:

'Education is concerned with the whole: whoever is educated knows how the world as a whole behaves. Education concerns the whole human being, insofar as he is capax universi, "capable of the whole", able to comprehend the sum total of existing things.'

Harold T. Shapiro, a former president of Princeton, makes the same point in another way in *A Larger Sense of Purpose*:

'...the most valuable part of education for any learned profession is that aspect that teaches future professionals to think, read, compare, discriminate, analyze, form judgments, and generally enhance their capacity to confront the ambiguities and enigmas of the human condition.'

Education, like leadership, must be open to all possibilities, and for that reason will always offer more than any individual can ever aspire to know. Education, like leadership, is a daily undertaking, because the learning curve can and must continue to climb throughout life as we understand more about the world and the part we are called to play in it. Education, like leadership, respects the Platonic principle from *Symposium* that says:

'The unexamined life is not worth living.'

Education, like leadership, is essentially about bearing fruits – strong character in the individual, and humane culture in the community or society.

Education, in line with the understanding of leadership put forward in this book, is the process by which human potential is brought to fruition through both the acquisition of knowledge and the development of the character of the learner. The age-old dilemma is a mirage — there is no conflict, because the two are complementary.

EDUCATION AS A LIFE-LONG ENTERPRISE

Education, then, is the process through which we come to know ourselves and the world at large, moving through stages from simple awareness to ever-increasing understanding, which is demonstrated by an ability to explain things and to make sound judgments on subjects as diverse as the meaning of life and the merits, if any, of reality television. Education, of which formal schooling is merely one aspect, begins at birth and ends at death. Although education necessarily involves a teacher-learner relationship, each learner encounters many different teachers through life: apart from schoolteachers, we learn from parents, friends, and even Mother Nature herself. This is why long before formal schooling begins, the inevitable inequalities of home life — the vastly varying degrees of love and socialisation, knowledge-building and character formation — set children on very different paths to the future.

Fortunately, a misshapen or brutalised mind may be awoken at the eleventh hour by an inspirational teacher, in either formal or informal encounters — perhaps in the pages of a book, the images on a canvas, the notes of a piece of music, or by Nature itself. No human soul is beyond redemption except by choice — education has to be driven by the learner; the teacher can only inspire and guide.

Throughout our lives our intellectual horizon can and must expand; in the end, it will be the measure of the education we have built for ourselves and of our understanding of life and the world, providing the intellectual foundation for our worldview. If at any stage in our lives it ceases to grow, it locks us into a permanently restricted perspective and impedes any further thinking for ourselves.

Mortimer Adler, in his educational manifesto, *The Paideia Proposal*, makes the case for a carefully defined compulsory schooling designed to promote democratic ideals. While many of the proposals remain controversial, the basic understanding of education on which the case is built is hard to refute if one believes in human rights and the dignity of all people:

'Basic schooling — the schooling compulsory for all — must do something other than prepare some young people for more schooling at advanced levels. It must prepare all of them for the continuation of learning in adult life, during their working years and beyond. How? By imparting to them the skills of learning and giving them the stimulation that will motivate them to keep their minds actively engaged in learning. Schooling should open the doors to the world of learning and provide the guidelines for exploring it.'

If this is true for all people, then it is more especially compelling for those who would lead – they must cultivate their own education and that of others.

MISEDUCATION AND MISLEADERSHIP — A SHORT HISTORY OF EDUCATION

There is a close relationship between culture — whether it be civilisational, national, or corporate — and education. Culture is the heritage of knowledge, ideas, beliefs and values, including such diverse elements as technology, political systems, manners, cuisine, and the arts, that has developed over time, and that inspires and enables people to live together in mutually rewarding social harmony. Leadership, by its very nature, must help shape culture, and this emphasises once more the connection between leadership and education.

There is considerable worldwide controversy over the nature of formal education. While much of the debate has been about methodology, it is primarily the disagreements relating to content that need to be dealt with here in regard to the education of leaders. (The methodological issues are, of course, important and will be dealt with later.) In considering the contentious issue of content, it is necessary first of all to briefly review the main themes of development in education theory.

As the quotation from Aristotle at the head of the chapter indicates, education has always been seen by civilised people as crucial to their survival. Western civilisation was built on a tradition of classical education reaching back to ancient Athens, where the goal was to teach men to be active and responsible citizens of the polis. The content focused on the liberal arts of grammar, rhetoric, and logic, which were designed to help men think for themselves and express themselves with clarity. Plato and Aristotle expanded this approach to develop a form of higher education that was devoted to the search for the truth about human beings and the cosmos through the study of philosophy and science. This provided a model for the emergence of universities in Europe fifteen hundred years later.

Rome readily adopted the Greek approach to developing active citizens, but also gradually came under the influence of Christianity during the period of the empire. The union of the Christian Gospel with Greek philosophy, the marriage of faith and reason, of ethics and knowledge, inspired scholars in the monasteries to keep the ideal and the content of Western education alive during the Dark Ages, and to prepare the way for the flowering of Western intellectual life in medieval Europe. The recovery in the twelfth century of many ancient Greek texts, especially those of Aristotle, Ptolemy and Euclid, from the lands conquered by Islam, together with the impressive contributions of Arab philosophers such as Averroes and Avicenna, provided an impetus to learning and to the birth of modern science in the West, leading to the rise of great universities in Bologna, Paris and Oxford.

The significant point is that the new knowledge was accepted and assimilated. It presented a challenge to medieval Christian culture, causing resistance from those who feared for the integrity and indeed the survival of the society that had emerged from the savagery of the Dark Ages. Yet the new learning still prevailed and the foundations of the scientific and technological civilisation of modern Europe were laid, thanks mostly to the efforts of the Franciscan and Dominican mendicant teaching orders. Their commitment to the new learning sparked the transformation of medieval culture and is a striking example of how effective the low-profile leadership of humble teachers can be.

The rediscovery of Aristotle did, however, narrow the horizons of Western learning, by encouraging a focus on science. Though the ideals of the humanist tradition of classical learning were kept alive in medieval vernacular literature and the feudal courtly culture, it was the revival of Platonic studies and the rediscovery of Greek poetry and drama in the Italian Renaissance that showed the need for education to develop moral character as well as intellect. So strong was this commitment to the humanist tradition that even the socio-political cataclysm of the Protestant Reformation failed to shake it, and both sides in the religious dispute continued to build education on Christian principles, Latin grammar, and the reading of classic literature.

The scientific and technological revolutions that swept over Europe in the centuries that followed naturally inspired industrial, agrarian, and economic revolutions, and also encouraged an overly-optimistic rethinking of existing social and political arrangements. There were, inevitably, profound implications for educational theory, and these set the stage for ongoing controversies. The French Revolution and the Napoleonic Wars introduced the ideas of liberalism and romantic nationalism, and it was the latter that prevailed in the development of educational theory. Liberal humanism, which saw the purpose of learning as the acquisition of knowledge and the development of culture, still echoed the classic humanist learning of past eras, but the romantic nationalism that still influences our thinking to this day was intent on producing people passionate about serving their nation. Socialist thinkers were quick to pick up on the lesson, and the control of education has been a cornerstone of state policy ever since.

Science and technology, and the type of economy that develops around them, demand ever-increasing specialisation and vocational training. Both represent a narrowing of focus which is inconsistent with the educational ideal of developing the full potential of each individual person. Efficiency and productive routine are goals that primarily require non-thinking functionaries rather than free-thinking individuals. That business and governments, from capitalist to socialist, tend to favour control over freedom is not surprising. This has greatly intensified with the increasing global competition for resources and economic advantage. An uncompromising commitment to economic efficiency requires a culture that extols that goal as the chief good and citizens who accept it as the first principle in their lives. This has persuaded governments to expand their power and influence over society, which, more than anything else, explains the rapid extension of state control over education in the past two hundred years.

However, the assumption that vocational training promotes economic efficiency is misguided. Specialised vocational training at school, narrowly focused on equipping a young person to perform a particular function, is not a practical expedient because it produces only narrow-minded clones who are resistant to change and who will inevitably need to be retrained again and again in our rapidly changing technological economy. By contrast, schooling that seeks to set young people on the road to fulfilment as whole human beings, preparing them to go on learning throughout their lives, makes them more open to change and more capable of adapting themselves accordingly.

State schooling entails a small group of people deciding how the great mass of people will spend their lives, and it represents a contradiction of the principles of leadership and education presented in this book. Predictably, millions died as the misleaders of the last century drove their social engineering projects forward with a cruelty completely at odds with the humanist ideals expressed in the art and literature of Western civilisation. And the threat of this continuing remains with us. While a number of educated people might challenge it, the great majority of trained functionaries are easily manipulated by the misleaders.

At a time when the ethical foundations of Western civilisation have been undermined over several centuries, the present crisis of freedom and democracy is a crisis of a culture desperately in need of education and leadership.

EDUCATION AND THE POST-MODERN LEADERSHIP CRISIS

Culture at any level must carry within itself the seeds of regeneration to ensure its own survival, and it is the responsibility of all leaders — parents, teachers, community and business leaders, and politicians — to cultivate the new growth. In Western culture over the past two hundred years weeds have been deliberately strewn in among the crops, and those responsible for the proper cultivation of the crops have abdicated their responsibility, in many cases even collaborating with the destruction of the harvest.

The modern mindset boasted that humanity, guided by science and reason, would sweep aside tradition to create a new world of peace and prosperity in which there would be no human suffering. The bloodiest and most destructive century in history demolished that misguided claim and ushered in the pessimism of the post-modern era, in which it is evident that neither capitalism nor socialism, if cut adrift from traditional morality, offer any humane answer to the question of how we might best live together.

In authoritarian states, the masters employ violence as the means to remain in power; in the decadent democracies of the West, the political parties of the centre are intent on extending state control over all aspects of life, holding their citizens in a constant state of anxiety and dependence on an increasingly ineffectual officialdom. These misleaders from both authoritarian and democratic states know that a properly educated citizenry would quickly expose them as charlatans, so to look to the state for constructive educational reform is totally unrealistic.

State education worldwide has been an expensive failure in terms of inspiring and enabling young people to develop their full potential. Comparisons between textbooks from the beginning of the twentieth century and the end expose the startling decline in standards for mathematics and for English comprehension and expression; and statistics from various countries indicate that many young people fail to meet even the emaciated educational standards of today. A significant percentage leaves school functionally illiterate. What is more, the abandonment of history, geography and classic literature in the name of 'relevance' has been a catastrophe for recent generations, who are now largely compliant and complacent in their confinement within the walls of immediate experience, living their lives in a meaningless eternal present. It is hardly surprising that young people in the West are bored and frustrated, and easily seduced by the latest fad.

All this tallies with my own personal and professional experience. The decline in standards in the brief period between my own schooldays and the time when I started my teaching career was marked, and the fears I expressed for the future of education have been fully justified in the decades that followed. Standards fell steadily through the 30-year period during which my wife and I had at least one of our four children in school, and my friends in the teaching profession endorse my perceptions. In my years in advertising and marketing, and subsequently, I have worked with hundreds of highly intelligent young people whose paucity of knowledge about the world was tragic. The gaps are often incredible — I recently encountered a university lecturer who knew nothing about the French Revolution, and a first-year university student who had no idea who Plato was. Quintilian is to all intents and purposes unknown in post-modern society. And one especially talented young advertising copywriter I worked with was unable to participate in a brainstorming session when an analogy involving Macbeth was proposed.

State schooling has been successful in producing an anti-intellectual, uninformed, unimaginative, self-centred, self-indulgent, and subservient work-force; but creating easily-manipulated pawns is not education in any sense of the word. Post-modern state education is specialised, vocational, and propagandist because what started out as a sincere attempt to ensure equality of opportunity, proper preparation for participation in democratic institutions, and formation and selection for the working world, quickly became the machinery of control for big business and the political establishment. The argument against the misleadership evident in state schooling put forward by many respected educationists and economists over many decades is expressed with some vehemence by Walter E. Williams, an African American professor of economics, in his book *More liberty means less government*:

'Public education has been a success — not for parents and students but for teachers, administrators, support staff, and politicians. Adjusted for inflation, per-pupil spending has risen from $2000 in 1960 to $5200 in 1990. As a result teacher, administrator, and support staff salaries have significantly increased. The pay-off to politicians, who bilk the general public to channel billions of dollars each year to the education establishment, comes in the form of the votes and support of a well-organised, well-heeled, politically-savvy education lobby.'

The claim that state schooling is designed to deliver a culturally-neutral education for all in preparation for citizenship and the world of work simply does not stand up. Participation in and understanding of democratic institutions is pitiful, and tertiary institutions and employers from all sectors of the economy have deplored the deficiencies of state schooling for decades. Far from being culturally-neutral, state schooling in the Western world, aided and abetted by Hollywood and the media, aggressively promotes the values of the post-modern welfare state: cultural relativism, anti-intellectualism, dependency, self-gratification, promiscuity, and cynicism. This post-modern Western culture is the antithesis of pluralistic; it is one of the most homogeneous cultures encountered in the history of humankind. The worldwide antipathy towards globalisation rests largely on fears of the debasement of rich cultural traditions, and MacWorld is a devastatingly apt characterisation of the phenomenon. G. K. Chesterton, in *The Common Man*, made plain what today's so-called educational authorities try desperately to conceal:

'…every education teaches a philosophy; if not by dogma, then by suggestion, by implication, by atmosphere. Every part of that education has a connection with every other part. If it does not all combine to convey some general view of life, it is not an education at all.'

I must repeat that the general view of life promoted in the state school systems of the post-modern West is of a secular Utopia in which a benevolent state machine controls and rectifies any and all afflictions of the human condition. This vision is unscientific, ideological, intellectually restrictive, and utterly inimical to human fulfilment. It is at the very heart of the leadership crisis.

Reading as the essential foundation

The most important fruit of one's education is one's worldview, the understanding of life and the world that is constructed over time from diverse cultural sources. It is even more important than the ability to think, because it provides the framework for constructive thinking. From the moment we are born, before we can think rationally, we are exposed to multiple cultural influences and to the more developed worldviews, both positive and negative, of other people. By the time we are six years old and capable of reasoning, the foundations of our own worldview will already have been laid, through instinct, intuition, and experience, and the quality of that foundation will determine the soundness of the edifice we build through the rest of our lives.

In my own case, by age six my worldview was riven with contradictions: the virtues of love, honesty, courage, obedience and a solid work ethic were in conflict with the realities of racism, egoism, alcoholism, abuse, and violence. By the time I was old enough to ask "Why?", I found myself having to negotiate a life that I would in later years describe as an Escher woodcut, full of bizarre traps and disturbing inconsistencies.

Any worldview not open to the ongoing search for truth and dialogue with other worldviews is not a humane worldview. Respect for truth and for the dignity of all people is essential to the choice of civilisation over barbarism. Tampering even slightly with such respect results in determinism — nature red in tooth and claw — and in the heartless utilitarianism of the survival of the fittest. To paraphrase Teddy Roosevelt, this world will not be a good place for any of us unless it is a good place for all of us.

Reading good books is indispensable to the tasks of developing a humane worldview and expanding one's intellectual horizons, but what constitutes a 'good book' is highly controversial, and any attempt to draw up a canon of essential texts would be challenged. Nevertheless, in the process of making the case for reading as the essential activity in education, an understanding of what is meant by 'good books' will become clear. The historian and poet, Robert Conquest, eloquently made the basic point about the need to read in *Reflections on a Ravaged Century:*

'For people can be educated, cultured and so forth without having been to university at all — as with dozens from Benjamin Franklin to Winston Churchill, from William Shakespeare to Einstein, to say nothing of the great women writers of the nineteenth century. Nor is this only a matter of genius. Even erudition is possible outside academe, a point illustrated perfectly by Gibbon himself, the greatest of historians, who did indeed attend Oxford briefly when fifteen years old, from which (as he tells us) he got nothing. What all of them had was, in the first place, reading'.

Interestingly, rates of literacy in the United States were higher at the end of the colonial period than they have been at any time since the advent of state schooling. Regular reading from the family Bible and the dedicated work of religious schools produced a population that was both literate and readily disposed to question government authority. Thomas Jefferson, in a letter to John Tyler, could speak confidently of the way forward for the newly established nation:

'No experiment can be more interesting than that we are now trying, and which we trust will end in establishing the fact, that man may be governed by reason and truth. Our first object should therefore be, to leave open to him all the avenues to truth. The most effectual hitherto found, is the freedom of the press.'

Freedom of the press is meaningless, however, without a literate and educated population who are aware of the possibilities and pitfalls of the human condition by virtue of their familiarity with the ideas that have shaped civilisation. Democracy itself depends on it. It was the development of the printing press and the rapid spread of literacy that made possible the gradual growth of representative government. *The Intellectual Life of the British Working Classes,* by Professor Jonathan Rose of Drew University, provides evidence to demolish the arguments of modernists and post-modernists who attack classic literature. Speaking of the working class autodidacts of nineteenth century Britain, Rose affirms what the poet Matthew Arnold saw all too clearly:

'(Arnold) was right to suspect that individuals within that class were pursuing, in the face of intimidating obstacles, a liberal self-education much as Arnold would have understood the term. Their motives were

various, but their primary objective was intellectual independence. For centuries autodidacts had struggled to assume direction of their own intellectual lives, to become individual agents in framing an understanding of the world. They resisted ideologies imposed from above in order to discover for themselves the word of God, standards of beauty, philosophical truth, the definition of a just society. There is nothing distinctively 'bourgeois' in this desire for intellectual freedom. If anything, it may have been strongest in people who had spent their lives following orders and wanted to change that. More than a few members of the educated classes supported this movement, but many others treated it as a serious threat to their own social position — which, in an important sense, it was.'

Rose makes it clear that if these self-taught working class people had been asked for a list of great books, their answer would have been no different from that of educated people of the middle and upper classes. He tells of the workhouse laundress Catherine McMullen being led from the letters of Lord Chesterfield, through Chaucer, Erasmus, Donne, and Gibbon to become the most successful novelist in Britain; as Catherine Cookson, her books sold more than one hundred million copies, and accounted at one time for a third of all books loaned by British public libraries. The Labour politician J. R. Clynes drew the inspiration that took him to deputy leadership in the House of Commons from the works of Shakespeare, and was described by a friend as:

"...the only man who ever settled a trade dispute by citing Shakespeare."

Elizabeth Bryson, raised in poverty in Dundee, was driven by the ideas and fiery prose of Thomas Carlyle to strive for a university degree, and went on to become an eminent physician in New Zealand.

The examples of autodidacts in Rose's and many other scholarly books, as well as the lives of scholars and authors such as Joseph Conrad and Pitirim Sorokin, underline that they were not confined to Britain. Statistics provided by Rose from a 1940 survey — that is, from a time when educational reform along state school lines was already having a negative impact on Western culture — give an idea of what has been lost.

'Even more impressive is a 1940 survey of reading among pupils at non-academic high schools, where education terminated at age 14. This sample represented something less than the working-class norm: the best

students had already been skimmed off and sent to academic secondary schools on scholarship. Those who remained behind were asked which books they had read over the past month, excluding required texts. Even in this below-average group, 62 percent of boys and 84 percent of girls had read some poetry: their favourites included Kipling, Longfellow, Masefield, Blake, Browning, Tennyson, and Wordsworth. 67 percent of girls and 31 percent of boys had read plays, often something by Shakespeare. All told, these students averaged six or seven books per month. Compare that with the recent NEA study Reading at Risk: A Survey of Literary Reading in America, which found that in 2002, 43.4 percent of American adults had not read any books at all, other than those required for work or school. Only 12.1 percent had read any poetry, and only 3.6 percent any plays.'

This book does not attempt to provide answers to the educational issues facing Western civilisation, but the nature of education and the means of furthering it are fundamental to developing leadership. What we read determines the content of our education, and until we return to the discipline of reading the books that have stood the test of time and have proved to be relevant in all times and all places, we will not emerge from the leadership crisis. If I were asked to name just ten essential books for leaders, I would perhaps suggest:

1. The Bible
2. Plato's *Republic*
3. Aristotle's *Politics*
4. Virgil's *Aeneid*
5. Livy's *Early History of Rome*
6. Shakespeare's *Julius Caesar*
7. Swift's *Gulliver's Travels*
8. Dostoevsky's *The Devils*
9. Bruce Catton's *This Hallowed Ground*
10. Jacques Barzun's *From Dawn to Decadence*

If Barzun's book is considered too recent to be a classic, indulge my prophetic pretensions — I believe its relevance will extend well beyond this time and place. In a more ambitious attempt to indicate my view on the essential reading for leaders, I have written another book — *An Educational Bridge for Leaders* — which contains 80 short excerpts from what I consider to be illuminating texts.

THE LEADER AS AUTODIDACT

Reading good books is a necessary condition for proper education, and therefore for leadership, but it is not a sufficient condition. Reading alone will not provide a properly rounded education. What else should leaders do to further their education?

It is important to consider the *methods* of teaching in addition to the content. The various methodological approaches in education not only guide the leader as autodidact in improving his mind, but also in providing different approaches to motivating people and developing their potential. The three types of knowing discussed in an earlier chapter each require different approaches to teaching and learning. Knowing that, or knowledge of facts, requires a combination of exposition followed by question and answer sessions and research projects. Knowing how, or skills-based technical knowledge in carrying out some specified procedure, requires coaching — that is, theoretical and practical instruction, followed by disciplined drill and practice in the procedures of the skill being learned. Knowing what, or knowledge of the appropriate ethical, emotional, or strategic response in a given situation, requires discussion in the form of the Socratic dialogue or the Scholastic disputation.

An autodidact must compensate for the lack of a teacher by finding substitutes in the form of books and any experts that he can engage in focused conversation, or can listen to and question at public lectures. The importance of the Socratic dialogue to any form of understanding of meaning, value, and ethical implications indicates the need for such serious conversation. Coaching, on the other hand, is less of a challenge for the autodidact because practising skills and drilling oneself is entirely possible (Roger Federer proved this), although drawing on the knowledge, skill and discernment of other people is still important — none of us is self-sufficient.

Books remain the foundation of learning. All three types of learning need to be facilitated by the reading of appropriate books in preparation and follow-up research. The American pragmatist John Dewey gave currency to the idea of learning by doing, which has been misinterpreted in our post-modern era. Dewey encouraged giving learners as much practical experience as possible, but plainly included the practical intellectual skills of reading, writing, and calculating. Reading up on a topic after a talk, and then writing down what has been learned is excellent practical preparation for thinking for oneself and expounding one's own ideas on the subject. But the greatest value of reading will always be the opening up of new horizons.

What should you, the leader as autodidact, do to improve your mind and your ability to bring the best out in other people? My scepticism regarding formulae notwithstanding, I have a programme for autodidacts and teachers that I call STRETCH, which provides a useful guide. It stands for Search, Think, Read, Experience, Try, Converse and Help:

- **Search** — curiosity is the spark that ignites education, searching for the truth about things in this life and the world, and your part in it. Asking questions is fundamental to learning, and the most important question is always "Why?".
- **Think** — education is not just about knowledge; it is about applying knowledge and plumbing the depths of understanding, which requires serious thought. Become a visionary and ask yourself: "Why are things the way they are?" and "How should they be?" Find time for quiet reflection every day.
- **Read** — history and classic literature above all. Reading is essential. Suffice to say that without it you are starving your mind and making yourself more susceptible to the machinations of the misleaders.
- **Experience** — take in the rich cultural legacy in world literature, art, music, film, architecture, science, and technology. Take the time to allow these works to address your emotions and your intellect, and think about their meaning, inspiration, and origins.
- **Try** — have a go at painting a picture, performing in a play, writing poetry, mastering a musical instrument, making pottery, sky-diving, riding a horse, climbing a mountain, creating a garden, or just taking more walks to be alone with Nature. Go beyond the safe confines of your life as it is.
- **Converse** — this is not easy in our world, where most people merely report events and talk about their own narrow lives. Find friends or acquaintances you can engage in real conversation, free enough to flow spontaneously, but guided by the ethos of the Scholastic disputation, with all concerned committed to listening and understanding others.

- **Help others** — involving yourself in the needs of others is a well-trodden path to wisdom. The needs in every community are numerous and there are multiple ways in which you can make a difference. Volunteering makes a difference not only in the lives of the people you help, but also in your own personal growth.

STRETCH is a means to establishing a lifelong process of education and personal growth. But it has to become a way of life, a habit; it cannot be turned on and off according to how one feels.

THE CHALLENGE FOR LEADERSHIP — REGAINING THE INITIATIVE

It is a paradox and a challenge that to resurrect real leadership we need leaders to re-establish real education. W. Somerset Maugham, in *The Summing Up*, gave us an emphatic direction for education and culture:

'The value of culture is its effect on character. It avails nothing unless it ennobles and strengthens that. Its use is for life. Its aim is not beauty, but goodness.'

He might have added, of course, that one of the platforms Western culture has been built on is the Platonic notion that truth, beauty and goodness are intimately related. However, exposure to classic art and literature, philosophy, and history provides no guarantee that it will produce leaders, as shown by the Nazi functionaries who combined a taste for classical music with an ability to work in the death camps. And it is manifested in more mundane fashion in the lives of lawyers, doctors, teachers, and other putatively cultivated people who fail morally both as parents and as professionals.

But, though human nature and individual personality are obviously significant influences on human behaviour, the quality of education, and the worldview that is shaped by it, will always be crucial. The criteria for a humane worldview given in an earlier chapter are, not surprisingly, the guidelines for a sound education. Anyone who aspires to leadership must start from there, and build their own education so that they might help inspire the education of others. It is a practical requirement and a test of commitment. Misleadership would scorn it. Civilisation's only hope is that leadership regains the initiative.

Education, glib and undefined, is constantly held up by politicians, the media and social commentators, as the panacea for all our social or economic ills. But if education is not about defining reality and finding the truth about our lives in this world, then it offers nothing. It is a meaningless concept, and politicians should stop promising to cure society of all its maladies by throwing more money at a state schooling system that offers only further decline.

Fr. Piero Gheddo, Director of *Mondo e Missione* and *Italia Missionaria*, a man who knows the suffering and the urgent needs of the poverty-stricken peoples of the Third World better than most Westerners, exposed the hypocrisy of the developed world in fueling the ongoing tragedy in Africa and other parts of the globe, in an interview with Zenit:

'Development is not only a technical and economic event, but stems above all from culture, from education: It is the work of individuals and not of money, it comes from people and not from machines, it is born through education, which is, however, a long, patient process, not accomplished by emergency interventions, but by living together with a people. We Westerners do very little for the education of poor peoples, and we never hear of the role of cultural and religious values that lead to development: It is a topic that is ignored by the mass media and the Western "experts" that favour economic and technical aid.'

The lesson for all those who aspire to genuine leadership is clear. We are not developing leaders because we are not cultivating the fulfilment of all human beings; in other words, because we are not truly educating people. There is no more eloquent way to conclude this discourse than with a quote taken from an address by Baroness Caroline Cox in 2009 on *What is at stake,* in which she reported the words of a man named Dinka, a tribal chief in Sudan:

"You gave us education. That gave us freedom to think for ourselves. You cannot give a greater freedom than that."

CHAPTER 7
UNDERSTANDING HUMAN NATURE

"I myself have become for me a profound question." St. Augustine

WHY ARE WE SHOCKED?

The historian Robert Bartlett recounts in *The Making of Europe* the story of an eleventh century dispute over booty between a group of Norman soldiers of fortune and the Greeks they were helping in the struggle against the rising tide of Islam. The Normans were notorious for their violent behaviour and were described by an Italian prince as "a savage, barbarous, and horrible race of inhuman disposition". When the Greek envoy entered the Norman camp to negotiate, he left his horse in the care of one of the mercenaries, who stood fondling the horse's head while the talks proceeded nearby. Suddenly, the Norman punched the horse's neck and the animal fell to the ground barely conscious. The shocked envoy was given an excellent replacement for his loss, but the message was clear: indiscriminate violence was a distinct possibility unless the Normans got their way.

The really interesting thing about the story is its ability to shock us as much as it disturbed the Italian prince who labelled such acts as inhuman. Are they really inhuman? Or are such acts all too characteristic of human beings? Names like Vendee, Nanking, Auschwitz, Gulag, Sharpeville, Belfast, My Lai, Cambodia, Rwanda, Darfur and the Twin Towers — the list is near endless — testify to the fact that the Normans were not some kind of human aberration.

Similar stories of violence appear in our daily news. A slighted teenager drives a car into a crowd of revellers; a rising teenage sports star kicks his ex-girl-friend in the stomach to terminate her pregnancy; a university lecturer murders his girlfriend, stabbing her two hundred and sixteen times, and then pleads that he was "provoked". Moreover, the public appetite for sado-masochism, as demonstrated by the violence depicted gratuitously in the media, calls into question the psychological state of our entire society.

Violence is by no means the only disturbing element in the human condition. The propensity of human beings for embracing irrational ideas, as in the cases of the followers of the Reverend Jim Jones of Jonestown and the adherents of the Moonie cult, would be less troubling if they were isolated social phenomena, but history is full of this type of behaviour. The current obsession with celebrity and the idolisation of the rich and famous, leads to lives wasted in triviality. The credulity of supposedly enlightened people in the face of silly and dishonest advertising is of serious concern and is ironic, given their contempt for the alleged gullibility of past ages.

Examples of human perversity are common: an eminent philosopher descends into madness, writing discourses that will obsess people around the world for the next century and beyond; an American president puts his family, his administration, and the country at risk for the sake of a tawdry sexual encounter. And no one has to look far to find similar sagas in their own lives or the lives of people close to them. Consider a self-assured, middle-aged man at the top of his profession, married, well-respected, and popular with his colleagues and clients, and with a reputation as a no-nonsense manager who has high expectations for his people — seemingly a model of success in his private and professional life. Then he is exposed as a participant in an internet pornography ring. His marriage breaks down, he loses his job and his pension, and he is sent to prison. What demons led him to endanger all the good things in his life for squalid self-gratification? The human condition is perplexing — we are, in every time and place, paradoxical.

But why are we shocked by these human realities? It is because we expect better of ourselves as human beings. We are not like other animals. We submit our every action to judgment and are aware of the tug of conscience in our lives — even hardened criminals try to justify themselves. G. K. Chesterton was typically astute when he reminded us that one thing we all agree on is that human beings are not what they were meant to be. This raises the important question of what we mean when we talk about human nature, because it must obviously include the capacity to go against our animal urges. The implications for leadership loom large.

LEADERSHIP AND THE SCIENCE OF HUMAN NATURE

If leadership is about people, then leading like you mean it logically requires a leader to be very knowledgeable about people in general, and about him or herself in particular, and wise in dealing with others. This means a leader has to be a dedicated student of human nature — something of an amateur, but well-informed, psychologist. As Henry Adams said in *The education of Henry Adams*:

'Knowledge of human nature is the beginning and end of political education.'

The old imperative of the Delphic Oracle, 'know thyself', is in fact what people naturally try to do, consciously or sub-consciously, effectively or otherwise. The answers that people give to their own psychological questions "Why am I so sad?", "What made me so angry?", "What will make me happy?" and "What is my life all about?" tell us something not only about the people themselves but also about human nature — what it means to be human. What makes psychology unique among the sciences is that it involves the knower trying to know himself. The scientist becomes the object of his own inquiry. This makes it the one science where we actually start with some valuable inside knowledge — often deceptive and easily misinterpreted to be sure — but revealing insights nonetheless. Yet this produces a paradox — that the one earthly creature equipped to know things far transcending his terrestrial home, seems unable to answer the riddle of his own existence. And we have been trying since the dawn of civilisation. Pascal gave the mystery classic expression in *Pensees*:

'What a chimera then is man! What a novelty! What a monster, what a chaos, what a contradiction, what a prodigy! Judge of all things, imbecile worm of the earth, depository of truth, a sink of uncertainty and error; the pride and refuse of the universe.'

This conundrum has weighed even more heavily on humankind over the past century as awe-inspiring material progress has coincided with cruelty of epic proportions. The failure of leadership in the twentieth century was the result of a tragic misreading of human nature.

WHAT IS IT THAT MAKES US DIFFERENT?

Trying to understand human nature and what it is that elevates us above the animal world has exercised the greatest minds in history.

Plato and Aristotle were convinced it was the power of reason that made us different, a view endorsed by later philosophers including Thomas Aquinas and Kant, who discerned a radical distinction between rational thinking and sense perception, that is, between conceptual and perceptual thought. Others, notably Hobbes, Berkeley and Hume, denied any such distinction, going so far as to reject the whole notion of abstract thought or the power of generalisation — the human ability to see the universal in the particular, using classifications like dogs, trees, and houses to understand the nature of different aspects of the world around us. The roots of their thinking went back to the nominalist philosophy of William of Ockham, who regarded any such universal concepts as mere names and not realities. For Ockham, any talk of pigs in general was nothing more than a convenient mental construct; for him it only made sense to talk of the particular beast in its concrete existence. The consequences of this controversy were significant, if only because it undermined the concept of human nature, stating that the only reality is the individual and his particular acts and feelings.

The common sense of the ordinary person in the street is justifiably dismayed by this kind of philosophical flummery. Nonetheless, nominalism fuelled the rampant individualism of today through philosophies trumpeting the sovereignty of the will of the individual, which inevitably erodes respect for other people. The most notorious of these philosophies, Nietzsche's will to power, influenced communism, Nazism, fascism and the existentialist ideas that encouraged such regimes as the Khmer Rouge in Cambodia, along with the less sensational but still terribly destructive undermining of personal relationships in the West today.

Nietzsche continues to be influential on both sides of the political spectrum, and large numbers of prominent writers, scientists, and academics embrace these views. Leadership, in the sense of helping people to be the best they can be, will never issue from such philosophies, only misleadership.

Returning to the distinction between man and animals, the debate ranges between those who see human nature as having the potential for the good life in community, and those who see it as "nature red in tooth and claw", which demands ways to ensure that individuals submit to social conventions. Hobbes, Adam Smith, Rousseau, and many others had their say, but it was Alexis de Tocqueville, picking up on a thread that runs through Plato, Aristotle and the Judeo-Christian tradition, who proposed that the real point of difference was that human beings worked to improve themselves throughout life.

This is an enormously important insight; but why do we seek to improve ourselves? Quite simply, it is because we have beliefs. Animals are locked into the here and now of immediate necessity, and act on instinct, without ever questioning their motives in behaving as they do. Human beings, on the other hand, live a life that far transcends present necessity, reaching back into a historical past and forward to an imaginable future. Our rationality does not exclude irrational impulses and non-rational decision-making and we all seem incapable of ever being satisfied with the way things are. We constantly change things in the belief that we will make them better. We believe we can improve on nature.

Our beliefs are intangible, fallible, often capricious, and even dangerous, though they can also be noble, far transcending any physical reality we have ever encountered, as for example when people talk about universal peace. We value some beliefs and condemn others because the human experience tells us that these abstract realities often have the power to dramatically influence our physical reality. The magnificent Rheims cathedral was built not by experts, but by the common folk of the town as a result of their belief; the current socio-economic transformations of China, India, Russia, and Brazil are being driven by beliefs, as is Islamic terrorism, and the demographic and cultural malaise in Western countries. What we ultimately do about climate change — if there is anything we can do — will be based on what people believe. Beliefs change our lives, and affect the lives of every other creature on the planet. And they provide irrefutable evidence of our human nature. It is hardly surprising that for ordinary people unencumbered by the intellectual perversities of academia, the reality of human nature and its potential for good or evil is patently obvious. And we ignore the lessons of past millennia at our peril.

A PRACTICAL GUIDE TO HUMAN NATURE

In *The Paideia Proposal* Mortimer Adler sets out some significant facts about human beings:

'Of all the creatures on earth, human beings are the least specialised in anatomical equipment and in instinctive modes of behaviour. They

are, in consequence, more flexible than other creatures in their ability to adjust to the widest variety of environments and to rapidly changing external circumstances. They are adjustable to every clime and condition on earth and perpetually adjustable to the shock of change.'

However, this merely scratches the surface of what we can say with real assurance about all human beings in all times and all places. If we take ten human babies, a mix of male and female from ten different cultures, and consider their future development, we can confidently predict, assuming they grow up to be reasonably healthy adults, that they will all:

- depend on the long-term devotion of adults for survival and development,
- move, to some degree or other, towards the fulfilment of their unique potential,
- experience the desire for affection, knowledge, achievement and affirmation,
- acquire language skills and reasoning capabilities, both abstract and sense-based,
- feel pain, both physical and mental, and reflecting on that pain, experience suffering,
- experience the hormonal upheaval and identity crisis of the teenage years,
- depend on the quality of education they receive for their development,
- have relationships, good and bad, with many other human beings,
- be affected by love (or its absence) from parents, siblings, friends, spouses, or lovers,
- want the exclusive commitment of a chosen mate, and children,
- experience insatiable yearning and the need for meaning and purpose,
- fear death, even though they know that all humans die.

Then take ten babies from ten different cultures two thousand years ago, and the same confident predictions would apply. Cultures may change, but human nature is a constant.

We can all, therefore, confidently expect to find common cause to some degree or other with all other human beings. The only conditions are a mutual acknowledgement that human nature is an objective reality, and a common commitment to finding the truth about ourselves and our world. This is a crucially important point because it establishes that there can be, for example, meaningful dialogue between Islamic groups and the West, given goodwill on both sides.

What then are the qualities of human nature, the factors that produce a creature destined for the experiences listed above?

1. **Self-consciousness** is the starting point. While consciousness is a fact in the lives of animals, in human beings it appears to operate on a different level, one involving awareness of the self. Self-consciousness is the reflexive, as distinct from reflective, power of the mind to understand, judge, and reason about its own acts, to know that it knows. Without the self-consciousness or self-knowledge of human beings, our planet would simply be a world of biological determinism operating at the animal level. From the start, it is apparent that we have an affinity with truth; to know that we are able to know reality implies meaning and purpose in the cosmos which we feel compelled to discover.

2. **Identity** flows from self-consciousness. The human being becomes an 'I' confronting the 'other', and identifies himself or herself as a unique individual. The 'self' identified is also aware of the framework of time and change, of past, present, and future. This phenomenon is the foundation of the human conundrum, the riddle of our origin and our destiny, and underlies our persistent need for self-esteem and the recognition of our worth on the part of others. Identity is a profoundly mysterious concept, as can be seen from a human version of the old riddle of the bicycle that over time has all its parts replaced, raising the question of whether or not it is still the same two-wheeler. Since the cells of our bodies are constantly being replaced, and the changes in our appearance and capabilities are plain to see, what in fact constitutes our identity? To whom does it belong? This has given rise to the philosophical quest to understand the human soul. In Book Four of *Republic*, Plato explained the human soul as being composed of intellect, passion and appetite. Thymos, the emotional part, which gives rise to fear and anger, came to be understood by later philosophers and psychologists as the human desire for recognition — we all

want who we are to be recognised and esteemed by others. Ernest Becker, in his Pulitzer Prize-winning book, *The Denial of Death*, explained this in terms of an urge to be heroic:

'An animal who gets his feeling of worth symbolically has to minutely compare himself to those around him, to make sure he does not come off second best. Sibling rivalry is a critical problem that reflects the basic human condition. It is not that children are vicious, selfish, domineering. It is that they so openly express man's tragic destiny: he must desperately justify himself as an object of primary value in the universe; he must stand out, be a hero, make the biggest possible contribution to world life, show that he counts more than anything or anyone else.'

3. **Free will** is the faculty that enables human beings to choose what to do and what not to do. It is the quality that renders us responsible for self-realisation; in other words, we have to accept what is given to us existentially, but are then free to make of ourselves what we will. Free will empowers us to change not only the physical realities of the natural world around us but also the biological realities of our selves, as when we choose to control our animal aggression or selfish instincts in the interests of what we understand to be higher claims to our allegiance.

4. **Intellect** lifts us above raw intelligence, or sense perception, memory and imagination. Intellect is the faculty of creative, conceptual, abstract knowing that provides the myriad possibilities for our free will to choose from, and is given expression in the multiplicity of human cultures and the achievements of science and technology. Again it must be emphasised that knowing, or having knowledge, means being in possession of the truth, understanding the reality of things. Our intellect, or the ability to know things in ways not given to other sentient creatures, therefore presupposes the whole idea of truth. The Jewish philosopher Martin Buber commented on the perversion of this human quality in his book *Good and Evil*:

'The lie is our very own invention, different in kind from every deceit that the animals can produce. A lie was possible only after a creature, man, was capable of conceiving the being of truth. It was possible only as directed against the conceived truth. In a lie, the spirit practices treason against itself.'

5. **Language** is the mysterious gift that enables the development of intellect. Despite the advances of modern linguistics, the mystery of the human ability for language has not been fathomed, All 'primitive' languages have been found to be built on syntactic structures as complex as those of any modern language. Language has been aptly described as a means of communicating something understood to someone capable of understanding, and it belongs to one specific species. It extends man's power of abstract thinking and analysis, enabling the processing of thought in logical sequences; it makes dialogue possible, opening the way for the self to pose the inevitable "Why?" to other human beings; this in turn leads to the human proclivity for giving reasons for actions taken, and therefore for morality and accountability in human relations.

6. **Belief** naturally arises from intellect, the power to know things and their potential. Belief, well-founded or otherwise, is a response to the "Why?" of our existence. We cannot not have beliefs. They shape human behaviour and culture, and consequently the world at large. Many are inspired by the sense of awe we experience in the face of the mysterious, as well as the angst arising from our existential dilemma, and the seemingly inexplicable yearning for we-know-not-what. The angst and the yearning can obviously be both cause and effect of negative as well as positive belief. Whatever the truth may be about us, we all somehow seem to seek fulfilment beyond our immediate achievements and circumstances, manifesting a desire to transcend a world where every attraction sooner of later proves ephemeral. We all have, it seems, an affinity with the infinite.

7. **Relationships** also distinguish human society from the animal world. Because we are rational creatures, our relationships must be built on truth, without which trust is impossible and the relationship becomes dysfunctional. The nature of human relationships will be considered in a later chapter, but we should note here that all individual human beings are confronted with a clear choice. If we choose to operate on the level of nature and the beasts, the results will be catastrophic because of the destructive capacity of our science and technology, however primitive or advanced it may be. On the other hand, we have the faculties that equip us to go against nature. Humans are the first and only

animal challenged by the concept of 'ought' in how they deal with others. And more than any other quality, it is the way we conduct our relationships with our fellows that determines our humanity.

These seven qualities provide the basis for an understanding of human nature and its potential for both good and evil. However, 'good' and 'evil' are themselves value judgments made by human beings, and in the climate of relativism in our world, many academics and other people would deny that they have any objective meaning. However, leadership, as opposed to misleadership, is not possible without the ability to identify and promote the good, and oppose what is evil. To do so requires that the understanding of human nature be taken further by exploring the concept of personhood.

PERSONALITY — WHAT IT MEANS TO BE A PERSON

What is meant by the word 'person'? The dictionary tells us that a person is a human being as opposed to an animal or a thing. Why do we need this additional descriptive of 'person' over and above that of 'human being'?

Our word 'person' derives from the ancient Greek 'prosopon' and the Latin 'persona', both of which originally signified the mask worn by an actor, and the etymology has deeper implications, which will be looked at in the chapter on relationships. For now we need only note that the word came to signify an individual with a particular role to play in the drama of life. Later, Roman law made 'person' a legal concept, the possessor of specific legal rights and duties. The Christian doctrine of the Trinity, God as three persons in one divine nature, put forward the promise of the perfectibility of humankind in community through the love of God, establishing firmly the meaning of the word for over a thousand years. Then the modernist thinkers of the Enlightenment looked for ways to understand personhood in supposedly more rational and scientific terms. This commendable curiosity unfortunately ignored the fact that personhood or personality is a philosophical or legal concept, while the idea of a human being is the scientific counterpart. Science has a great deal more it can discover about human nature, but we have to rely on our metaphysical resources to decide what it means to be a person.

Over the course of the modern era the concept of human nature was gradually pushed aside in favour of the existential fact of the individual person, increasingly understood as the autonomous 'self' seeking 'authenticity'. In time, Sartre, among others, could plausibly define personality as something each of us has to invent for ourselves.

This led to the self-absorbed individualism that makes for precarious relationships, and to presumption and despair. For generations, people have been encouraged to see themselves as separate and responsible only for self-fulfilment, and to loudly insist on their personal rights rather than their human rights, forgetting that without the latter, the former have no philosophical justification.

The quest for self-fulfilment has led to a marked increase in the incidence of mental disorder and social pathology. It has given rise to what has been labelled the 'pastiche personality', described by Kenneth J. Gergen in his 1991 book *The Saturated Self: Dilemmas of Identity in Contemporary Life:*

'The pastiche personality is a social chameleon, constantly borrowing bits and pieces of identity from whatever sources are available and constructing them as useful or desirable in a given situation.'

The pastiche personality precludes the possibility of personal integrity, preventing human beings from finding self-fulfilment. However, this search for what it means to be a person has led back to an explanation of why personality is a complementary concept to that of a human being. 'Human being' emphasises our participation in the fellowship of humankind; 'personality' emphasises our unique potential to play a particular role in the drama of life. Neither is dispensable as each defines an aspect of being human.

As previously stated, the quality that sets us apart from other creatures is the potential to rise above our animal nature and to become something better. This was seen by Martin Buber and expressed in his classic work *Good and Evil:*

'In a period of evolution, which generally coincides with puberty without being tied to it, the human person inevitably becomes aware of the category of possibility, which of all living creatures is represented just in man, manifestly the only one for whom the real is continually fringed by the possible. The evolving human person I am speaking of is bowled over by possibility as an infinitude. The plenitude of possibility floods over his small reality and overwhelms it.'

As packets of potential we are always a work in progress, always at a stage in the journey to true fulfilment. Plato saw the origin of our condition in the attraction we feel for the true, the good, and the beautiful. He said we are emotionally unsettled when we experience beauty because we have lost the perfection intended for ourselves, and our lives have become an endless quest to somehow retrieve it. The inexplicable longing for a fulfilment we cannot define for ourselves makes every encounter with beauty a disturbing reminder that something is missing in our lives. Beauty challenges our complacency and compels us to use our human creativity to achieve the wholeness we yearn for.

This is related to our affinity for truth, our deep dissatisfaction, and our yearning for the good. And so arises the peculiar form of purpose known only to human beings as individuals, as persons.

The purpose goes beyond immediate needs; it is transcendental, calling us to be what we are not at the present moment. The old quest for authenticity that dominated so many lives throughout the nineteenth and twentieth centuries was at least an admission that we are not what we were meant to be, which is why we admire and idolise other human beings who we identify, often erroneously, with the true, the good and the beautiful. The young child copies his father in speech, behaviour and tastes; the U2 fan dresses like Bono, cultivating his hairstyle and mannerisms; the ambitious young executive mimics the behaviour of his ruthless CEO; the sincere Buddhist emulates his master; and the committed Christian strives in imitation of Christ.

We have already considered the reality that all people are religious about something; it is interesting to further reflect on the fact that what we worship is what we want to be like. As we are told in Matthew 6: 21:

'For where your treasure is, there your heart will be also.'

What we choose to regard as our treasure is an intensely personal, sovereign decision that only we as individuals can make, even when we are influenced or coerced by others. Inevitably we can all make bad choices, and the first and most elementary error we can make is to settle for a purpose less than transcendental. The British essayist Theodore Dalrymple, who as a doctor dedicated himself for many years to the treatment of mental disorder and social dysfunction, is quite emphatic on the matter in his books *Life at the Bottom* and *Our culture* – what's left of it. A declared non-believer himself, Dalrymple makes clear that without a transcendent purpose, material comforts will not prevent the slide into boredom and social dysfunction.

There is an intimate link between the unique potential of the individual human being, deeply conscious of his exclusive identity, and the singular transcendent purpose, within the context of community, to which he feels called. And this is the basis of personhood or personality, as distinct from 'character'.

Before the next two chapters, which deal with character and with the dynamics of human relations respectively, a brief review of the development of personality and its component parts is appropriate (see Figure 7.1).

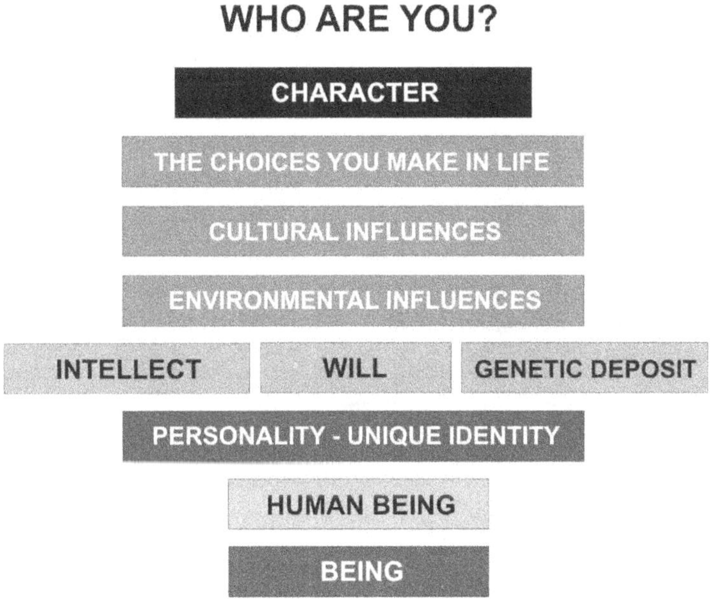

WHO ARE YOU?

CHARACTER

THE CHOICES YOU MAKE IN LIFE

CULTURAL INFLUENCES

ENVIRONMENTAL INFLUENCES

INTELLECT — WILL — GENETIC DEPOSIT

PERSONALITY - UNIQUE IDENTITY

HUMAN BEING

BEING

Figure 7.1

Our starting point is being (at the bottom of Figure 7.1). I am — that is, I exist, or have being. The kind of being I am is a human being. It follows from this that I am also a person, a distinct personality, a particular identity, with a unique genetic deposit, a free will, and an intellect that allows me to understand concepts, judge ideas and facts, and reason about cause and effect. This defines the potential I possess from the start of my life in terms of intelligence, sense perception, physical stature and prowess, emotional and affective disposition, and somatic urges. Exerting pressure from all sides on my personality are the complicating external factors of environmental and cultural influences, completing the framework in which I am called to make the daily choices that will determine the shape of my character, or the stamp that I put on my personality by virtue of my own free will.

The complex and dynamic interplay between all these elements makes a mockery of this or any other formulaic description of human psychology, and character itself becomes a factor in shaping personality. But too many textbooks and treatises, and even dictionaries, fail to make the distinction between personality and character, and consequently confuse the issue of personal development. This simple matrix is intended merely as a guide and a means to avoid this confusion.

THE IMPLICATIONS FOR LEADERSHIP

As a person I am aware of the fact that my universe is inhabited by other human beings to whom it is only reasonable to accord the status of personhood as well. My life is inescapably one of relationships, and whilst this essential aspect of being human is dealt with in depth further on, we should at least note here that identity and meaning can be developed in no other framework. Our destiny is forged in the heart of community with other human beings. In the words of Martin Buber, again writing in *Good and Evil*:

'Man as man is an audacity of life, undetermined and unfixed; he therefore requires confirmation, and he can naturally only receive this as an individual man, in that others and he himself confirm him in his being-this-man. Again and again the Yes must be spoken to him, from the look of the confidant and from the stirrings of his own heart, to liberate him from the dread of abandonment, which is a foretaste of death.'

From these relationships the idea of personal responsibility emerges quite naturally, as does the notion of morality. The philosopher Hans Jonas pointed out that responsibility — that is, the acting out of respect for the rights of others — is the core concept in ethics. This would indicate that human freedom, essential to personal identity, can only grow in proportion to the extent that responsibility is present. Jonas, along with Alasdair MacIntyre and other thinkers, is suggesting that whatever way we look at it, we are dependent on and responsible for other people. The implications for leadership are plain. All human beings as persons are accountable for what they do and the impact it has on others. If leadership means inspiring and enabling growth in others for the good of the community, then all of us are required to exercise self-leadership in the first instance. That, of course, is a salutary reminder that education, a process only persons can undertake, is a responsibility and not a privilege.

THE ESSENTIAL MYSTERY

The science behind our understanding of human nature and the philosophy of personality nevertheless still leave us with an incomplete picture of ourselves. Everyday concepts — such as zero or nothing, being and non-being, infinity, life, consciousness, and purpose — remain profoundly mysterious, with self-consciousness the most unsettling.

What do we mean when we talk about 'my left foot' or 'my brain' or 'my feelings' or 'my thoughts'? Who am I? The mystery of body and soul is impenetrable. Albert Einstein was frank in his admission that science could never explain the universal human experience of the 'now', a basic concept profoundly elusive for proponents of artificial intelligence. Science still has possibilities that are awe-inspiring, but like all human capabilities, it also has its limits. Stephen Hawking has retreated from his prediction that a grand unified theory of everything was only a matter of time. Those who scoff at mystery, who speak not as men and women of science but as proponents of the philosophy of scientism, have not even resolved the private issues of their own personalities. Through the intellectual decisions called beliefs, they, like the rest of us, are obliged to take a stand on how they intend to conduct themselves in relation to external reality, including other human beings. And that is inescapably an act of faith.

Looking at my own intellectual development, I see that despite all the knowledge I have accumulated in my search for a broader understanding of life, I am confronted by unfathomable mystery when I try to answer Kant's three questions. The only intellectually satisfying, and indeed existentially practical solution to self-knowledge I have found is in my faith. No doubt this is why the majority of humankind is still committed to one or other of the great religious traditions.

In this regard, the practices of the Nazi regime were revealing. Following the Wehrmacht's invasion of Poland in 1939, special SS brigades were sent in to slaughter Jews, community leaders, and others who might have organised resistance. Significantly, in order to gain promotion, all senior officers in the SS had been required to renounce their religion.

Before they could be dispatched to commit these inhuman acts, they had to have their own humanity dismantled, and the removal of belief in transcendental truth was the essential starting point.

Many atheist authors, including Richard Dawkins and Christopher Hitchens, would argue that religion has been and is still the cause of terrible violence. Predictably, they cite the Crusades, witch-burnings, and Jihad amongst other events. However, their logic is flawed and their arguments specious: religion, just like science, can be perverted and abused by the misguided and the malevolent. The development of cruel and destructive weaponry for killing fellow human beings and the irresponsible methods of exploiting the environment are just two of the abuses of science in our time. Religion, science, and all other human pursuits can be used for evil or for good, but in themselves they are neutral — it is human nature that holds the key to how they will be developed and deployed.

If human nature is a myth, as Sartre suggested, if there is no essential truth about human beings, then concepts like equality, justice, and freedom lose all meaning. In this sense, it is the truth that sets us free. Wherever falsehood reigns, there is only misleadership — the tyranny, exploitation, manipulation, and human degradation that has characterised many governments worldwide in the past century.

Leadership as defined in this book is entirely consistent with empirically verifiable human nature and personality in that it is always ready to ask the existential "Why?" and the creative "What if?". Those are the questions that constantly remind us of the awesome responsibilities we bear in this strange and beautiful cosmos.

CHAPTER 8
BUILDING CHARACTER

"We cannot remake ourselves without suffering; for we are both the marble and the sculptor."
Alexis Carrel, Nobel Prize winner for Medicine

MAKING A STAMP ON WHO WE ARE

Having a firm mental grasp of human nature and personality is essential for effective leadership, but understanding what human beings do with the inherent potential is even more important. The way we use the advantages of our human nature and the unique genetic deposit given to each of us determines our character, the self-chosen stamp we put on our developing personality. And though personality and character are always forged in the furnace of social frameworks, with the influence of others intruding at every point, in the final analysis the shape of character is inevitably a matter of personal responsibility.

Misleaders would dispute this as they regard human beings as malleable and manipulable, to be shaped into whatever they require for their projected schemes. The Russian novelist Chingiz Aitmatov once related how Stalin ordered a live chicken to be brought to him and how he stripped the terrified and pain-stricken bird of its feathers in front of his cronies. He then placed it on the floor, took some bread crumbs in his hand, and enjoyed the amazement of his lackeys when the injured chicken staggered after him when he moved. Stalin told the meeting that people could be ruled the same way — by controlling them through fear and food.

He ignored the countless examples of resistance to tyranny, from Thermopylae to the Battle of Britain, and among the millions of his own people whom he chose to murder or incarcerate in the Gulag archipelago. That many others failed to oppose the evil of the Stalin regime should not be too hastily condemned, but rather remembered with compassion, bearing in mind the unconscionable violence unleashed on people in that brutal system. The historian Robert Conquest, in *Reflections on a Ravaged Century*, shows how the inhuman treatment perverted the character of perpetrators and victims alike. He quotes the British author Edward Crankshaw, who had first-hand experience of the social impact of Stalin's '*Utopia*':

> 'This is a milieu almost impossible for the foreigner to present to his own countrymen. I have had to work with such officials in war and peace. Their sycophancy, their barefaced lying, their treachery, their cowardice, are so blatant, their ignorance so stultifying, their stupidity so absolute, that I have found it impossible to convey it with any credibility to those fortunate enough to never have encountered it.'

Ultimately, we are all what we choose to be, and the harmful consequences of imprudent or perverse choice are plain for all to see in a world struggling for answers about the human condition. Two case studies from my files illustrate the centrality of character in shaping the lives of individuals and communities. In each case, names and certain other particulars have been changed.

CHARACTER COUNTS

Andrew was a successful advertising executive who was headhunted to work closely with me and my creative team on a major multinational account. He was highly experienced, knowledgeable, urbane, charming, and easy to like. The clients responded with enthusiasm to his appointment, and I felt sure that he would be an excellent colleague, and even a good friend. However, within the first month, cracks began to show.

Many years later, I reflected on something Andrew had confided to me over a drink one evening. He told me that he had a morbid fear of losing his earning capacity and being reduced to living as a "bum". This largely explained what followed.

David, the agency CEO, was a misleader — sly, spiteful, and a bully; and in Andrew he found someone vulnerable to his aggression and his whim. After a few client meetings, Andrew's deference to David had already alerted the senior executives of our major account that the former carried no real authority, and that their main contact at the agency should be the boss. Andrew's considerable abilities were insufficient to save him from a de facto demotion to the status of an always amenable messenger, and, hounded by his fear of financial catastrophe, he tried slavishly to please his boss.

Subsequently, frustrated by developments, I chose to leave the agency. Andrew stayed on until the agency fell to a hostile takeover and he was one of the many casualties. A man well qualified to make a success of any marketing enterprise, he had wasted four years pandering to someone of greatly inferior ability. However, he then took up another senior position at a well-respected multinational agency. Unfortunately, Simon, the CEO there, exhibited many of David's character flaws.

Andrew again found himself playing the roles of emissary and gopher for his distinguished boss, who even sported with his employees outside of normal working hours. For example, Andrew would occasionally receive evening phone calls from Simon, summoning him to provide menial assistance in some domestic issue such as repairing a defective awning in a rainstorm while his boss continued entertaining guests. Andrew could have resigned to make a better career elsewhere but his fears held him back.

Then Simon suddenly disappeared, reportedly taking off to some South East Asian destination, and the agency collapsed soon afterwards. I tried to help Andrew secure a new position, but was caught unawares when he unexpectedly accepted a job offer that had come out of the blue from an agency in Kuala Lumpur. It seems his greatest need was for someone to protect him from his fear of destitution.

The second, contrasting, case concerned Naran, a man placed in my leadership programme by his general manager, who hoped to persuade Naran that he had done the right thing by withdrawing a spur-of-the-moment resignation. Naran was a highly-qualified scientist who exemplified the social isolation that many creative people drift into. Wrapped up in his own work, he gave the impression of aloofness, and he was having difficulty working effectively with other people in the laboratories. The 360-degree assessment prepared for him prior to the leadership programme was brutally disparaging. He was apparently impatient and intolerant of failure in his peers and the people who reported to him, and the lack of respect he showed for them had created many enemies; a staff petition had led to the loss of his team management responsibilities. He was now working alone, interacting with others only as and when it was necessary.

Naran was very reticent in the first seminar, but he was plainly a decent man who had for understandable, if not justifiable, reasons allowed a debilitating alienation to develop between him and the people he was meant to work with. His disdain and intolerance for others, perhaps unconscious but still reprehensible, was now being returned with a vengeance. The seminar led him to reflect on his position and he sincerely regretted his failure to provide the leadership with which he had been entrusted.

Naran willingly shouldered the blame for the situation, even though his peers and team members bore some responsibility too. Refusing to excuse his failings by reference to the short-comings of other people, he seemed genuinely inspired to try to change the way he conducted himself in relations with others.

The rapid transformation Naran brought about in himself was astonishing and helped spark an equally unexpected willingness on the part of his colleagues to start afresh. Reportedly, he became committed to helping people with their needs and was always open to the ideas of others. He had become what he had always had the potential to be — an inspirational leader, even though he no longer had a team.

Within a short time, however, he was installed as leader of an expanded team, and at the company's annual conference, almost six months to the day after the first leadership seminar, he was awarded a prize for outstanding leadership within the organisation. Naran, through difficult choices made in uncomfortable circumstances, had driven the change, rebuilding his character to become an effective leader.

Suffering and redemption

The lives of the hundreds of people on my leadership programme all reflect to some degree or other the central themes of the stories of Andrew and Naran: suffering and redemption. Suffering is one of the inevitabilities of being human — wealthy or poor, we all sooner or later experience it, and our suffering may be exacerbated, if not caused, by the circumstances put in place to preclude suffering. The post-modern nanny state, with all the backing of science and technology, bureaucrats and psychologists, is built on the lie that government action can somehow eradicate suffering.

Without suffering there would be no human development. Human creativity and achievement are often inspired by or involve suffering, as is demonstrated by examples from the sublime — an Admiral Nelson, an Edith Stein, or a Gothic cathedral — to the ridiculous — this author's laboured attempts to keep age and weight at bay by jogging on painful knees. In *God at the Ritz,* Lorenzo Albacete, a priest and physicist, reflects on the place of suffering in human life:

'Suffering compels us to think through the great questions of life. In fact, real thought cannot occur without suffering. Creative thinking, which expands our existential horizon, is a plea to the source of meaning and sense. That is what distinguishes creative thinking from speculation.'

He goes on to explain that we do not suffer because we feel pain, we suffer because we ask "Why?", "Why is this happening to me?" and "Why must I endure this?". Suffering involves our self-conscious reflection on the pain we are feeling, including likely duration and future implications, and perhaps nostalgia for better times. And the suffering "Why?" frequently ushers in the creative "What if?", and new possibilities emerge, holding out the promise of redemption. In human experience, suffering presages redemption.

Redemption is perhaps the most powerful and enduring theme in Western literature, as seen in the Biblical stories of Israel, St. Paul, and the Prodigal Son, and in characters such as Sydney Carton; (the dissolute barrister in Dickens' *A Tale of Two Cities*), the tumultuous Dmitri in Dostoevsky's *The Brothers Karamazov,* and Jean Valjean in Victor Hugo's *Les Misérables.* The contemporary movies *Cinderella Man, Blood Diamond, Hotel Rwanda, Crash,* and *Grand Torino* indicate that the post-modern malaise of meaninglessness is unlikely to smother this primeval human yearning.

The lives of nations are also often laid out in terms of suffering and redemption: slave-holding America redeemed by the immolations of the Civil War, Poland restored through the sacrifices of Solidarity, South Africa lifted up by the spirit of reconciliation espoused by Nelson Mandela, and modern Japan reconstructed through the support of her former foes and the virtues of her own ancient tradition.

A tawdry episode in British politics occurred in the 1960s when John Profumo, Secretary of State for War in Harold Macmillan's cabinet, was found to have been using the services of the call girl, Christine Keeler. The fact that Keeler was concurrently involved with a Russian naval attaché, and this at a time when the Cold War was at its height, elevated the case from a salacious social indiscretion to a possible breach of national security. Profumo's political career was ruined and the affair almost certainly contributed to Macmillan's Conservatives losing the next election. However, the disgraced aristocrat redeemed his reputation by working for charity at Toynbee Hall in the East End of London for the rest of his life. He started as a toilet cleaner and ended up as chief fund raiser.

Profumo bought his redemption not with money or position, but with sincere regret, humility, and a commitment to helping marginalised people. The same John Profumo who betrayed and hurt many people went on to serve and lift up many others. The difference between these two parts of his life was character, the stamp each human being puts on his own personality through the choices he or she makes.

Suffering and redemption show that human nature has the potential for both good and evil, and personal fulfilment will always ultimately be determined by the free choices we make as we negotiate the challenges of this life. But what is good and what is evil? And how is a leader to confidently promote what is good for people, and oppose what is evil?

CAN WE KNOW WHAT IS GOOD FOR US?

People use the concepts of good and bad all the time —discussing economics or politics without recourse to them would be impossible; and our laws and conventions must of necessity make the distinction between what is good and what is bad. Life itself requires us to recognise that, in terms of our survival, health, prosperity, personal fulfilment and so on, some things are good for us and some are bad. And there seems to be some close affinity between the good, truth, and beauty, just as there is between the bad, falsehood, and ugliness. The post-modern mind, however, shuns such concepts as mere value judgments; that is, choices made by individuals according to personal taste, opinion, or whim. Where did this divisive notion arise?

Over the past two hundred years, with the growth of a more materialistic mindset in the West, the economic term 'value' (originally employed in relation to 'goods and services' which carried some or other 'value in use' or 'value in exchange') has been allowed to usurp the word 'good'. By the 1960s, academia and the media were replacing the term 'moral judgment' with the phrase 'value judgment', and both had come to bear a pejorative meaning. The Logical Positivist School of philosophy, though subsequently disavowed by some of its own proponents, had persuaded many in the West that there was a clear distinction between 'facts' and 'values' when it came to knowledge. They asserted that 'facts' were empirically verifiable and applicable to all, while 'values' were dismissed as mere personal opinion not to be foisted on other people or society in general.

This resurrected the controversy as to whether good and evil are objective realities or simply the subjective judgments of the individual, and it opened the door to the irrational moral relativism so pervasive in the post-modern West. Consider the absurdity of denouncing the imposition of one's personal morality on others, but simultaneously expressing outrage at the moral turpitude of those who wage war and torture prisoners. Regardless of political affiliations and philosophical standpoints, we all know when bad things have been done, and we know too the good that needs to be interposed.

A PRACTICAL EXAMPLE

In a heavyweight boxing match some years ago former champion Mike Tyson, frustrated by the pugilistic skills of his opponent, Evander Holyfield, resorted to biting his rival's ear. It was a sensational moment in professional sport, and the incident and its aftermath provide an intriguing example with which to analyse our understanding of good and bad.

We can state categorically that Tyson's behaviour was a transgression of the spirit of sporting competition, a breach of the rules of boxing, an illegal act inviting criminal charges, a violation of his contract, and a clear instance of cheating fight fans who had paid the substantial ticket prices to see the contest. Everyone, except perhaps very young children, unscrupulous defence lawyers, and the avant garde of academia, would confidently use the word 'bad' to describe what Tyson had done, and they would feel no inclination to engage in any philosophical review of their judgment or the word used to express it.

Physical and possibly emotional harm was done to Tyson's opponent, but harm was also done to society at large by such a violation of the standards of civilised behaviour. Quite apart from the invidious example provided for the young and the impressionable, which would include many of his own friends and family, Tyson's action was a challenge to the social conventions without which no functional human relationship is possible. In a barbarian community, his behaviour might have been applauded; but it simply has no place in civilised society. It was bad; that is, it was not good!

He also did serious harm to himself. Apart from the damage done to his reputation, his credibility, and his career, he undoubtedly suffered from the hate and rage in his mind and the torment of trying to conceal the frailty and pain. Like all of us, in his own way he would feel the need for answers to Kant's three questions, but every damaging act would push him further away from finding enlightenment and peace. Instead, he would be descending progressively into meaninglessness. The destruction of a human being, Mike Tyson or anyone else is bad. And we know it is.

What could save Mike Tyson? How could he be helped to turn away from behaviour that is harmful to himself, others, and society at large? Psychologists, social workers, and human resources specialists would probably respond that Tyson should undergo therapy, an anger management programme, rigorous training in people skills, or specialised treatment with appropriate drugs. But they would merely address symptoms of the problem — his feelings of anger, frustration, resentment, and the remorse that follows being caught — but not the problem itself: his worldview and the negative attitudes that flow from it, such as lack of respect for other people, dishonesty, malevolence, cowardice, cruelty, and foolishness. The only way to save someone like Mike Tyson is to help them change the way they see this life, and their attitudes to themselves, to other people, and to the world they are part of.

The Tyson affair reminds us of a lesson left to us by the ancients: our well-*being* depends on our well-*doing*. In other words, it depends on us doing the right thing, on doing what is good. And what we do stems inexorably from our worldview and our attitudes.

THE GOOD LIFE AND ITS DENIAL

In August 1963, Martin Luther King Jr. delivered his famous "I have a dream" speech from the steps of the Lincoln Memorial in Washington DC to a massive civil rights march. His inspirational message deliberately echoed the stirring words of Abraham Lincoln one hundred years earlier, when that great president had, on the Gettysburg battlefield, rededicated his country to the ideals proclaimed almost another one hundred years before in the American Declaration of Independence of 4 July 1776. In every crisis in its history, the United States has been able to look back to its roots and draw strength from its founding principles, and the words of that document remain for all humankind a useful guide in understanding the good that we seek:

'We hold these truths to be self-evident, that all men are created equal, that they are endowed by their creator with certain unalienable rights, that among these are life, liberty, and the pursuit of happiness. That to secure these rights governments are instituted among men, deriving their just powers from the consent of the governed. That whenever any form of government becomes destructive to these ends, it is the right of the people to alter or abolish it, and to institute new government, laying its foundation on such principles and organising its powers in such form, as to them shall seem most likely to effect their safety and happiness.'

What the Americans did was revolutionary, but the ideas by which they justified what they did were not; they were the distillation of wisdom, drawing from Greek philosophy, the Jewish scriptures, and the Christian Gospel, and what had been built upon those philosophical foundations by thinkers such as Locke, Hume, Smith and Montesquieu (even though some of them rejected the Judeo-Christian revelation).

By 'happiness' the Founding Fathers meant not transient pleasure, but personal fulfilment, perfection, or integrity, which in turn implies many other 'goods' necessary for that fulfilment. Happiness happens to be one of the most carefully studied concepts throughout history; people have naturally always wanted to know the secret behind personal fulfilment.

Aristotle told us that our prime objective should be to live our lives well — to pursue a good life. He noted that living well involved gaining possession of all those things which enable a person to be fulfilled, things that by our very nature we need rather than desire, but things that all human beings ought to desire. And he specified health, strength, energy, and the physical pleasures we all enjoy, as well as the external means to secure those goods, such as food, drink, exercise, rest, clothing, shelter, and freedom. In addition, he emphasised our need for knowledge, friendship, love, self-esteem, honour, and the cardinal virtues understood by the ancients to be prudence or practical reason in making decisions, courage, justice, and temperance or self-control. Philosophy ever since, as well as modern psychology and most ordinary people, has found Aristotle's prescription to be a good guide.

Aristotle's ideas and the principles expressed in the American Declaration of Independence also tally with the understanding of human nature espoused in the preceding chapter, and the lessons that persistently emerge from the pages of history and classic literature. Accordingly, we can list with some confidence the good things that necessarily promote the well-being, or the perfection, or the fulfilment of the human person. Obviously, since we are creatures limited in this life by the constraints of time and space, the scope of our personal potential, and also the realities of our socio-economic circumstances, our acquisition of these good things, the things we ought to pursue, can only ever be relative in terms of the ideal and also in terms of what may be achieved by our fellow human beings.

All of us as human beings need and ought to pursue these good things: freedom, meaning, purpose, knowledge and a commitment to truth, love and respect for and from other people, and therefore healthy relationships, mental and physical health, security, prosperity, and the virtues that will provide the mental strength for the quest. By contrast, the bad things we ought to avoid are the polar opposites of the good: enslavement (to ideology, other people, drugs, self-indulgence, fantasies, etc.), meaninglessness, purposelessness, ignorance, dishonesty, hate and contempt for and from other people (and therefore dysfunctional relationships), mental and physical illness, insecurity, poverty, and the vices that will progressively corrupt the mind.

In any workplace, home or community where the good things are absent, human well-being is to some degree or other compromised, and that is true in different ways for all people everywhere. Moreover, the discrepancies between individuals and between communities all over the world, particularly in health, security, and prosperity, can be discouraging. However, intellect and free will enable people to overcome all sorts of disadvantages, and embracing the virtues identified by the ancients and endorsed by modern science can compensate for most circumstantial deficiencies and bring personal fulfilment closer in other ways. Some of the happiest and most productive people I know have disabilities and/or rather meagre material resources.

ATTITUDES MAKE ALL THE DIFFERENCE

How we see reality and what we understand life to be about gives rise to the attitudes we adopt to ourselves, other people and the world around us. Attitude is a word used frequently by most people in the social give-and-take of daily life. But when asked to define the word 'attitude', only a small percentage of people in my experience confidently asserts that an attitude is a mindset or a state of mind. Most people struggle to understand that attitudes are more a matter of nurture than of nature, and helping them get a grip on how attitudes develop inevitably requires practical examples.

Because attitudes shape human behaviour and determine the quality of human relationships, people need to understand them, how they arise, and how they impact on our lives. I have tried to provide an understanding accessible to the many different audiences I address: people in the retail sector, real estate agents, accountants, scientists, the teaching fraternity, advertising and marketing professionals, and managers from many other areas of commerce and industry, as well as from government agencies. It is no easy task.

I am profoundly conscious of the complex interplay between genetic predispositions, emotions, appetites and affective realities, knowledge and fallible human reason, as well as external influences. What follows makes no pretence of being a scientific explanation of the human psyche. It is a simplified overview of human attitudes and their impact, but one that has proved enlightening and useful in the lives of people from many different backgrounds and circumstances. I have been encouraged over the years to find confirmation of the basic accuracy of this generalised sketch in reputable textbooks on philosophy and psychology.

A TALE OF REDEMPTION

If an attitude is a state of mind formed in relation to oneself, other people, and the world around us, then it obviously develops from sense perception or experience, including all learning, formal and informal, which we respond to rationally through our intellect, emotionally through our feelings, and affectively through our appetites or desires. Our responses become states of mind that express how we regard someone or something, and how we intend to conduct ourselves in dealing with them. The following is an example from personal experience.

Growing up in Rhodesia, I was raised to be racist; I had not been born a racist. The experiences of my infancy and youth, in our home, in the community and society at large, put out an unequivocal message: white people are superior to black people. The fact that the two races were segregated, the socio-economic and educational disparity between them, the fact that most black people we encountered were in menial positions, and the lack of respect accorded them by white people, reinforced this core message. Of course, I also witnessed acts of real kindness towards black people on the part of many adult whites, but naively took that to be further evidence of our racial superiority.

As the winds of change swept through Africa, it was clear that conflict between the races was inevitable. Mau Mau atrocities in Kenya and events in the Belgian Congo struck fear in the heart of colonial society. The misguided and misinformed moral justification, the feelings of fear, anger, and anxiety, and the desire to hang onto a pretty idyllic lifestyle, all reinforced the racist worldview I had developed over the years, including the attitudes of arrogance, contempt for black people, and frequent hatred, bigotry, intolerance, and hostility towards critics of colonialism and those who wanted to change our world. The fact that these attitudes were in open contradiction of my Christian beliefs and the otherwise mostly positive values of respect and responsibility instilled in me by my parents and Rhodesian society, was testimony to the perversity of human reason and our proclivity for self-deception.

This example of racism is a good one, not only because it illustrates the development of a widespread attitude, but also because it has in my case been exorcised. Racism diminished me as a person and stunted my intellectual, emotional, and spiritual growth. Removing it freed me to pursue genuine fulfilment. The many people who guided and supported me in changing my attitude have already been mentioned and I owe them a lifelong debt. They were my teachers in a long process of education that in the end was necessarily driven by me. Ultimately it was my choice between good and bad. Racism and the behaviour that flowed from it was inimical to my own development, a destructive force in the lives of the African people, and noxious to Rhodesian society and the world at large.

A word about evil – if you ask me whether it is evil wilfully and without provocation to show contempt and hatred for another human being, or to violate their potential through physical maltreatment, enslavement, economic exploitation, sexual exploitation, ideological indoctrination, or any other form of abuse, I can only answer yes, yes, yes! If we desire human progress, it has to be for all people, not just some. This does not mean support for some vast utopian social engineering project to ensure a universal equality of outcomes; on the contrary, it stands in defiant opposition to any scheme that reduces people to nondescript social units, just as it rejects the exploitation of the many by a few, or a minority by a misguided majority.

There are of course countless examples that can be raised on this simplified model for understanding attitudes and how they develop. But even though we may know the good things required by all human beings, can we confidently assert what are good and bad attitudes?

WHAT ARE GOOD ATTITUDES AND WHAT ARE BAD?

The writer Ralph Waldo Emerson made this statement in his journal in 1836:

'The difference between good and bad, better or worse, is simply helping or hurting.'

In the light of the definition of leadership put forward in this book, Emerson's axiom seems to offer a straight-forward rule of thumb for distinguishing between good and bad, or positive and negative attitudes. It is this: good attitudes promote well-being, while bad attitudes cause harm. They either promote the well-being of oneself, other people, and the world around us, or they cause harm to oneself, other people and the world around us. They are either constructive or destructive.

If this is indeed the case, then it follows that we should be able to identify the good and the bad attitudes. The lists shown in Table 8.1 are in no way comprehensive, but they do provide a very useful guide to those mindsets that promote well-being, in the left-hand column, and those that cause harm, in the column on the right.

GOOD/POSITIVE ATTITUDES	BAD/NEGATIVE ATTITUDES
Caring	Selfish
Honest	Dishonest
Benevolent	Malevolent
Self-controlled	Licentious
Hard-working	Lazy
Adventurous	Complacent
Accountable	Irresponsible
Curious	Credulous

Confident	Cynical
Persevering	Submissive
Creative	Narrow-minded
Cooperative	Uncooperative
Decisive	Wavering
Generous	Greedy
Friendly	Hostile
Respectful	Contemptuous
Hopeful	Despairing
Courageous	Cowardly
Cheerful	Bitter
Charitable	Cruel

Table 8.1

Each column has an inner consistency: there are no attitudes that would sit comfortably if moved to the other column; the attitudes listed in the first column are near polar opposites of those in the second column; the positive attitudes listed on the left reflect the conclusions reached by the proponents of emotional intelligence; and those same attitudes are essentially the ones that have been traditionally associated with good character in people.

In *The Pursuit of Happiness* Dr. David G. Myers, another of many scholars whose conclusions encourage me in my approach, defines the elements of the good life thus:

'Happy people… are strikingly energetic, decisive, flexible, creative, and sociable. Compared to unhappy people, they are more trusting, more loving, more responsive…Happy people tolerate more frustration. They are less likely to be abusive and are more lenient…they are more loving and forgiving and less likely to exaggerate or over-interpret slight criticism. They choose long-term rewards over immediate small pleasures…Moreover, in experiment after experiment, happy people are more willing to help those in need.'

The two lists also help to illuminate the distinction between attitudes and emotions. For example, I might feel desire (my emotion) for a family heirloom, and either be caring or selfish (my attitude) towards my sister, whose emotional need is greater. My emotional reaction to a stranger might be suspicion about his intentions, but I may choose either an attitude of friendliness or one of hostility. I might feel uncertain about the possible outcome of a business venture, but make up my mind to be decisive rather than wavering. Despite our focus on attitudes and how they shape character, it is necessary to have at least a working understanding of emotions and their impact on behaviour.

GETTING A HANDLE ON EMOTIONS

The loose way in which we use words, diluting the ability of language to give accurate expression to our thoughts, is a serious problem when trying to understand human emotion. Psychologists and philosophers still argue over definitions and categories of emotions, and many dictionaries are less than helpful. In order to provide a degree of clarity, here are three definitions from respectable sources. The first is from Webster's *New World Dictionary of the American Language*:

'1. a) *Strong feeling; excitement* b) *the state or capability of having the feelings aroused to the point of awareness* 2. *Any specific feeling; any of various complex reactions with both mental and physical manifestations, as love, hate, fear, anger, etc.*'

My only disagreement with this definition is over its categorisation of love and hate as emotions, but that issue is dealt with later. The second definition belongs to the philosopher Mortimer Adler and is from *Intellect: Mind over Matter*

'…*emotion is a passion that the body suffers and we consciously experience when a complex set of bodily reactions occurs: changes in respiration and pulse, changes in epidermal electricity, increases of blood sugar and adrenalin in the blood due to reaction on the part of the glands of internal secretion, papillary dilation or contraction. In short, an emotion is a widespread, violent bodily commotion that is consciously experienced and accompanied by strong impulses to act in a certain way.*'

Adler goes on to assert, incorrectly in my view, that anger, fear, and erotic love, by which I assume he means lust, are the only real emotions, with all others being derivatives or states of the will. The fact that he contradicts himself in this regard by identifying grief and depression as further possibilities tends to detract from an otherwise compelling discourse.

The third definition comes from Daniel Goleman, in an appendix to his 1995 best-seller, *Emotional Intelligence*.

> *'In its most literal sense, the Oxford English Dictionary defines emotion as 'any agitation or disturbance of mind, feeling, passion; any vehement or excited mental state.' I take emotion to refer to a feeling and its distinctive thoughts, psychological, and biological states, and a range of propensities to act. There are hundreds of emotions, along with their blends, variations, mutations, and nuances. Indeed, there are many more subtleties of emotion than we have words for.'*

Inspired by the work of Paul Ekman at the University of California, who discovered a trans-cultural recognition of facial expressions for fear, anger, sadness, and enjoyment, Goleman goes on to list the psychosomatic states he sees as possible core emotions, specifying anger, fear, sadness, enjoyment, love, surprise, disgust and shame. He acknowledges that the matter is complex and scientifically unresolved, and one can see why when he tries to tease out the derivatives of each of the core emotions.

Identifying mental states like hostility, self-pity, despair, wariness, friendliness, trust, adoration, contempt, disdain and scorn as emotions in my view, is wrong-headed suggesting as it does that these are natural feelings and that any behaviour flowing from them must therefore be natural and even acceptable. Take a positive one, such as friendliness, and consider the implications if that mental state is taken to be an emotion — it would mean that unfriendliness, its opposite, would also be natural, and that the way I treat others would depend on how I am feeling at any given point in time. Even though these mental states, and many others, may be accompanied by actual emotions manifested by mental and bodily upheavals — for example sweating, laughter, a grimace, or the shakes — they are quite emphatically attitudes rather than emotions. And there is a good reason for making this assertion.

ATTITUDE IS A STATE OF MIND CHOSEN BY AN ACT OF WILL

Understanding human nature and how to motivate people requires the ability to distinguish between attitudes and emotions, between where we can make a decisive difference and where we will struggle to make a change. It all depends on human free will.

I may feel dislike or even disgust for a person or their behaviour, but whether I adopt an attitude of hate towards them is another matter. Hate is not felt, it is directed; what I feel is some form of dislike or revulsion or anger, but the hate I project towards the other person is chosen by me, consciously or sub-consciously, but chosen nonetheless. I do not have to hate anyone. I can voluntarily overlook my involuntary emotional responses and choose instead to love the person, helping them to become more likable. The example of love is instructive.

Love is not liking, or affection, or attraction, or sexual desire, though in the complexities of human motivation, these emotions no doubt play some part in what we mostly think of as passion, and what Plato in *Phaedrus* called "the divine madness". The ancient Greeks showed much greater wisdom than modern society in explaining the concept of love. They said that there were four types of love: storge or familial affection (for example, between parent and child); philia or friendship as opposed to mere acquaintance; eros or romantic love, of which sexual attraction is an obvious spur (though many men and women have throughout history betrayed those they claim to love through promiscuous sex); and finally, agape or unconditional love, the perfection of love, actively willing the true well-being and fulfilment of the person loved, even and especially if it involves self-sacrifice.

A woman may feel disgust and disappointment at the behaviour of one of her children, but choose to love them regardless and to work for their redemption and fulfilment. A man may shock and anger a friend through some selfish act, yet find the friend chooses to love him through forgiveness and support as he tries to mend his ways. A husband may be emotionally tempted to sleep with a beautiful colleague, but choose instead to love his wife as he ought to by being faithful. The emotions are there in every case, but the choice to strive for the real good of the person loved is an act of will. Love is attended by many different emotions, but is in itself an attitude, an act of will, a freely chosen mindset.

A further example is the mindset we call confidence. Contrary to popular belief, it is an attitude, and not a feeling. The word derives from the Latin 'cum' for 'with', and 'fides' for 'faith' or 'trust'. It means 'with faith' or 'with trust'. In our relations with other people, try as we may over many years, none of us is ever able to fully understand the innermost hopes and motivations of even those special people with whom we are most intimate. We can never be completely sure what is in their minds — we simply have to trust them, have faith in them, treat them with confidence. That is why a relationship is broken or becomes dysfunctional when one person is unfaithful or violates the trust of the other. Without choosing to be confident in the honesty and goodwill of other people we can have no meaningful relationships.

Similarly, when it comes to each of us as an individual, we need the self-confidence that enables us to act according to the requirements of any given situation, regardless of whatever feelings we may be experiencing — fear, nervousness, frustration, or shyness. Every day, people all over the world make speeches in public, learn to ride a bicycle, play golf, tackle daunting projects, and ask members of the opposite sex for dates. They overcome their feelings, their emotions, by choosing to act with confidence in themselves. Confidence, like love and all other attitudes, is an act of will.

In short, feelings just happen — they are psychosomatic events; but we can freely choose our attitudes. We alone of all creatures can choose to ignore our feelings or go against them. And we can do so because we have free will, the faculty of choice, and the intellect to help us make judgments as to the right attitudes and the right behaviour.

When psychologists in the twentieth century told us to trust our emotions and 'go with the flow' they were often mistaking habitual attitudes and cultural mindsets for spontaneous, and therefore 'authentic', emotions. People suddenly felt 'liberated' and 'empowered' to act on what were frequently destructive attitudes misconstrued as emotions, or real emotions like lust, desire, and anger that decent human relationships and civilised society require us to control.

Control and, especially, self-control are rather unpopular concepts in our free-for-all world. However, armed now with a functional understanding of the dynamics of attitudes and emotions, we can consider how these shape character, the stamp each of us imprints on our personality.

THE ELEMENTS OF GOOD CHARACTER

Good character, if there is such a thing, can only be a truth about reality. Goethe, quoted in Josef Pieper's *The Four Cardinal Virtues* put it this way:

> *"All laws and rules of conduct may ultimately be reduced to a single one: to truth."*

A person with no commitment to the truth about reality, the way things are, and the manner in which he has his being, would have no idea of how good character, or indeed any kind of character, should be defined, let alone pursued. In order to achieve the good in life, a person must first have a sound knowledge of reality, in other words, he or she must actively seek the truth.

When it comes to promoting leadership as opposed to misleadership, once we acknowledge that truth is indispensable, we can confidently build on our understanding of human nature and the good things it needs, our knowledge of helpful and harmful attitudes, and our simplified working model of the dynamic interplay of emotions and attitudes. We can then proceed to identify the essential qualities of good character. Earlier, mention was made of the need for personal virtue if people are to achieve the fulfilment they seek. The cardinal virtues were listed as prudence (or practical reason in decision-making), courage, justice and temperance (or self-control), and it is notable that each is an attitude. In fact, it is easy to see how all of the positive attitudes listed in the first column of Table 8.1 relate to one or other of these four cardinal virtues:

Prudence is a word that is not used much nowadays; if it is, the meaning is taken to be 'caution', even 'timidity' or a shrewd, self-seeking, no-risk attitude. This is unfortunate because our society has lost an appreciation of the most important of the cardinal virtues — the one from which the others grow. Prudence is the ability to make the right decisions in everyday life. It is practical wisdom that grows with experience and knowledge of reality. Hence, courage, justice and temperance all depend in the first instance on prudence. Their opposites — cowardice, unfairness, and a lack of self-control — all work against the good of people and our world, so violating prudent judgment. Prudence demands honesty with ourselves and others, openness to truth, a willingness to listen to all points of view, and clear-minded rationality when we are caught unawares by the vicissitudes of life. It is an attitude to life that has to be deliberately chosen and cultivated. The enemies of prudence are thoughtlessness, laziness, negligence, irresponsibility, credulousness, and blindness to the plain truth. Good character cannot be built without prudence.

Courage is the ultimate commitment to truth — the willingness to sacrifice all for what we know to be right and good. It is an implicit acknowledgement that a person recognises a principle higher than himself. People can only decide what that principle is for themselves on the basis of a knowledge of reality, on what they see to be the truth. Courage is required in life precisely because we are vulnerable and not self-sufficient; we have to take risks. If we were not vulnerable, we could never be brave. Hence we are called to be courageous, to take a stand on principle in our homes, communities, workplaces, society, and the world at large. When we shrink from what we know to be right or good, we stain our character, and our personality suffers a loss in our quest for integrity and fulfilment. Modern psychology and ancient wisdom agree that the source of many mental illnesses is the egocentric anxiety that values personal security above all else and refuses to risk injury or loss to self in any circumstances. Good character demands courage.

Justice might not sound like an attitude, but that is precisely what it is. It is the commitment to give other people their due as human beings, which of course requires the prudence to decide what is just and the courage to stand by one's decision. Truth, or knowledge of the reality of things, is quite clearly a prerequisite of justice. Our word 'justice' comes from the Latin word for 'right' or 'law', implying once more that there is a standard that is above the self and that is binding equally on all, the powerful and the weak, the rich and the poor. Thomas Aquinas, in his *Commentary on the Book of Job*, states the age-old threats to justice:

'Justice is destroyed in twofold fashion: by the false prudence of the sage and by the violent act of the man who possesses power.'

The false prudence of unscrupulous politicians and businesspeople, the sophists of our day, and the violence that threatens the whole world to some degree or other, underline how an attitude of injustice characterises this age of misleaders. An attitude of justice, sincerely desiring and promoting the obligations and protection of the law (both natural law and positive law) to apply equally to all, is essential to good character and needs to be cultivated by every individual. Justice should not, however, be a legalistic attitude, but should be tempered by compassion and mercy.

Temperance is another word not much used or understood today, and most people would associate it with abstinence from alcohol. Temperance, however, comes from the Latin 'temperare', which means to put the different parts of the whole, the person in this case, in proper order, or to build integrity. We are correct in thinking of temperance as self-control or self-discipline, but wrong when we think of it as puritanical or afraid of exuberance and the pleasures of life. Pleasure is a proper part of personal fulfilment. Developing one's potential involves avoiding over-indulgence and enslavement to destructive habits, attitudes, and behaviour. Temperance requires unselfish self-preservation and self-assertion, developing one's full potential within the context of society and the world. It is intemperate, or self-destructive, to use one's freedom and intellect to push for one's own self-preservation, self-assertion, and self-fulfilment without due regard for other people, the community, and the environment.

THREE ESSENTIAL ATTITUDES TO ADD

If the cardinal virtues of prudence, courage, justice, and temperance are necessary for human beings to build good character, there are three further virtues or positive attitudes that are essential to personal fulfilment. They relate to Christianity's three theological virtues of faith, hope and love; the best aspects of Western civilisation reflect their influence, and one does not need to be a Christian to recognise their centrality to the good life. This is not a book of Christian apologetics nor is it an attempt to proselytise, and for that reason I have chosen to deal with these virtues or foundational attitudes of good character under the headings of 'confidence', 'aspiration' and 'love'. Retaining the word 'love' was inescapable, because there is no other word that will suffice.

Confidence has been explained in part already. It views life and the world in a positive light and is the source of all constructive action in regard to oneself, other people and one's environment. Economists agree that confidence is essential for any economy to thrive. This applies equally to any human endeavour. We can only develop and prosper through strong trust or faith in each other and in ourselves. It is the first and ongoing task of a leader to build confidence in people, and that can only be done if they can see meaning and purpose in their lives, underlining yet again the importance of objective truth. The attitude opposed to confidence is cynicism, a disease of the soul that has reached epidemic proportions today. Cynicism says, "believe nothing, trust no-one, and disparage everything"; it is both the seed and the fruit of misleadership. Leadership involves a contest between confidence and cynicism, and the triumph of the former is the clearest indicator of a leader's progress.

Aspiration is the natural fruit of human free will and intellect — the two things that enable us to initiate and drive changes in ourselves and our environment in the quest for a better life. Blaise Pascal, in *Pensees*, expressed the inevitable challenge for all people in developing their character:

'The future alone is our objective.'

Because our lives are from the start centred on turning possibility into actuality, on driving potential to fruition, on setting objectives and seeking fulfilment, aspiration becomes a defining attitude. Parents must inspire this in their children, teachers must ignite it in their pupils, and leaders must ensure it is a strong influence in the lives of their followers. G. K. Chesterton once observed that the two enemies of hope are presumption and despair, two attitudes rampant in our society with its emphasis on rights rather than responsibility, and its notion that we somehow deserve things we have not worked for. The despair that follows any disaster, disappointment, or other adversity is destructive of character. Resolution and courage are required. If we allow disappointment, fear, and frustration to kill aspiration, we are resigning ourselves to failure and regression. Aspiration is the proper response to the challenges of life, and it provides encouragement to all the other virtues.

Love, in the meaning used throughout this book, has previously been explained: it is the intentional state of mind that actively wills and works for the well-being and fulfilment of the person on whom it is focused. The frequently accompanying emotions of affection, desire, joy, excitement, sadness, anxiety, and disappointment can distort it, even changing it to an attitude of possessiveness, seeking the gratification of the self rather than desiring the best for the other. Similarly, jealousy is an attitude sparked by the uncontrolled emotions of desire, frustration, and anger. Love's importance lies in the fact that no person can be fulfilled without it, both the giving and receiving of it, and those two actions underline the fact that it is an act of will, a personal choice, rather than a feeling. This is further established by the definition of love provided by St. Paul over two thousand years ago in his *First letter to the Corinthians*:

'Love is patient; love is kind; love is not envious or boastful or arrogant or rude. It does not insist on its own way; it is not irritable or resentful; it does not rejoice in wrong-doing, but rejoices in the truth. It bears all things, believes all things, hopes all things, endures all things. Love never ends.'

It has been said that love is a verb rather than a noun; it is active rather than passive, actively pursuing the well-being of others, heedless of the cost to self. To this end, it is through love that we transcend our selves, recognising a higher principle inextricably associated with truth. It puts one in harmony with oneself, with other people, and with the world; it is the most important attribute a leader can have. Over time I have come to regard respect as the starting point for love because true respect for the dignity of another person will always demand that you act in their best interests.

Personal integrity can only be built on these seven attitudes, and all the other positive attitudes listed in Table 8.1 depend on them. A quick perusal of the list of negative attitudes reveals that they are all harmful to personal integrity. Choosing the positive attitudes is how we build character — each individual person's self-chosen, constantly evolving, moral identity.

Leading like you mean it is a matter of character

Eight hundred years ago, Thomas Aquinas provided an analysis of corrupted human nature, identifying four principle failings known to all human societies: weakness when challenged by hardship or danger, ignorance when hard decisions have to be made, malice towards other people, and intemperance or giving free rein to self-gratification. These are the failures of character that all leaders are called to counter in themselves and in the people they lead by cultivating positive attitudes and behaviour.

Good mental health can be seen as being attuned to the realities of life, having an objective understanding of the challenges and possibilities of one's environment, as well as one's own abilities and limitations. Regrettably, this definition excludes a large number of people today — a situation that is due to the decades-long inculcation of counterfeit self-esteem in the young through unwarranted praise and the erosion of standards, and to the pervasive ethos of victimhood that encourages people to lay the blame for failure anywhere but at their own door. Professor William Damon in *Greater Expectations* explains the need for proper character development:

'Self-esteem is a meaningless concept without a firm grounding in substantive achievement. Like happiness, it can be gained only indirectly,

not through its own pursuit, but through dedication to activities, talents, skills, and purposes beyond the self.'

Every act of will and every choice we make in relation to how we will conduct ourselves in life stamps our personality in a particular way, defining our character or the sort of person we have chosen to be. To lead like you mean it demands constant attention to developing one's own character and to inspiring the growth of good character in others. Leading like you mean it is about *people*, and therefore it is about personality and character, which are the building blocks of community and culture.

CHAPTER 9
BUILDING FULFILLING RELATIONSHIPS

"Human nature will not change. In any future great national trial, compared with the men of this, we shall have as weak and as strong, as silly and as wise, as bad and as good." Abraham Lincoln

RELATIONSHIPS AND TRUTH

Understanding people and their motivations is a primary focus of leadership, but the reality is that we can only do this by studying the individual person in the context of his social arrangements or relationships. Isolated from his perpetual dependence on other people in every area of life, the individual becomes inexplicable.

To state the obvious, everything that we know about human nature, personality, and character applies to every single person we ever come into contact with. They all need freedom to flourish, all yearn for fulfilment, all experience pain and suffering, and all seek redemption, even if they often do so through behaviour that will cause them and others further grief. Tragically, throughout life most of us remain largely unaware of the deep thoughts and feelings of others, even the people closest to us. Consequently, we inhibit our own growth to the same extent that we fail to be sensitive to the needs of others.

The first-hand knowledge we have of our own experiences loses its value unless we have a genuine commitment to find the truth about our lives in the context of our relationships. The philosopher Alasdair MacIntyre in *Dependent Rational Animals* underscores this, saying:

'But genuine and extensive self-knowledge becomes possible only in consequence of those social relationships which on occasion provide badly-needed correction for our own judgments. When adequate self-knowledge is achieved, it is always a shared achievement. And because adequate self-knowledge is necessary, if I am to imagine realistically the alternative

futures between which I must choose, the quality of my imagination also depends in part on the contribution of others. The virtue that is indispensable for achieving both the required degree of self-knowledge and the ability to resist all those influences that make for self-deception is of course honesty, primarily truthfulness about ourselves, both to ourselves and to others.'

Distortion of the truth is where dysfunction arises in relationships. So what causes the human propensity for distorting the truth?

THE TROUBLE WITH RELATIONSHIPS

The Emperor Frederick II, who ruled the Holy Roman Empire between 1220 and 1250, has been variously described as the precursor of the Machiavellian Renaissance prince and as an early model of the enlightened despot. He once conducted an experiment to try and discover the natural language of humankind. He had a group of babies isolated from hearing any speech at all until they should develop their natural language. The babies were otherwise well cared for by wet nurses, but the women had to do their work in complete silence, never exposing their charges to any communication, verbal or otherwise. Every one of the babies died. They might just as well have been deprived of food and drink. The lesson is clear: if we cannot relate to other people, our lives become unsustainable.

There is a terrible irony here: we cannot live without other people and yet it seems that all too often we find it well-nigh impossible to live with them. In *No Exit*, Jean-Paul Sartre spoke for many when he declared:

"Hell is other people."

Over many years running team and leadership programmes, whenever I have surveyed participants on the greatest source of stress in their lives, most have responded, "Other people!". This widespread agreement with Sartre reminds us of the paradox of the human condition — the potential for social harmony, but the persistent failure to achieve it. And it is only in the context of relationships that we can examine the fatal flaw.

Relationships cover all social bonds: family, friendship, acquaintance, neighbourhood, community, team, business and organisation, and society itself. And dysfunction seems to be the rule rather than the exception. The worldwide phenomenon of jokes about men, women, sex, marriage, mothers-in-law, children, work, bosses, lawyers, doctors, accountants, used-car salesmen, and politicians, to name but a few, indicates that most people accept that human relationships are messy affairs.

This is unsurprising given the complex problems confronting 'me' within 'myself' — my capabilities and frustrations, my aspirations and anxieties, my desires and inadequacies. The interaction of those antagonisms with the equally enigmatic people I mix with domestically, socially and professionally — multiplies the complexity. Little wonder that getting relationships right at every level of society is so difficult.

THE DELUGE OF DYSFUNCTION

In a recent book, *Cahokia: Ancient America's Great City on the Mississippi*, Timothy Pauketat, an anthropology professor at the University of Illinois, has disposed of the myth of benevolent and non-violent primitive societies, a concept still cherished in ideological enclaves. Pauketat has revealed inhuman practices (and it is significant that we should describe them that way) the like of which have scarred every area of human settlement around the globe at some time or other. The inhuman practices are a worldwide *human* phenomenon — not an American or Mesopotamian or African or Asiatic or European phenomenon, but a universal falling away by human beings from what they are capable of being.

Cahokia, once a city of twenty thousand people, was situated on the Mississippi quite close to what is today St. Louis. It seems to have been the urban centre of a vast twelfth-century empire not unlike those of Central and South America. Cahokia and its empire were ruled by a political and religious elite who practised rituals reminiscent of the Aztec and Inca cultures, and some of the peoples of the ancient Mediterranean world. Human sacrifice was carried out on a scale formerly believed to have been confined to the more well-known cultures to the south. This malevolent social arrangement might be explained by many different factors, but it was indisputably destructive of human potential and of fulfilling human relationships (as are all other civilisations, including more advanced ones, to some degree or other).

An example is provided in Joseph Conrad's *Heart of Darkness,* which is a disturbing reflection on the inhuman consequences of the 'Scramble for Africa' that was given impetus by the Congress of Berlin, orchestrated by Bismarck in 1884. The European powers laid claim to vast tracts of territory in the 'Dark Continent', drawing arbitrary boundaries that bore no resemblance to the traditional tribal and ethnic divisions, and for the most part enslaving or reducing to serfdom the indigenous populations. One initiative in this land grab saw the great Congo basin become the possession of the Belgian King. As with other imperialist nations, Belgium claimed to be bringing civilisation to the primitive and barbarous inhabitants, but the real motives were international prestige and economic advantage. Such was the great lie of European imperialism.

Conrad's novel captures the contradictory and self-serving attitudes of white civilisation at the heart of the imperialist ideal. Kurtz, the central character, is an agent for a Belgian trading company and seems to be a paragon of nineteenth century European values — intelligent, cultured, and dedicated to bringing the benefits of a superior civilisation to the benighted savages of Africa. Yet during an ivory expedition, he makes himself ruler of one of the tribes and implements a regime of unrestrained cruelty.

The narrator, Marlowe, is appalled by the cultural backwardness of the natives, and approves of the spread of civilisation through the troubled expanses of Africa, though he is emphatically a proponent of doing things the British way. Yet far from being critical of Kurtz's demonic transition, Marlowe applauds the Nietzschean act of will that has swept aside the fraudulent facia of civilisation to reveal the inner truth about humankind — the heart of darkness. Kurtz's acts throw into stark relief the dishonesty of the other characters and of European civilisation itself.

My own experience of the contradictions of colonial society and the arrogance of imperialism endorse the unpalatable truth not only about the injustices visited upon the peoples of Africa, but also about tendencies in human behaviour. Whether the relationships are political, social, economic, or domestic, they are generally rendered dysfunctional to some degree by the treatment of the other person as inferior, dangerous, or useful as a means to an end.

People like to believe that their personal attitudes and behaviour are independent of the nature of the society they are part of. Nothing could be further from the truth, as history bears testimony. In *Christianity and History* Professor Herbert Butterfield expresses the matter thus:

'The plain truth is that if you were to remove certain subtle safeguards in society many men who had been respectable all their lives would be transformed by the discovery of the things which it was now possible to do with impunity; weak men would apparently take to crime who had previously been kept on the rails by a certain balance existing in society; and you can produce a certain condition of affairs in which people go plundering and stealing though hitherto throughout their lives it had never occurred to them even to want to steal. A great and prolonged police strike, the existence of a revolutionary situation in a capital city, and the exhilaration of conquest in an enemy country are likely to show up a seamy side of human nature amongst people who, cushioned and guided by the influences of normal social life, have hitherto presented a respectable figure to the world.'

Butterfield exposes the absurdity of the common belief that we are by nature civilised beings. In fact, the virtues of Western society were the result of a long and painful process of social and political experimentation, philosophical inquiry, education, discipline and sacrifice. Maintaining those virtues is a personal responsibility, and Butterfield recalls Thomas Carlyle's contention that every man in France was responsible for the horrors of the French Revolution. He uses the analogy of an expensive watch destroyed by the presence of a minute grain of sand in the mechanism to illustrate the vital relationship between the personal and the public commitment to deal justly with others.

THE ROLE OF CULTURE

The human proclivity to treat others in ways we know to be wrong is caused in large measure by culture. Cahokian behaviour, for example, would have been driven to a great extent by Cahokian culture. Congolese attitudes would have been strongly influenced by Congolese tribal culture. And the Marxist-Leninist indoctrination that blanketed Eastern Europe after World War II had obvious effects on the character of many people. People had their sense of individuality repressed, and lived lives subject to the whim of their Soviet masters. Scarred by incessant fear and uncertainty, and the humiliation of repression, they developed a propensity for dishonesty and betrayal, not unlike the victims of gangster rule anywhere in the world. Bereft of hope and meaning, they often became informers for the rogue state that stifled their humanity.

The cultural pressures of the post-modern West's brew of individualism, consumerism, and rapidly morphing technology, have been intensively researched over several decades, and many conclusions reached early on have proven remarkably prescient. The 1979 classic *The Culture of Narcissism* by Christopher Lasch provided a description of emerging approaches to relationships that matches with alarming accuracy the cases I encounter almost daily:

'Beneath the concern for performance lies a deeper determination to manipulate the feelings of others to your own advantage. The search for competitive advantage through emotional manipulation increasingly shapes not only personal relations but relations at work as well; it is for this reason that sociability can now function as an extension of work by other means. Personal life, no longer a refuge from deprivations suffered at work, has become as anarchical, as warlike, and as full of stress as the marketplace itself... The recent vogue of 'assertiveness therapy', a counter-program designed to equip the patient with defences against manipulation, appeals to the growing recognition that agility in interpersonal relations determines what looks on the surface like achievement.'

These views are echoed by many commentators who are well aware of the increasing pressures bearing down on people in their relationships. Family breakdown, the disintegration of neighbourliness, the pressures of work or of no work, financial insecurity, and the loss of religious faith and moral certitude, are all taking their toll. And they occur in the context of a world in which terrorism, war, famine, pandemics, and environmental disaster are given as much immediacy by the media as the constant threats of theft, violence and vandalism that haunt our cities. Unsurprisingly, this has led to an endemic loss of confidence in the future and a growing willingness to play the game of life according to Darwinian rules of survival.

Contemporary research is already uncovering worrisome social trends in the lonely legions of Twitter, MySpace, Facebook and YouTube users. It is hardly surprising that this technology-driven form of social networking might lead to superficiality, capriciousness, deceitfulness, bullying, and more of the desperate loneliness-in-a-crowd behaviour that haunts post-modern society. Culture is not a straitjacket, however; all societies have people who manifest greed, pride and cruelty, and others who exhibit love, justice and courage. Culture is an obvious influence on worldviews and therefore on the attitudes and behaviour that determine character, but the choice remains that of the individual person.

THE ELEMENT BENEATH CULTURE

The enduring threat posed to all human relationships is an element lying beneath culture that reveals itself in all people and all times. This element predisposes people to deal with others without respect for their innate dignity as persons. It is the element at the heart of the human conundrum — our potential for the good, and our propensity for the bad — and is seen in all the social contradictions of freedom and slavery, wealth and poverty, peace and war, knowledge and ignorance, health and disease, charity and crime, companionship and loneliness, love and hate, respect and contempt, loyalty and betrayal, truth and falsehood. We see the results of its influence in the media every day in the corrupt politician, the dishonest businessman, the manipulative lawyer, the unprofessional doctor, the unfaithful husband, the violent criminal, the drug addict, the sports cheat, the soccer hooligan and wherever human relationships are not what they should be.

The element in question is human pride, or hubris.

Let me clarify immediately that this does not mean the justifiable feeling of pride in achievement on earning a promotion, or watching a daughter receive her Master's Degree, or enthusing as a grandson takes his first steps. That kind of response is natural and healthy, a response more accurately described as a feeling of euphoria or elation. The human pride under discussion here is not a feeling but an attitude, a freely chosen act of will. It is the attitude that says: "My will is the most important thing in the world", and urges a person to try and make the world conform to his own desires. It neither recognises nor respects the equal dignity of others, regarding them instead as objects to be used. It is radically inconsistent with love, and destructive of all relationships.

Other harmful attitudes naturally arise from this root mindset of pride — contempt for others, cynicism about life in general, despair in the face of hardship or misfortune, complete selfishness in terms of material and sensual gratification, and personal security, and having one's way at all times. It is a disease of the soul, with the malformed and out-of-control ego derailing reason and refusing to countenance the truth about oneself and the world. It is wilful self-delusion and enslavement to the lie of self-sufficiency. Knowledge of reality and acceptance of truth, the way things are, are indispensable to wholesome human relationships, yet it is somehow within our nature to resist them.

Every society known to history has in some form or other held up the injunction to treat others as you want to be treated yourself as the guiding principle for all human relations, though few have lived up to it. Its universality and conscience-tugging rightness have led to it being called The Golden Rule, and its enduring moral power rests on the recognition of the equal human dignity of all people. Hubris refuses such recognition.

THE BITTER FRUITS OF HUBRIS

As a fallible and flawed human being, I have over many years struggled to come to terms with my own propensity for hubris, and now accept that, in my case at least, shedding it demands renewing the struggle daily. The insistent desire for personal recognition provides a constant temptation to promote self at the expense of others. The pursuit of self-justification often involves making judgments about others without even beginning to understand the dynamics of their lives, and frequently condemning them as wrong, inferior or even evil. Self-justification lures one into the lie, the refusal to face up to the truth about oneself and the world.

In a fit of honesty I once measured myself against the criteria posed by the psychotherapist Louis Tartaglia in his book *Flawless*, which examines the ten most common psychological disorders he has encountered in his patients over many years. These common human perversities were certainly reminiscent of my experience with other people, but not mental states I had, in my hubris, ever considered applicable to myself. They are:

- Addicted to being right
- Raging indignation
- Blame and resentment
- High anxiety
- Intolerance
- Self-pity
- Self-centredness
- Lack of self-confidence
- Cynicism
- Dishonesty

I am ashamed to admit that I did not emerge from the exercise with much credit. All ten of these character flaws, which clearly belong to any list of negative attitudes, applied to me to some degree in the way I conducted myself in relations with others. These states of mind are harmful to mutually rewarding relationships, and I had, of course, always been alert to such flaws in other people. But now I had them staring me in the face as I looked in the mirror. Tartaglia wisely emphasises that the most practical thing to do when you encounter these character flaws in other people is to address your own.

The truth I finally confronted about myself was the hubris that I had been guilty of during my years as a teacher, but which I allowed to run completely out of control in my career in advertising. I became so obsessive about winning advertising awards and becoming a creative director that I deceived myself into believing that my genius was going to transform the industry, and that everybody else shared my assessment of my abilities. Completely blind to my own inadequacies, I saw each new success as confirmation of my destiny, and when the offer to become a creative director materialised, my euphoria was tempered by a certain resentment that it had not come sooner.

My first appointment was a disaster. The CEO and several members of my staff showed hostility and deceit, actively politicking to bring me down, but those were, ironically, much the same attitudes and behaviour I had employed to secure the position. Naturally, I failed to see this at the time, believing myself to be the blameless victim of a malignant conspiracy, but the experience at least forced me to reflect on what I might have done differently. On the next three occasions when I served as creative director, I did make a significant difference to the performance of each of the agencies concerned, but I did so posing as and acting like a guru, never showing much respect for the ability of others.

The greatest influence I was ever to exercise in my advertising career came when it seemed to be all over. At the age of forty-seven I found myself with no job and few prospects, given a rapidly transforming industry that was suspicious of old hacks. A poorly-paid position as a senior writer for a new retail agency was all that seemed available. Taking up the job with my confidence in tatters and my expectations low, I resolved to unleash all my creative energies and extensive experience to rebuild my career.

However, a retail sweatshop was hardly the right environment for producing award-winning creative advertising. My days were filled by helping harassed account executives meet absurd deadlines, mentoring younger writers and art directors, and trying to encourage justifiably cynical colleagues to respond to an endless stream of mundane briefs with a never-say-die inventiveness. By the time I resigned, five years later, from what was by then a very successful agency, in addition to holding down a new position as account director on several multinational brands, I was also giving weekly seminars on advertising, marketing, and life in general to a large group of young people from all departments, plus staff from the brand-development agency on the floor above.

By corralling my hubris I had found greater fulfilment in my work and my relationships than ever before. But unchecked, it can still break out, and I have learned that I need to reflect daily on my attitudes to others and to myself so as to keep it under control. Though my journey to redemption had started emotionally, intellectually, and spiritually some years before, the challenges of those five years were a watershed in my life. And it all turned on a determination to find the source of my inadequacies in relations with others.

WHY HUBRIS IS OUT OF CONTROL

The hubris of humankind has been a feature of all cultures from the earliest days of civilisation, but we live at a time when it has become an epidemic. In an era when scepticism and cynicism are rampant, this virulence is explained largely by the close affinity hubris has with untruth, and the strange reticence we all feel when it comes to disclosing our innermost feelings. In his book *Sincerity and Authenticity* Lionel Trilling quotes Oscar Wilde in expounding on this disconcerting human enigma:

"Man is least himself when he talks in his own person. Give him a mask and he will tell you the truth."

It is hard to find any area of human relations where pragmatic deceit is not at work. Can a father tell his children he is deeply afraid that the airliner in which they are travelling is going to crash? Can a young man tell his fiancé that he is sexually aroused by her best friend? Can an employer tell a job applicant that she feels put off by his looks and manner, or his bad breath? Can an inspirational CEO admit to his team that he no longer believes in the vision he held up for them and is seeking another position?

The Russian philosopher, Nicolas Berdyaev in *The Destiny of Man* gives a thought-provoking explanation of how untruth has become so ingrained in social, political, economic, and spiritual life that it has come to be seen as morally good. I have already given some indication of how the lie of racial superiority was used to justify colonial culture, and similar institutional deceit is easily exposed in Nazism, Marxism, market capitalism, libertarianism, scientism, political correctness, environmentalism and all closed systems of thought. Berdyaev also levels the same charge against the various Christian Churches, and he is justified whenever any church or religion refuses to take into account all known truth about reality. Ideology has, in fact, become the classic example of the lie in the twentieth and twenty-first centuries, and it is based on the utilitarian thinking that says the end justifies the means. Berdyaev points out the dangers to democratic society:

'Politics is the sphere in which the discrepancy between ends and means reaches its maximum; it therefore admits of the greatest falsity. Thus parliament is a means for bringing about public welfare which is supposed to be the aim of democracy. But parliamentarianism with its rival parties, each of which strives for power, applies false means to achieve its ends at any cost and at the same time forgets those ends and becomes an end in itself. Parliamentary politics are permeated with lies which are essential for securing the majority of votes at elections. Power is a means of realising the good of the state, of the nation, of civilisation, of humanity. But power always tends to become an end in itself and to replace all other ends.'

To suggest that the common good, or the national good, is somehow completely in congruence with the standpoint of a particular political party is patently nonsense. It implies that the architects of party policy are omniscient, infallible, and utterly selfless, and that people and the world at large are so many machines, utterly predictable in the way they behave. This highlights the inevitable conflict between genuine democracy and ideology. It also sheds light on our predicament in trying to build relationships on truth.

Our difficulties with hubris and untruth in the post-modern West have been exacerbated by the erosion of traditional values over the past several centuries and the gradual emergence of the self-sufficient individual as the social ideal. In what is often called 'the therapeutic society', the influence of waves of new schools of psychology has permeated our culture. 'Values clarification' in schools encourages young people to choose for themselves the attitudes and behaviour they will adopt in their relations with other people. This sweeps aside the wisdom of the ages and nourishes hubris in uninformed and impressionable minds.

With the deliberate dismantling of parental authority, the exaltation of permissiveness and promiscuity, and the equating of consumerism with the meaning of life, the message of our culture to the young is anarchic and confused, but relentlessly seductive. Their over-stimulated hubris is usually carried over into adulthood and, naturally, the workplace. It erupts in all manner of anti-social pathologies, and the ensuing alienation, frustration, anxiety, and self-doubt presage the ruinous spite, rage, and self-destructive behaviour so prevalent today.

The people afflicted are, of course, superficially controlled by the social and political elites through the soft controls of human resources management — nominally participative, empowering, and consensual, but in reality constraining, manipulative and Machiavellian. However, the smouldering rage is volatile and flares up with increasing frequency. The rapid growth of the security industry and the proliferation of gated communities is damning evidence of the real crisis facing the Western world — the need to renew civil society, to make living together possible once more. This will require addressing the hubris of one and all — the arrogant elites and also the self-indulgent citizens who scream for their rights while eschewing their responsibilities.

The widespread mental disorder psychologists call narcissism and the socially destructive mindset the philosophers call nihilism are merely hubris that has been fanned out of control from infancy to adulthood by a complex host of factors. It is an attitude that one is free to reject at any time, although it is far from simple to do so, because it can only be successful if love is present; and hubris and love are incompatible.

BEING CLEAR ABOUT BEING TRUTHFUL

It has already been acknowledged that being completely truthful in all situations is difficult: we all bend or conceal the truth quite often in our daily lives. What then is truth, and what does it mean to be an honest and trustworthy person?

Truth is *being* — it is everything that is, or everything that exists. It is reality in its totality, including intangible things such as thoughts and ideas, and ironically even lies. The existence of a lie is indisputably part of reality, but it is interesting to note that untruth has no being in itself — it is contingent upon the existence of truth in the first place, because it is a denial of that truth. The truth about anything, then, is the reality of its being, the way it is, in relation to the reality of everything else that exists or is.

By way of definition, we may then say that truthfulness, or living in truth or honesty, is being completely open to the reality of all being, of all that is — oneself, other people and the universe at large in all its seemingly endless diversity.

According to this understanding, without truth there can be no goodness, freedom, justice, beauty, or properly ordered human relationships. The good of a human being can only be identified in the light of the truth about human beings. The freedom due to any person depends on the truth about human freedom. Justice derives its meaning from the truth about human rights and responsibilities. The beauty of anything, regardless of the ongoing philosophical controversies in the deeply-troubled world of art, can surely only be judged according to the truth of what it is. This enables us to affirm the essential beauty of a barren, drought-stricken landscape, an excessively salivating bulldog, an aged and dying man, or an awkward, pimply adolescent. Such an understanding of beauty leaves all the space as may be required for personal taste. The words of Keats in *Ode on a Grecian Urn* are entirely apposite:

> *"Beauty is truth, truth is beauty — that is all*
> *Ye need know on earth, and all you need to know."*

Truth as it has been defined here plainly extends way beyond human knowledge, and always will, for the simple reason that we can never traverse the infinite distance between being and non-being. The exciting implication is that, theoretically, the prospects for scientific discovery are practically limitless, and if we were ever to reach the edge of the cosmos, what would we find — empty space? Space is not nothing — if light can penetrate it, then presumably particles are present or something is waving. We can have no conception of non-being — consider only the configurations necessary to programme nothing into a computer. So the definition acknowledges the inescapable part that mystery must always play in human life.

The definition also helps us appreciate that our personal knowledge, which is always limited to some extent, makes us vulnerable at various stages in life in the face of new knowledge we might find unsettling or even threatening. Thus it would be harmful to a six-year-old child to have the reality of the threat of nuclear annihilation spelled out to him. It would be discouraging for employees to be given access to confidential information about financial matters they can do nothing about while management is handling the matter ethically and efficiently anyway. And it would have undermined Ernest Shackleton's efforts to escape the merciless Antarctic winter if he had shown his crew anything less than a complete conviction that his desperate measures would be successful.

By nature, we often find truth disagreeable and for all human beings acceptance of our personal inadequacies and radical dependence on others requires a long and gradual journey to emotional maturity throughout adolescence and often deep into adulthood.

We should never shut out or deny something simply because it does not suit our own ideas, desires, or ambitions. We should instead direct our attitudes and behaviour to promoting the good of the world in which we live, according to our always expanding knowledge of reality. In his essay *A Brief Reader of the Virtues of the Human Heart* the philosopher Josef Pieper lays down the bottom line for humanity:

'All duty is based on being. Reality is the basis of ethics. Goodness is the standard of reality. Whoever wants to know and do the good must direct his gaze toward the objective world of being, not toward his own sentiment *or toward arbitrarily established* ideals *and* models.*'*

If love means wanting and actively seeking the good of the other, then love becomes the standard by which we have to measure our relationships. And love too depends on truth. We can only love according to truth because in order to love someone we have to know the truth about them, what is good for them and what is bad for them. If I say, for example, that for you to help me in defrauding the tax department will be good for you because it will make you rich, I am lying. I am saying that money is the supreme good and that deceit and theft, and the harm they cause to others as well as to one's self are all justifiable means to that end. We know what is good and bad inasmuch as we know reality and refuse to corrupt that knowledge with our own self-serving distortions and evasions.

HOPE FOR RELATIONSHIPS

Once we understand the real meaning of truthfulness and accept our own existential need to be honest, the possibility of successfully addressing the challenge of living in harmony with others opens up to us. The word 'dysfunctional' itself automatically asserts that there is a functional state from which relationships have deviated. It suggests that while wrong choices have brought about bad experiences, there is a right way to conduct relationships that would be for the good of all.

Moreover, as we have already seen, being a person has no meaning outside the context of relationships. The etymology of the words 'prosopon' and 'persona', as mentioned in the chapter on human nature, emphasises this fact. The first comes from the ancient Greek words for 'look towards'; the second is a Latin compound which means 'sounding through'. The human person is made for relationships. Nicolas Berdyaev in *The Destiny of Man* neatly encapsulated the verdict of philosophy and the human sciences:

'Personality from its very nature presupposes another — not the "not-self" which is a negative limit, but another person. Personality is impossible without love and sacrifice, without passing over to the other, to the friend, to the loved one. A self-contained personality becomes disintegrated.'

This is the extension of the oldest problem in philosophy, that of the One and the Many, into the sphere of human interaction. What must have precedence — the individual or the community?

Each of us is defined by the nature of our relationships with other people. For example, I am a husband, father, son, brother, grandfather, friend, associate, acquaintance, and a South African-born ex-Rhodesian who has become a New Zealand citizen. Every other descriptive that may be applied to me likewise reflects the reality of who I am in a social context — cultivated, complex and cantankerous. Even my taste for red wine and good books unavoidably involves me in a variety of social commitments. Within the realm of those commitments, what may I expect of others and what may they expect of me?

Christopher Lasch in a postscript entitled *The Culture of Narcissism Revisited* echoes the wisdom of the ages when he declares:

'The best hope of emotional maturity, then, appears to lie in "a recognition" of the need for and dependence on people who nevertheless

remain separate from ourselves and refuse to submit to our whims. It lies in a recognition of others not as projections of our own desires but as independent beings with desires of their own. More broadly, it lies in acceptance of our limits. The world does not exist merely to satisfy our own desires; it is a world in which we can find pleasure and meaning, once we understand that others too have a right to these goods.'

Every person is an end in himself or herself, and never the means to anybody else's ends. Yet every person is radically dependent on the others. Once we accept this, the problem of the One and the Many is resolved by the reality that the fulfilment of each depends on the fulfilment of the other. The rampant individualism and concomitant hubris encouraged in the West for so long is detrimental to the well-being of individuals as well as the community. It lies at the heart of the ever-increasing social pathologies that blight our homes, neighbourhoods, and workplaces. The urgent task of leadership is to re-establish the proper equilibrium between the One and the Many.

The West seems to have forgotten that the rights of the individual depend entirely on the concept of human rights, which in turn requires a scientifically grounded understanding of human nature and an adherence to the principles of natural law.

Because the Nazis perpetrated their barbarities with complete constitutional and legal sanction, the only legal platform on which the Nuremburg trials at the end of World War II could proceed was that of natural law. It is also true that if the laws of the state were indeed the sole standard, then many people would adopt the attitude that being caught was the only crime, and trust, the cement of any successful society, would be removed. As C. S. Lewis reminded us:

"a good society requires good people, and laws can't make people good".

Civilisation is the attempt by humankind to rise above biological determinism, to say no to 'nature red in tooth and claw', to rise above mere animal nature. The purpose of civilisation is to build the ethos, ideas, attitudes, and behaviour that will inspire and enable the good of one and all, the individual and the community. In this sense, a truly humane civilisation would in theory provide the basis of a civilisation for all humanity, one in which all cultures could flourish side by side. Of course, such a civilisation would require all cultures to affirm and practise the essential conditions for a humane worldview as laid out in Chapter Four. Those same principles should logically extend to all forms of human relationship.

BOUND TO GROW

There is a double truth in the insight that we are 'bound to grow': firstly, that we are tied together to enable us to develop our personal potential, and secondly, that we are certain to flourish in the context of good relationships. The purpose of human relationship is human fulfilment, and people who enter into a relationship without a commitment to the fulfilment of the other, render their own fulfilment impossible. They may temporarily satisfy their hubris or biological urges, but they will corrupt their own character as well as the relationship. We are only bound to grow if we have the sincere intention to build relationships instead of using them for selfish ends. How do we do that?

Given a commitment to a humane worldview, a character being built on virtue and the consequent reining in of hubris, healthy relationships become a real, if still challenging, possibility; except for one factor – other people – and they are essential to any relationship. They too would need the same three qualities, and in a world where the development of narcissistic personalities is state-sponsored and also considered commercially de rigueur, the incidence of such people will predictably be low. This is also the root of our trouble in producing leaders. And it is the challenge for all those who feel called to lead.

Can we inspire people to turn their lives around and start building more loving families, more nurturing communities, workplaces with more genuine team spirit, and a nation dedicated to being a good place for one and all? Can we help to renew society through relationships built on trust rather than intimidation? All the great teachers have taught us that the only way to change another person is to love them.

In practical terms, how do we love others and encourage them to respond in kind? The guidelines have always been there in loving families and caring communities in every time and place, and there are just five of them:

Empathy is the kind of understanding of other people that hubris precludes. It is the ability to think and feel like the other person, to vividly imagine their hopes and fears, their pleasure and their pain, to put yourself in their shoes. That, of course, is only possible if you respect them as someone with a dignity equal to your own, free, and gifted with a unique potential and yearning for fulfilment like every other person on the planet, regardless of personal attributes and circumstances. The better you know someone, the more accurately you will be able to empathise with them, but our common humanity makes it possible for us to imagine the fear of a stranger being mugged or the distress of a starving child on the other side of the world. Empathy is not an emotion; it is an act of will that requires us to suppress our own feelings and to imagine those of the other person. Empathy is a willed coming out of ourselves in order to know what it must be like for a fellow human being in a particular situation, whether a spouse, a child, a colleague, a customer, or a stranger. It is an attitude that must be taught in the home and the school, and is best developed through stories of people in other times and places, underlining yet again the value of history and classic literature. It goes without saying that empathy can only be based on the truth about the other person. Empathy helps suppress hubris and opens the door to compassion.

Compassion is sharing in the suffering of another person. It too is a willed state of mind, an attitude. It should never be confused with pity or feeling sorry for the other person, which is usually superficial and easily turned into disgust or contempt. The test of compassion only comes in concrete situations where we demonstrate our willingness to share the other person's suffering by our actions – spending time at the bedside of a dying person (especially if he or she is not a close relative or friend); putting one's personal safety at risk in going to the assistance of someone who is being attacked; visiting a prisoner in jail fully conscious of the wrong they have done; giving time and money in helping the poor and needy; offering friendship and hospitality to a person suffering from loneliness; devoting time and expertise to help a colleague remedy poor performance in their work; interrupting one's own busy schedule to assist someone whose car has broken down. Compassion requires a potent brew of all the virtues, not least of which would be courage, as well as the social awareness and decisiveness that come with prudence. It is a reflection of the goodwill or respect for the dignity of other people that forms the necessary foundation for any social arrangement, and its hallmark is service to others. Nothing could be further from it than the shallow sentimentality, rife in post-modern minds, that never goes beyond tears and talking. Compassion helps to promote a healthy sense of humour.

Humour and the laughter it generates is one of the great joys of human nature. The old English saying 'the maid who laughs is half won' is a piece of folk wisdom that can be applied to all relationships. Where there is no laughter, human nature is being repressed and not fulfilled. But, like all blessings, humour can be corrupted and become a curse, as when people laugh at the suffering of others. I am far from being prudish or priggish when it comes to dirty jokes, sick humour or dark comedy, but the very names we give to these categories should warn us of the attendant dangers. The humour that swamps the media today, utterly dependent as it is on profanity, promiscuity, and abusiveness, all of which are inimical to healthy relationships, is a perversion of one of our most essential attributes for building them. Jean Paul Richter's observation that the person who laughs too much is actually profoundly sad, seems particularly apposite today.

The key to all healthy humour is our sense of irony, susceptible unfortunately to cultural repression, but always at the disposal of the individual who chooses to seek fulfilment in truth rather than in ideological proscriptions. Irony recognises the frailty, fallibility, and false pride of all human beings, enabling us to laugh at ourselves and others when we take ourselves too seriously, as creative comedies from Lysistrata to Seinfeld illustrate. It is the antidote for hubris and inspires the humility we all need in accepting our inadequacies and our radical dependency on the goodwill and support of other people. In this sense, humour prepares us to be forgiving.

Forgiveness is one of the most difficult sacrifices any of us ever have to make, and for that reason it is not something that is easily found in these narcissistic times. We struggle to embrace forgiveness because it is offensive to hubris. Yet forgiveness is the only way for us to remove the cancer of hate, rage, and resentment that can destroy any hope of personal fulfilment. Forgiveness is therapy for the offended; contrition is therapy for the offender. Blood vengeance, historically seen in the carnage of the blood feud and later in the more equitable though still barbarous eye-for-an-eye philosophy, was a dominant attitude in primitive society and is a by-product of hubris, which is naturally unable to tolerate any offence to the ego. Whenever civilisation loses its moral compass, bloody vengeance emerges once more to torment the soul of humankind. And so it is a familiar theme throughout history, as attested by cultural icons from *Hamlet* to *High Noon*. The alternative to vengeance is forgiveness, without which fully humane relationships are impossible. Forgiveness demands empathy, compassion, a sense of irony, and all the strength of character we can muster in the moment when we are called on to forgive. It also demands patience, the acceptance that each of us is a work-in-progress, and a willingness to endure inconveniences and offences while waiting for potential to bear fruit as a fully integrated personality. Forgiveness makes it possible for us, in the face of human weakness and folly, to offer others our faithfulness.

Faithfulness is the commitment we make to be true and trustworthy in relationships. It is the commitment to be empathetic, because you can only be true to someone you understand, to be compassionate, to appreciate the irony in each other's failures, and to be unfailingly forgiving, persevering through all vicissitudes for the sake of the relationship. Faithfulness is the unfailing support and solidarity that engenders confidence and hope now and in the future, enabling us to believe in and trust one other in all things. It is the acid test for integrity — personal, community, corporate, and national — and it is sobering to reflect on the fact that we are defined as individuals by the quality of our relationships. Life is a learning process — learning how to be what you should be. It involves a commitment to the truth about yourself and others, and to letting others know that what they see is who you are, and that what you say is what you mean. Roger Scruton in *Gentle Regrets* explains the profound significance of human faithfulness expressed in a vow:

> *That we can make vows is one part of the great miracle of human freedom; and when we cease to make them, our lives are impoverished, since they involve no lasting commitment, no attempt to cross the frontier between self and other.*

THE CHALLENGE OF RELATIONSHIPS

Since leadership is about people, and people are incomprehensible outside of their social bonds, building effective relationships is inevitably the essential challenge for leaders. For misleaders, on the other hand, effective relations are not a concern since they seek rather to manipulate and exploit people, and to misuse relationships as a means to their own ends. But all of us, susceptible to hubris as we are, can be tempted at times to mislead; only a resolute will to overcome that fatal flaw will enable us to be the leaders our world so desperately needs.

Building fulfilling relationships

Applying the five guidelines of empathy, compassion, humour, forgiveness, and faithfulness is made more difficult by the fact that our networks of relationships are inescapably complex and relentlessly dynamic, changing as the people involved and their circumstances change. For example, parents shape their relationship with each other and their children within the web of social ties that includes family, friends, people from school, people from sports and cultural clubs, the community at large, and more; and the quality of their lives depends on the quality of those relationships. For leaders in the world of work, the picture becomes even more complicated. Figure 9.1 shows a simplified template for an organisation's relationship map, indicating why leaders have to devote so much time and energy to people issues. In a very real sense, every circle on the map represents an individual or a group of people that the organisation needs in order to add value in some way or other to their operation.

ORGANISATIONAL RELATIONSHIP MAP

Figure 9.1

If the circles were laid out like links in a chain, it would provide a graphic representation of the organisation's value chain, and whenever a link in the chain failed to add value, the entire chain would be weakened. This is why the culture of an organisation is critical to its effectiveness, because corporate culture reflects the character of the organisation and how it conducts itself in relationships. If the culture does not reflect the same virtues as those for individuals, few of the people involved would be likely to follow the necessary guidelines, and the weak links in the chain — dysfunctional relationships — would be spread throughout its length.

Tragically, that seems to be the experience of most organisations today. Personal integrity and respect for other people are scarce commodities in the Western world, as is evinced by political corruption, commercial greed and dishonesty, social perversity, widespread cheating and violence in sports, all manner of social pathology, and the chronic instability of relationships.

What a world of opportunity it is for real leaders — for people who can see beyond the suffocating cynicism and fatalism in the corridors of business and bureaucracy to a better future built on genuine human relationships. It will be no easy task, and never could be, because we are capricious and self-centred human beings trying to live together with so many other capricious and self-centred human beings. And each one must be treated as an individual; to deal with everybody in the same way is to deal unfairly with most of them, because we are all different, yet all deserve respect as persons, not as part of a group. The problems people have in relationships rarely arise as a result of poor people skills, but are almost invariably the result of negative attitudes. And anyone with all the skills to be completely effective in relationships might still use them for evil rather than for good.

The challenge is what it has always been: a life and death struggle between hubris and love. A challenge that can only be addressed by each of us as individuals, making the right personal choice.

The reality is that to change all your relationships and the whole world for the better immediately, you only have to change one person — yourself. Self-leadership has to be the first step.

CHAPTER 10
Leaders unleash creativity

"We looked at peace and security as a problem to be solved and not as a work to be made." Dorothy Sayers

The mark of humanity

Some fifty years before William the Conqueror defeated the Saxon king Harold at the Battle of Hastings in 1066, a young monk at the abbey of Malmesbury, inspired by the legend of Daedalus, tried to prove that it was indeed possible for a human being to fly. The intrepid Eilmer devised pairs of wings that he attached to his arms and legs, and launched himself off the tower of the abbey, sailing through the fresh English air for some two hundred metres before coming to an abrupt stop in a crash-landing that broke both his legs and left him crippled for the rest of his life. The rather undignified denouement of his enterprise notwithstanding, Eilmer resolved to try again, convinced that all he needed was a tail for greater stability and manoeuvrability. His abbot did not share Eilmer's pioneering spirit and grounded the world's first aviator for life.

Significantly, drawstring toy helicopters made for years thereafter by inquisitive medieval people helped to keep alive Eilmer's belief that the air and wind power could be harnessed for human flight; the dream of Daedalus lived on. Flying was evidently no longer regarded as magical, but as being well within the scope of human reason.

Eilmer typifies the inventiveness of people in the Middle Ages, who for centuries were dismissed as backward and superstitious. Medieval Europe was in fact prolific in its technical progress, and the intellectual flowering of the twelfth and thirteenth centuries contributed very significantly to the scientific revolution and the development of democratic ideals. Anonymous 'Dark Age' inventors transcended the impotent agricultural and transportation technology of Roman civilisation with innovations like the rigid, padded harness, which enabled a horse to pull as much as an ox, but much faster; the horse-shoe; the three-field system of cultivation; a swivelling front axle on carts; the widespread exploitation of water-power and wind-power (with the consequent ability to reclaim vast tracts of land from the sea), and the pioneering of commercial aquaculture.

Medievals also gave us painting in oils on canvas, musical notation, the pipe-organ, the harpsichord, and the violin, the literary inspiration of Dante, Chaucer, and Langland, the intellectual ferment of universities, and the majestic beauty of the deplorably misnamed Gothic architecture, as well as double-entry book-keeping, bills of exchange, and the beginnings of free-market capitalism.

The creativity of ancient societies was, of course, also remarkable, and is most spectacularly demonstrated by their monumental building projects, including the walls of Jericho, the pyramids, Stonehenge, and the largest building project ever — the Great Wall of China. But this ignores even more important intellectual breakthroughs like writing, mathematics, astronomy, agriculture, and much, much more.

All this creative activity is a good illustration of the reality that the urge and mental capacity to reorder the natural world to make human life better is an attribute common to all societies, albeit in different degrees and with widely variable results.

And the fruits of the human intellect go far beyond these achievements in every direction. From papyrus to pantomime to the Periodic Table of Elements; from Sanskrit to sonatas to skydiving; from crochet to croquet to cuisine; from iambic pentameters to impressionism to the internet, human creativity exhibits a global cornucopia of cultural achievement. Intellect, the culture-creating part of the human mind is incessantly at work wherever human beings are active. However, human ingenuity, like all human characteristics, is misused at least as frequently as it is deployed for the good of humankind. But we simply cannot not draw on the very resource that typifies our human nature. The human intellect is a problem-solving phenomenon, constantly evaluating the way it finds the world and pondering how it might change things for the better.

It is a creative power in search of challenges.

Directed by hubris, it is dangerous; guided by love, it is the hope of humanity.

THE INFLUENCE OF CHARACTER AND CULTURE

The French scientist and philosopher Blaise Pascal, who among his other achievements produced the first basic computing machine, provided many insights into the human condition and its potential for good and evil. In *Pensees*, he told us:

'It is not man's nature always to go in one direction; it has its ups and downs. Fever makes us both shiver and sweat. The chill is as good an indication of how high the fever will go as the heat itself. It is the same with human inventions from age to age, and with good and evil in the world in general.'

Any proper understanding of our creative ability can only be built on a deep awareness of this dual potential. Creativity is humankind's great advantage in the ongoing task to procreate and prosper on this planet, yet the quality and application of our creativity is inevitably determined by character and culture. Leaders are called to ensure that human creativity produces what is best for people everywhere and for the environment, while misleaders, as they have done throughout history, either repress or pervert creativity. The examples are endless, but a few representative cases deserve consideration.

The European Middle Ages provide a telling comment on both medieval and modern culture. The renewed interest in and understanding of the Middle Ages is scarcely more than nine decades old; previously, the modern era, which was born in the Renaissance and the Scientific Revolution, and defined most forcefully in the eighteenth century Enlightenment, blinded itself to the achievements of their predecessors on which they so obviously built. As one of those whose education was distorted by this manifest obscurantism, I am frequently shaken by revelations from recent research (research that could have been conducted hundreds of years ago).

Misinformation has corrupted our understanding and attitudes for far too long. We have always been led to believe that women's rights were suppressed before the emergence of enlightened ideals in the modern era. That the repression of women, wherever and whenever it has occurred, has deprived civilisation of the creative energies and output of half of humankind, is beyond dispute, and in the Western world at least, it has only been during the last century that women have gradually shaken off the fetters that constrained them for so long. So what was happening during the four hundred years of the modern age before that? And what was the reality in the medieval period? A few facts are in order.

In the classical period of ancient Greece and Rome — a time greatly admired by the savants of the Renaissance and the Enlightenment, women were indeed kept in the background and subjected to the control of their fathers and husbands. The picture presented by the Dark Ages is dramatically different. For example, there was the barbarian warrior queen Boudicca, who taunted the men of her tribe when they showed signs of preferring subjection by the Romans to risking their lives for freedom. Similarly, the Byzantine emperor Justinian's wife, Theodora, wielded massive influence over her husband and the empire, saving his throne on more than one occasion through her resolute defiance in the face of danger.

The French historian Regine Pernoud in *Those Terrible Middle Ages,* delighted in informing her contemporaries of some long-ignored historical facts: the first book on education known to have been published in France was written by a woman, Dhuoda, in the ninth century; the queens of medieval France were crowned, like their husbands, in Rheims Cathedral; and Eleanor of Aquitaine was one of the predominant political figures of her age.

Women also exercised extraordinary authority in the Church during the Middle Ages, and abbesses often administered vast territories, with full respect shown for both their spiritual and temporal power. Heloise, the famed mistress and wife of the scholar Abelard, and a great scholar herself, was one of many women whose careers provide a more balanced picture of medieval attitudes. One of the most widely read encyclopaedias produced in the Middle Ages was written by the abbess Herrad of Landsberg, and the intellectual contribution to posterity of women like Hildegarde of Bingen and Gertrude of Helfta, also help to expose the mendacity of much modern scholarship. Well-preserved medieval records show that women worked and ran their own businesses in all sorts of fields — as merchants, millers, hairdressers, doctors, apothecaries, plasterers, copyists, and more. There is even evidence to show that women served as crusaders. So when did the position of women change?

Pernoud argues that the reintroduction of Roman law in Europe brought the freedom enjoyed by women in the Middle Ages to an end.

The surge of interest in classical culture that followed the discovery of the Aristotelian texts and their translation from Arabic into Latin led to the renewed study of Roman Law. The Renaissance itself was built on a fervent admiration for all things classical, and consequently a rejection of all that followed the collapse of classical antiquity. Roman Law, with its entrenchment of the authority of men through the legal concept of the paterfamilias, was steadily brought back to replace the Common Law that had developed over so many centuries. The freedom and rights of women and children were gradually curtailed through the first three centuries of the modern era, and modern culture for the most part deprived itself of the feminine genius. It was left to the heroic efforts of the few to keep the ideal alive and to work for the restoration we are still living through today. Culture is a very significant factor when it comes to creativity.

Another example of Pascal's insight can be drawn from more recent events: a report in the German journal *Der Spiegel* a few years back bemoaned the failure of development aid to make any meaningful difference in the lives of the people of Africa, its intended beneficiaries. The incompetence and self-interest of the aid agencies and the donor governments of the developed nations in misdirecting the finance and contributions in kind were seen as significant factors, but the greed and corruption of the recipient African governments and their unrestrained use of power were identified as the main reasons for the failure. Der Spiegel went on to tell the story of an agent for the German Society for Technical Cooperation, a man by the name of Hendrik Hempel. He led the impoverished people of a state-owned farm in Northern Eritrea to reorganise and rebuild the agricultural facility so as to reclaim the wilderness created by years of war. The people were inspired to create an enormously productive green haven in the otherwise desolate landscape.

Unfortunately, Hempel's success provided an embarrassing contrast to the regime's persistent failures. The government and its lackeys refused to draw lessons from the more productive project — instead they forced Hempel's farm to accept an unsustainable influx of former guerrillas from abandoned state-run projects, and he was obliged to walk away from the beacon of hope he had built amidst deprivation and despair. Where Hempel had held up an inspiring vision and unleashed the creative energies of impoverished people in pursuit of the goal, the misleaders in the regime could see no further than their own arrogance and avarice.

This familiar pattern can be seen wherever a culture of creativity confronts a culture of repression and exploitation. Mugabe's gangster government in Zimbabwe is destroying what should be a thriving modern economy; the hopeless malaise has nothing to do with race, but everything to do with a culture horribly distorted by tyranny and the hubris of one man and his cronies. But then every nation on earth should ask itself whether its people are genuinely inspired to use their innate creative abilities in search of the good life.

In *The Mystery of Capital,* Third World economist Hernando De Soto has revealed the cultural quagmire that is choking the efforts of poor people in the undeveloped world to improve their lives. These people — from divergent racial and ethnic backgrounds in Peru, Egypt, the Philippines, Mexico and Haiti, among others — are extraordinarily inventive and thrifty. However, the corrupt and capricious power wielded by their governments and the absence of formal property rights means their economic assets can never be turned into capital.

It took De Soto's researchers six hours a day for two hundred and eighty-nine days to get legal certification for a small one-person business in Peru. Registration costs amounted to $1,231. To acquire legal approval to build a house on state-owned land the team worked for nearly seven years, wading through over two hundred administrative procedures in fifty-two government offices. Obtaining legal title for the piece of land required them to negotiate more than seven hundred bureaucratic stages. Arbitrary authoritarian regimes fear nothing more than poor people becoming prosperous and educated, because that spells the end of docile submission to tyranny. A culture that smothers human potential is not a humane culture, and will never prove to be creative in anything other than evading regulation. It is significant that many poor people in Third World countries slip naturally into the extra-legal black-market economy that slowly destroys the official economy, and at the same time all hope of a society built on truth and justice.

This repression of the natural creativity we all possess as human beings can be as readily revealed in the culture of families, schools, businesses, and communities as it can in the lives of nations. Children all over the world enter school severely handicapped because their parents never told them stories or read to them. Children all over the world give up on maths because some lazy teacher has told them they lack the ability or because they have heard their parents laughing about their own inadequacies in the subject when they were at school. Employees all over the world keep their ideas to themselves or even give up altogether on thinking inventively about their work because of management disdain or a rigid corporate culture where people are not allowed to make mistakes. Homeowners in neighbourhoods all over the world have descended into passivity in the face of rising rates of crime and social dysfunction because of their despair over official incompetence and indifference. These negative cultural impacts are unnecessary, as demonstrated by the many inspiring creative responses that result from more positive stimuli.

However, culture is not the sole determinant of the quality of creativity, because creativity in the first instance is a personal phenomenon rather than a social phenomenon. This is why character plays the same influential role in the individual person as culture performs in the life of society. The best way to understand this is to examine the nature of human creativity itself.

WHAT IS CREATIVITY?

Over many years of studying, practising and speaking about creativity, I have used a particular demonstration that seems to convey with compelling force exactly what human creativity involves. Consistently arresting, this simple demonstration is not just an astonishing physical feat, it is also a concrete illustration of the creative process. It is not my own, and I regret that I am unable to give credit to whoever devised it originally.

The demonstration involves a glass bottle, a fork, a spoon, and a matchstick. The task is to somehow balance the eating implements and the match on the rim of the bottle with contact restricted to a single point (see Picture 10.1). Remarkably, because I am certain that I am not the only person in the world who has performed this trick for others, only once has someone in my workshops seen it done before.

Performing the feat involves connecting the eating implements by weaving the lip of the spoon between the prongs of the fork to create a metal arc. Then one end of the match is hooked through the prongs at the centre-point of that arc, and the other end is placed on the lip of the bottle so that the handles of the implements are suspended on either side. The physical reality has to be seen to be believed, and even then belief is strained. Though there is obviously a simple scientific explanation for the phenomenon, it does not detract from the truth that our cosmos is a strange and wonderful place.

Picture 10.1

How does this demonstration illustrate the process of human creativity? Perhaps it is best to first define human creativity. Consider the following prescriptions from some famous creative people.

"An idea is a feat of association." Poet Robert Frost

"Thinking is connecting things, and stops if they cannot be connected." Author G. K. Chesterton *in Orthodoxy*

"Lateral thinking is restructuring patterns and provoking new ones." Creative guru Edward De Bono in *Lateral Thinking*

"Creativity is to see what everyone else has seen and to think what nobody else has thought." Nobel Prize-winning physiologist Albert Szent-Gyorgyi

"Creativeness often consists of turning up what is already there. Did you know that right and left shoes were thought up only a little more than a century ago?" Advertising guru Bernice Fitz-Gibbon

Each of the definitions is itself a creative insight, but all say essentially the same thing — that physical and mental reality in all its multifarious manifestations, whether familiar or strange, presents itself in forms which people, through the use of free will and intellect, may choose to look at in different ways, and even to reconfigure so as to change reality. Admittedly limited and fallible, the human mind nonetheless has the power to shape the future. If you believe that life has meaning beyond self-gratification, it implies an awesome responsibility; if you do not believe it, you are equipped to do a great deal of harm to your fellow human beings and the environment.

The fork, spoon, match, and bottle trick illustrates various aspects of the definitions above: it shows 'a feat of association' that involves 'connecting things'; it 'connects unconventionally', so 'restructuring patterns'; and it provides evidence of someone thinking 'what nobody else has thought'. Humour, greatly beloved of all human beings, provides another telling example of this re-ordering of reality by the human mind. Any joke provides a ready illustration, as in the following:

'Back in the Middle Ages, a knight found himself stranded in a foreign land when his horse died. Further tormented by some very inclement weather, he sought refuge at the first inn he came across, and he inquired of the inn-keeper whether there was a horse he might purchase. The inn-keeper was unable to help, but the knight noticed a mangy-looking St. Bernard hound sleeping near the bar. He asked if he could buy it as at least some sort of replacement for his deceased steed. The old inn-keeper seemed very reluctant, looking first at the aged canine, and then at the howling tempest outside. After a long pause, he said to the anxious knight: "Sorry sir, but I would not send a knight out on a dog like this".'

A video clip on YouTube recently provided another engaging demonstration of creativity understood in this way. The Slovenian jazz and popular music choir, Perpetuum Jazzile, perform *Africa* by Toto, providing almost all of the accompaniment one would normally expect from an orchestra, as well as the vocals. Even more impressive is the simulation of a thunderstorm, which is performed as an introduction to the song. The choir uses only their hands, thighs and feet, snapping, slapping, stamping, and clicking them to produce a convincing audio representation of a high-veld thunderstorm, including the rain and rolling thunder. The choir credits Kearsney College in South Africa with the original idea, and while one is astonished by the virtuosity of Perpetuum Jazzile, the creativity of the mind that first saw the possible connections of an assortment of unaided human percussive techniques to produce a thunderstorm is awe-inspiring. The familiar things around us wait on the human mind to discover ever new ways to use them.

In these terms we can see human creativity at work in masterpieces such as a Modigliani painting, a Paul Simon song, a Francis Ford Coppola movie, a Jane Austen novel, a Leon Krier building design and the human genome project. It is plain that creativity thus defined is equally exemplified in all our cultural developments: in computers and credit cards, mobile phones and muesli bars, zippers and zoos, post-it notes and pinot noir, iPods and in-line roller skates, and so on. The same process is demonstrated by great sports stars, such as Christiano Ronaldo, who use the same equipment and the same conditions to produce results that the rest of us can only emulate in vastly inferior fashion, if at all. But we are all creative, because we are all human beings, and we all have free will and intellect. Given the right cultural environment, the only question is whether or not we choose to use our creative faculties.

Unleashing creativity

The mathematician and philosopher Bertrand Russell once described the creative process as starting with a problem or puzzle, leading to the hard work of focussed thinking, followed by a break in which the unconscious mind is left to reflect on the problem, and then the sudden revelation of the solution.

I must confess that I struggled to write the previous section without using the words 'problem' and 'solution', so ingrained has their usage become in our everyday conversation. Given Russell's otherwise excellent description of the creative process, it is appropriate to repeat the cautionary remarks made regarding formulae in an earlier chapter. Complex human issues cannot be reduced to simple mechanical processes that are susceptible to resolution by applying some 'scientifically-proven' problem–solution formula.

Problem–solution approaches are, more often than not, wishful thinking. For example, crime is not a problem with a solution; it is the symptom of an extremely complex set of social issues not amenable to any one-dimensional quick fix. Traffic congestion is not a problem to be solved; it is an inconvenience arising from another complex maze of social issues involving historical choices and developments, cultural attitudes, economic drivers, political interests, and more. Defective education is not a problem to be solved; it is a threat to human well-being that has grown out of still further complex political and economic choices about which maths and science can have little to say because the issues are philosophical. All these uncomfortable social circumstances in the end require the seldom easy task of reconciling human disagreements.

That said, Russell's description is still a valuable guide to what we need to do when we are confronted by the challenges of life. He identifies five stages in what he would call problem-solving but which is better described, in equally simple terms, as improving things or making things better. The five stages are: encountering an inconvenience, becoming irritated enough to do something about it, thinking hard about it in a disciplined and focused manner, allowing the subconscious mind time to address it and, finally, enjoying the eureka moment when the way to dismantle, overcome, reconfigure, or transcend the inconvenience becomes apparent.

For Russell and most other great thinkers, the inconveniences in life — the puzzles, the enigmas, the conundrums, the challenges — are what spark our creative impulses. Without them, life would have no meaning, no purpose, no quest. In *All Things Considered*, G. K. Chesterton proclaimed:

'An adventure is only an inconvenience rightly considered; and an inconvenience is only an adventure wrongly considered.'

To the creative human intellect, life is an adventure; confronting challenges, wrestling with difficulties, overcoming obstacles, and reconciling ourselves with others is what we are naturally called to do from birth. A baby still too young to crawl, lying on its back on the floor, perhaps spots something that takes its fancy. The affections are kindled and the mind kicks into gear, directing the hands to stretch towards the object of desire, and in time the child will roll over, probably unwittingly on the first occasion, and will achieve the initial stage of mobility over distance. A year later, the same child will toddle towards whatever catches his eye, and if he cannot reach it, he will quite likely pull up a chair in order to take possession of the treasure. If his mother lifts him off the chair and places the object further out of reach, the child may well wait until his mother is out of sight before launching another vertical assault on the prized item.

The five steps identified by Russell would all have been in play during such a common domestic experience. Quite spontaneously, the child would have gone through the creative thinking process highlighted by the definitions of creativity and by the fork, spoon, match, bottle trick — weighing relevant data, making possible connections, trying to see different possibilities and, quite probably, after a certain amount of frustration, hitting upon a course of action.

Any society in which people's creativity is repressed, distorted or denied, is manifestly a fundamentally inhuman society. The unique potential of each unrepeatable human life can only be developed by unleashing the individual person's innate creative energy in the quest for personal fulfilment. Unleashing creativity in others is what leaders are called to do to improve things, to make things better, to help the individual and the group (the one and the many) achieve the fulfilment they seek.

BREAKING THE SHACKLES OF CONVENTION

In the chapter on education I criticised the inadequate and often pernicious contribution of state schooling to the future of human life. I believe our deeply troubled world desperately needs proper education to break the shackles of conventional thinking and to find ways to promote genuine human progress. Not surprisingly, developments in education around the world throughout history, both positive and negative, hold valuable lessons for leaders in any walk of life.

Education, theoretically at least, aims at human fulfilment in individuals and society at large. In a very real sense, control of the means of education is control over the way people think and what they believe. This is why it has come to be monopolised by the state, whether democratic or authoritarian, and why it is often corrupted by ideology. But this perversion of the ideal of education has prompted many wonderfully creative responses in different parts of the globe.

In *The Beautiful Tree* Professor of Education James Tooley describes how while working on a commission for the World Bank's International Finance Corporation he studied private education in developing countries and stumbled on a fact that is apparently well-known by officialdom, but either ignored or suppressed. In the slums of Hyderabad he discovered what he was to witness repeatedly in many other Third World nations: how entrepreneurial teachers, sometimes uncertified and always working with minimal resources, have set up makeshift private schools that increasing numbers of poor people choose for their children in preference to free state schools. The failure of state schooling to provide real education drives the poor to patronise the impoverished private schools where inspired leadership and human ingenuity seek to give children some hope of developing their unique potential.

These under-resourced private schools face many serious challenges, not the least of which are teaching methods and curriculum content. Nevertheless, their creative response has greatly improved lives and communities. Tooley is justifiably excited about the creative possibilities:

'Rather than new Big Plans, I want to point to the general ways in which we can start small and work our way up — and by 'we' I mean thousands of small-scale philanthropic and aid agency projects, working hand in hand with thousands of small-scale educational entrepreneurs — trying different approaches, building on what works, and rejecting or modifying what does not. So many little bits of information are out there in the market, known only to parents, children, and entrepreneurs, that can move the solutions forward.'

Back in the 1970s, I knew a secondary school principal in Rhodesia who was increasingly concerned about the lack of a healthy balance in the lives of his students and teachers. Neil Jardine was an outstanding academic and sportsman, but he deserves to be remembered more for what he achieved as a creative educationist in improving the lives of young people and their families. His creative idea was the integrated day, which scheduled all school-related activity to be completed between 7.30am and 5.00pm each day. Classes, homework, sport, and culture all became part of the regular timetable, leaving students free after 5.00pm for family time and recreation. For the teachers, all their classes, counselling, preparation, marking, administration, and coaching were likewise time-tabled activities and their time after hours was given back to their families and their leisure. The system, attacked by traditionalists and scoffed at by the cynics, worked brilliantly. Certainly, sometimes teachers had to mark books after hours, and pupils occasionally had to catch up on work at home, but working after five was the exception, not the rule. The result was more balanced and productive lives for all concerned.

Neil's experiment was not a solution to a problem, it was a creative response to a complex set of social circumstances that had developed over a very long time. Gradually, over many years, pressure had been brought to bear on children, their families, their teachers, and even the community at large, as a result of the inordinate demands placed on them and the resultant lack of balance in their lives. The integrated day was an attempt to encourage and to help all people restore that balance.

It was a radical idea, some would even say utopian, and its initial success did not mean that everyone lived happily ever after. In fact it was Neil's greatest task to try and encourage people to change their attitudes and deeply ingrained beliefs; and inevitably many never made those changes, but continued to oppose the new system. Nevertheless, it was a creative response to a demoralising social situation that most people simply endured fatalistically, never interrupting their life on the treadmill to ask whether there was a better way to integrate schooling into the life of the community.

There are countless examples of creative thinking of this type in the world of business, too: the names George Eastman, Walt Disney, Ingvar Kamprad, Anita Roddick, Akio Morita, Soichiro Honda, Steve Jobs, Ricardo Semler, Estee Lauder, Michael Dell and Sam Walton immediately spring to mind. The architects of Amazon.com exemplify for me the ingenuity of the entrepreneur — they created a virtual bookstore that offers a better experience for many shoppers than a conventional bookstore does. That, it seems to me, is the key to creativity in business and probably in any other field — making life better in some way for other people.

The most successful businessperson I have known personally was Colin Adcock, a man who headed up Toyota South Africa for many years. He had been poached by Toyota from their advertising agency, where he had created a happy and productive culture that obviously impressed the automobile giant. Three things stood out about Colin: he wanted fresh thinking and new ideas, and surrounded himself with bright, talented people who he gave the freedom and responsibility to flourish; secondly, he was fanatical about details, reminding one of Carlyle's comment on Frederick the Great that genius is "the transcendent capacity of taking trouble"; and finally, he showed sincere interest in people — his staff, his suppliers, stakeholders, and customers — often dealing personally with customer complaints. That he won the national Businessperson of the Year Award several times was no surprise.

My own favourite story of creativity in business is the story of Muhammad Yunus in Bangladesh. He won the Nobel Prize for his efforts in setting up Grameen Bank to provide micro-loans to poor entrepreneurial people to help them develop their business pursuits. As a Professor of Economics, Yunus was inspired to look beyond the comforts of his life in academia to the plight of the poor, and his first venture in micro-financing came when he loaned $27 to forty-two women who made bamboo furniture in the village of Jobra. Micro-loans have since helped the poor in many Third World countries to escape the trap of usury that holds them in economic servitude.

Yunus's book *Banker to the Poor* is a testimony to the astounding potential of human creativity and to the power it draws from love and respect for the dignity of all people. It is an outstanding example of true leadership.

CHARACTER AND CREATIVITY

It would be silly to suggest that all the creative people mentioned were paragons of virtue, driven in their endeavours purely by love for their fellow human beings. Ingvar Kamprad, for example, had to apologise for his onetime support for Nazism — an aberration that would be hard for anyone to shake off in terms of character or reputation. There are many more stories in history of people of genius who had deeply flawed characters — Byron, Cellini and Gauguin are notorious examples. Every one of us has character flaws, which we may choose either to wrestle with and try to overcome, or to simply give free rein to, regardless of the consequences for ourselves and other people.

That said, the contribution of character to creativity remains fundamental. Inventiveness or creativity is a human quality of not only the intellect, but also the will — our faculty to choose what we will and what we will not do. Most people hardly even begin to explore the possibilities at their disposal by virtue of their creative potential, and the failure is seldom one of the intellect, even in non-academic people, but rather of the will.

For example, most people believe that they have no artistic ability and are unable to draw anything. But, at an advertising seminar in Chicago back in the 1980s this was shown to be false. I was part of an audience who the speaker introduced to a book entitled *Drawing on the Right Side of the Brain*. The author, Betty Edwards, demonstrates how she has taught many people to draw with a skill they never dreamed they possessed.

I have since tried the approach in workshops, with excellent results. I ask the group to draw a chair, and they all generally put pencil to paper almost immediately. Their renditions reflect the poverty of the image in their minds. I then ask them to try again, but I do not let them start drawing for ten minutes, during which time I encourage them to look hard at the chair so that they begin to see the form, the proportions, the colour, the light and shade. The difference this makes to their second attempts is remarkable.

This human potential has been shown for decades through the success of sportspeople using creative visualisation techniques. In my years of coaching rugby and water polo, I worked with many boys whose lack of coordination had led their parents, their peers, and often themselves to write them off as hopeless in their chosen sport. I cannot remember a single case, out of hundreds, in which a boy who applied himself to learning the skills, and persevered through the unavoidable frustrations did not succeed in developing the required repertoire. Such is the importance of the will.

The reality about any creative endeavour is that it will involve a challenge (which will be intimidating to some degree) as well as sustained effort and the frustration that comes with hardship, failure, or a lack of rapid progress. This means that the person who wants to use his creativity will need to have aspiration, confidence, courage, self-control and practical wisdom, plus all the positive attitudes that flow from them, such as patience, perseverance, cooperation, commitment, accountability, a spirit of adventure, and so on. Strength of character was similarly involved in designing a Gothic cathedral, in painting the ceiling of the Sistine Chapel and in composing musical masterpieces in spite of being deaf.

To the extent that these qualities of character are missing, any creative enterprise will be compromised. Given human weakness and the stress that accompanies creative work, it is hardly surprising that the myth of the artistic temperament is so pervasive in our culture — but it is not that people of talent lack self-control and respect for convention, rather it is that their frequently frustrated passions spill over into eccentric or anti-social behaviour. And, of course, like the rest of us they are prone to fits of hubris.

And what about love? If we affirm the equal dignity of all people, it is logical that the purpose of our creativity is to improve this world for all people. As has been suggested, respect may be seen as the starting point for love, because true respect for the dignity of another person will always demand that you act in their best interests. A survey of the great works of art, science, and technology throughout history seems to endorse this view, and where unintended consequences such as environmental degradation or social dysfunction have resulted, the essential cure is always the same — sincere commitment to the well-being of all people, and the willingness to take action.

War, of course, appears to be an exception. War is the field in which human ingenuity has over the millennia been most persistently driven to deliver new possibilities to humankind. The astounding advances in strategy, weaponry and other technology, logistics, architecture, energy, transport, medicine, and much more, which have sprung from the spilling of human blood, are undeniable. The technological revolution of the latter half of the twentieth century grew out of World War II, the Cold War, and the epidemic of smaller conflicts that swept the globe, and the consequences are still unfolding.

The fact that many of the technological breakthroughs were made by murderous regimes likewise appears to undermine the argument that love inspires creativity. However, these monstrous states carried in themselves the seeds of their own destruction, just as the lethal technologies the West has developed to keep enemies at bay are inherently dangerous to our own civilisation. Human ingenuity can be used by hubris as well as love, by misleaders as well as leaders, and whenever an ideology can only prevail through violence, it is a culture of death rather than a culture of life. The innate contradiction will, in fact, destroy it sooner or later. The demise of the USSR in 1989 was a spectacular example, and the radically unstable Western world could easily become another.

I am no pacifist. I believe that self-defence and support for the innocent and persecuted in our world are responsibilities never to be taken lightly, but I also know that war can never bring peace and security; only love and forgiveness can do that. Civilisations have fallen throughout history, and they fall when they are not built on love. So in the end it seems that when it comes to human ingenuity, love will always trump hubris.

Creativity and strategy

The incidence of war raises a further question: What is the relationship between creativity and strategy? The science of strategy is believed by many to have grown out of the art of war, but this can only be true if the very first thing that human beings did was to fight among themselves.

War is essentially just another human activity, similar to agriculture, architecture, or athletics, albeit more existentially arresting and logistically complex. Its most famous philosopher, Clausewitz, saw it as nothing more than a duel on a larger scale. In *On War* he famously said:

> *"War is a continuation of policy by other means. It is not merely a political act but a real political instrument."*

As with any other human activity, war challenges human beings to find more effective ways to organise and carry out what they intend to do, and this calls into play their natural creative abilities. So strategy, in effect, is a creative plan to achieve certain specified objectives; developing a strategy is nothing more than finding inventive ways to improve things, to make things better. In business, that generally comes down to discovering different ways to add value and to outdo the competitors in the marketplace. The renowned Japanese business strategist Kenichi Ohmae in his book *The Mind of the Strategist* defines strategy as a superior matching of corporate strengths to consumer needs than that of your competitors. Significantly, he makes it clear that strategy involves precisely the kind of creative thought that has been discussed here, saying that it is:

> *'...the ability to combine, synthesize, or reshuffle previously unrelated phenomena in such a way that you get more out of the emergent whole than you have put in.'*

Since all human beings have creative ability, it follows that all human beings can be successful strategists if they choose to use the potential at their disposal. Again, because it is hard work, involving frustration and even suffering, most people prefer to leave this type of thinking to others. Far too many are duped into believing that some two-hour skills-training programme will provide them with a magic formula to make strategic thinking quick and easy, so that they can 'solve' all their 'problems'. There is no easy way out. Strategy, like any creative pursuit, demands conscious and sustained effort.

There are a great number of books on strategy, Ohmae's being one of the best, but any leader wanting to improve his ability in developing innovative strategies would do well to read history books, which are replete with stories of attempts to make a better world. Three good choices would be Jean Gimpel's *The Medieval Machine*, Doris Kearns Goodwin's *Team of Rivals* and Niall Ferguson's *Empire*.

Averse as I am to quick-fix formulae, when it comes to creative thinking, there are expedients to help ensure that one does not sit staring out of the window, sucking on a pencil, and waiting for lightning to strike. The earlier chapter on thinking contains relevant advice because creativity and strategy require us to will our minds to engage in both intuitive and rational thought. Then, in the quest to move beyond frustration in the direction of fulfilment, the issues can be driven forward in a variety of ways:

Analogy is the freeway of human ingenuity, and our use of this device is completely natural, as can be seen in the universal use of metaphor and simile to describe things. Analogies provide us with endless opportunities for seeing things in different ways, for breaking familiar patterns and for generating fresh connections. Biomimetics, or using natural phenomena as analogies for human technology, is currently one of the most exciting frontiers of science and we have seen the fruits for years in such things as aeroplanes, aerodynamics in car design, flippers for swimmers and divers, and Velcro, which was inspired by burrs on a family pet. A particularly memorable example is the mess-free rubber glue dispenser dreamt up by a 3M engineer for whom it was analogous (no pun intended) with the rear end of a horse, which never requires toilet paper to keep it clean.

Reframing the question is a very fruitful means of generating ideas and new ways of seeing things. Asking the right questions, framed in the right way, is a fundamental approach to discovering the reality of things, and the more we know, the more unexpected connections we are able to make. But there are always different ways of asking the same thing, and every time we reframe the question in another form, previously unexplored aspects of the issue or phenomenon are exposed. The marketing manager of a world-leading brand of sewing machines told me once how they had regained their old ascendancy in the marketplace by reframing a question. Instead of their engineers asking themselves, "How do we design a market-leading model?", they posed the question, "Why does a sewing machine have to look like a sewing machine?" The result was a revolutionary new product.

Brainstorming is a tried and tested stimulator of human ingenuity, and I am constantly surprised to find how seldom it is employed in the workplace and how poorly it is implemented when it is used. The logic is compelling — the more minds that are brought to bear on a challenge, the more knowledge there is to draw on and the more connections can be generated. The exercise must be done on a flip-chart or a whiteboard, and it should be light-hearted and free of the constraints of rationalisation, thereby liberating people to react spontaneously with whatever thoughts are sparked in their mind by what their team-mates say. Bearing in mind that some of the most valuable insights in any organisation will come from the people at the coalface, brainstorming provides every chance of creative alternatives to the status quo. An even better reason for brainstorming is the fact that it can be a wonderful team-building exercise which encourages people to feel empowered and appreciated.

The SWOT Analysis remains one of the most effective strategy development tools available, and once again it amazes me that so many organisations seem to neglect it. Brainstorming the strengths, weaknesses, opportunities, and threats that define the reality of any organisation, can reveal a host of unknown or forgotten possibilities and inspire people to think more deeply and laterally about the current circumstances and the potential to improve things. Again, it is a powerful team-building exercise. The only caveat that should be noted is that people are often tempted to address the opportunities quadrant as if it were a continuation of the list of strengths, and the threats quadrant as if it were an extension of the information contained under weaknesses. Opportunities and threats should be understood as external factors or contingencies for which the organisation should be prepared; for example, new government regulations might either present an opportunity or pose a threat; an outbreak of bird flu might raise a threat to one country, but provide opportunities for another; the development of new technology might be assessed as either an opportunity or a threat.

Empathy is always a potent aid to human ingenuity, and the fact that it remains largely untapped provides ready-made opportunities all over the world. Getting inside the heads of others — customers, suppliers, stakeholders, and competitors — is the surest means of achieving strategic insight and finding ways to reframe the question. Empathy is under-used because it is hard, demanding as it does all those virtues that are the elements of strong character. Hubris and self-centredness seem to come more naturally to all of us, and the opportunity for growth — personal and corporate — goes begging.

Books on strategy and publications such as the *Harvard Business Review* provide many other ways to approach strategy; for example,

3M's strategy-by-storytelling, scenario planning, driving-forces mapping, and process management, all of which have their own merits. However, bringing one's own natural creative ability (increasingly better equipped through ongoing education) to bear on an ever-expanding understanding of a business, the developing market, and all the people in the value-chain enables any challenges to be met far more effectively. But it does require the will to change things for the better.

The following is a list of basic questions which also help prevent the slide into inertia that often occurs when people try to tackle a strategic challenge:

- **Where are we?** This is the time to define reality.
- **Where do we want to be?** This requires the definition of a vision.
- **What are our strengths?** This demands an analysis of the potential for competitive advantage.
- **What are our weaknesses?** Total frankness is essential — honesty pays dividends.
- **How do we get where we want to be?** This is the hard part, requiring focused creative thinking.
- **What are our options?** This reframes the previous question to provoke further thought.
- **What are the other possibilities?** This further reframing helps drive through the frustration.
- **What are the trade-offs?** There are no win-win situations — the trade-offs must be identified honestly.
- **What are the risks?** Failure is a real possibility — identification of every risk to be taken is necessary.
- **What special insights do we have?** This involves sifting through all insights for the real gems.
- **Does everything fit?** Strategic integration is essential —all contradictions need to be eliminated.

Human creativity is only realised through action and a strategy has no value while it remains an idea — even one on paper. Holding oneself and others accountable by means of a written action plan, listing tasks, responsibilities, and deadlines, is what is required to make things happen.

LIVING THE ADVENTURE

The wonder we feel at the grandeur of the cosmos and the mystery of life is a trustworthy guide to the purpose of human existence. The inescapable reality for every human life is the personal experience of change over time, and the constant awareness of growth and decay in ourselves and in the world around us. This leads logically to our recognition of potential and actuality — the potential of an acorn to become an oak, a cub to become a lion, and a human baby to become, well, almost anything — and we rightly affirm the concept of progress, even though we often select the wrong path. And we thus derive our sense that there are right ways and wrong ways to do things, leaving us always vulnerable in our quest for fulfilment as self-determined beings within the determinism of the natural world.

Chesterton's characterisation of life as an adventure is a challenge to all of us to take charge of our own destiny, to refuse to be passive pieces on someone else's chessboard. Creativity is the expression of our intellectual prowess, our freedom, and also our radical dependence on others, the distinctive qualities of our human nature. And it can only be seen in action, even if the action taken is merely a clever riposte to an opponent in a debate. Left dormant, creativity impoverishes human life through frustration and boredom; misdirected, it destroys human life through perversity.

If leadership is the human activity that inspires people to be the best they can be in mutual pursuit of a better life for all, then creativity is indispensable and must be cultivated in both the leader and the people being led. Recruitment advertisements that claim to be seeking 'creative' people are often silly and superficial; sometimes they are plainly mendacious. Most organisations are insincere in calling for creativity and they frequently appoint pliant people who are well-versed in the vocabulary of political correctness and corporate conformity.

Recently, a gifted manager who had been through my leadership programme obtained a well-paid position in a large government department. E-mailing me from her office, she confided that in terms of remuneration and conditions the job was the best she had ever had. Yet she was deeply unhappy. Intelligent and energetic, she has always impressed me as being predisposed to unleash her own creative ability as well as that of others, but this has become the root of her problems. She has very little to do and although she has quickly identified many systems and procedures that could be improved, as well as many opportunities to boost morale and efficiency, she has become reticent about proposing them. The first few encounters with her boss made it clear that she is expected to quietly accept the status quo and to do as she is told. She now faces a real test of her leadership: should she choose the comfort and security of a job that offers no prospect of personal growth other than part-time study at the university, or should she resign and accept the risks inherent in seeking a position that will respect her as a person rather than as a functionary?

I have over the years worked with many inspirational people who have elected to take the latter course, and predictably they have gone on to better things. Sadly, I know many more who have clung to a security that has all too often proved to be ephemeral. The challenge of life is inexorable change; the required response can only be the creativity so clearly seen in the great cultural achievements of humankind, and also in the more mundane triumphs of ordinary lives. And the criterion of creativity has to be respect for the dignity of all people. G. K. Chesterton perhaps said it best when he compared art with morality, saying that both required drawing the line somewhere.

Leaders and Misleaders

CHAPTER 11
QUO VADIS?

"Not everything that counts can be counted and not everything that can be counted counts." Albert Einstein

NO DIRECTION

Where are you going? Quo Vadis? If we put the question to the world, there is no answer. If we put it to the Western democracies, the answers are less than convincing given the political, social, economic, cultural, and environmental crises facing them and the world at large. If the question is asked of the corporate world, the endemic short-termism and greed of many of the people in authority, along with the corruption and inefficiency of the government agencies responsible for regulation, mean that the only visionary answers will come from isolated pockets of creativity and compassion. Talk to ordinary people and the mood is almost universally one of profound concern for the future.

If we do not know where we are going, that is as clear an indication as any that we have a critical shortage of leadership. In a world where misleaders appear to outnumber leaders in all areas, what is to be done? It is certainly not a matter of learning leadership skills — that is being done in every sector to no avail. What is required is the resolution of courageous men and women who will pick up the gauntlet and lead like they mean it.

Where are you going? You are called to lead yourself, lead your family, provide whatever measure of leadership you are required to contribute in your workplace, and (as a citizen of a democratic state in which sovereignty allegedly rests with the people) in your community. Only you can answer the question, and that is the first thing a leader would do.

No Going Back

Looking back on the halcyon days of an idealised past is a common human response to the onset of difficult times, and amidst the turmoil and uncertainty of our times, the very last thing any of us should be contemplating is a turning back of the clock. History has moved on and so must we.

One hundred and seventeen years after the sack of Rome by the Visigoths under Alaric, and fifty-one years after the abdication of Romulus Augustulus (the last emperor in the West) the imperial throne of the Eastern Roman Empire was ascended in AD 527 by a man whose mission was to restore the empire to its past glories. Justinian proved to be one of the most remarkable rulers of history. However, his principal objective of returning Rome to its former dominance remained an extravagant and unattainable vision.

The codification of Roman law was one of the most significant cultural achievements in all history, and the benefits have been enjoyed by societies in Western Europe, Russia, and the wider world. This was inspired and driven by Justinian. His economic reforms ushered in a period of great prosperity, and arts and letters flourished under his regime. The magnificent Hagia Sophia in Constantinople was his achievement, and it inspired architects in the empire and beyond for centuries thereafter. The slaughter of some thirty thousand people by his troops in quelling a dangerous insurrection was a serious blot on his record and even from a position of empathy for very different times it is impossible to justify. However, in the overall context of his reign it is still clear why posterity has acknowledged him as a great ruler. Yet when it came to his central ambition, he failed.

The successes of Justinian's generals in recapturing most of Italy, large stretches of the former empire in Africa, and a substantial foothold in Spain, while at the same time managing the Persian threat in the east, amazed his contemporaries, but were never likely to endure. Justinian was not dealing with the challenges that had faced Diocletian and Constantine; his was a totally different world —more complex and capricious, it was simply not susceptible to old expedients. The eminent French historian Henri Daniel-Rops in his history *The Church in the Dark Ages* sums up the widely held opinion of Justinian's remarkable reign:

'It had been a great reign; there is no doubt of that. For a period of more than thirty years, men had witnessed a remarkable phenomenon: in every field of human activity — politics, economics, arts, letters, and the law — the imperial philosophy had regained possession of the world. Justinian was the last of the great Roman emperors. But this success was exceptional and paradoxical. It depended on the action of a few vigorous personalities, and on the skilful utilisation of various favourable circumstances. It could not be, and it was not to be, lasting. Justinian's empire crumbled away with astonishing speed after his death. Autocratic, hieratical, and bureaucratic, Byzantium was not in fact capable of regaining control of the West and of undertaking its restoration. It did not slow up its decline into barbarism; in one sense it speeded it up, by completely destroying the tentative assimilation achieved by the Ostrogoths. Compared with some of the Goths — Totila, for example — it showed itself to be a force of the past, extremely poor in new ideas.'

The lesson provided by Justinian's failure has not always been heeded, and many people have paid the price of trying to go back to a past that can never be recovered.

No Easy Answers

If there is no going back, it is also true that there are no easy answers to the challenges of leadership in trying to move things forward either. Some may argue that the guidelines for leadership given in this book are altogether too black and white, and neatly stacked, but the clear identification of ideals should never be misconstrued as targeting the unattainable, and as therefore being impractical. It is true that all human beings are fallible, inconsistent, contradictory and capricious, and that living and working with other, equally contrary, people is arduous. But as has been shown, our animal nature is infused with a transcendent mind, and our affinity with the transcendent is precisely why we set up ideals (truth, beauty, goodness, and love) and pursue them; it is also why we are forever seeking better ways to organise our lives together. In *The Closing of the American Mind*, Professor Allan Bloom reminded us of this quintessential human challenge:

'Man is the particular being that can know the universal, the temporal being that is aware of eternity, the part that can survey the whole, the effect that seeks the cause.'

And he went on to point out why we set the standards that we persistently fail to live up to:

'Utopianism is, as Plato taught us long ago, the fire with which we must play because it is the only way we can find out what we are.'

The age-old paradox of the human person is the reason why there are no easy answers and why leadership is the Herculean labour that we all know it to be. In any social arrangement, from the simple to the complex, there are inevitably claims and counter-claims for priority, preference and precedence. Trying to provide satisfaction for all of these claims seems likely to remain forever a pipe-dream. What is the best way forward in this time of crisis?

As something of a long-time Anglophile, I was deeply saddened by Peter Hitchens' book *The Abolition of Britain*, which charts the decline of that once-great nation and the loss of Britishness. Coming from a country that no longer exists — Rhodesia — I could empathise strongly with the author's emotional polemic. (And it does not take much intellectual effort to extend the same feeling of compassion to the Bantu, the Maori, the Aborigines, the Native Americans and the other dispossessed peoples around the world.) Hitchens expresses his pain thus:

'Routine, tradition, and unchanging surroundings keep habits and ways of thought alive. Disruption, demolition, novelty and innovation destroy custom and certainty. For the very young, the ambitious, and especially for those whose deep desires are frustrated by the invisible chains of an ordered society, change is always healthy and good and desirable. But for those with painfully earned skills, for those who seek security in an ordered way of life, change is a mixed curse, bringing confusion and even fear along with novelty and freshness. Whether the British people liked it or not, they were destined to spend the next three decades dancing and twitching and leaping to the beat of rapid and unstoppable change, a beat that was to grow faster and wilder with each passing year.'

Hitchens is, of course, aware that most generations in Britain and elsewhere have had to grasp the nettle of change to some degree. Following the triumph of William the Conqueror at Hastings in 1066, the English did not have an English-speaking ruler for three hundred years. The English Reformation, the Civil War, the Glorious Revolution, the Industrial Revolution, and many more events, subjected Hitchens' forbears to changes every bit as cataclysmic as those recent generations have had to endure. Yet his point cannot be simply brushed aside, any more than can the appeals of millions of unjustly treated people around the world.

The pages of history and current media headlines reveal monumental injustices, but serious harm is also inflicted every day on large numbers of those in the workplaces of our supposedly civilised society. I once consulted over several years with a large manufacturing corporation as it was transformed from an over-staffed, technologically-retarded, and rather complacent job-for-life dinosaur into a lean, efficient, high-tech, commercial powerhouse. In my role as leadership coach, I witnessed first-hand the full panorama of human triumph and tragedy.

Most of the senior executives flourished financially and in their personal development as businesspeople, though often at the cost of either stress-related illness or domestic upheaval. In a few cases character changed noticeably for the worse. This pattern was repeated across perhaps thirty percent of the middle managers, but the other seventy percent for the most part drifted into cynicism and resentment, suspecting that sooner or later their long-standing careers would be sacrificed in the ongoing restructuring and in the quest for utilitarian efficiency. The cynicism and resentment spread downward into the rank and file of the corporation, where suspicion and anxiety were already widespread in the face of the relentless changes. Inevitably, the unbroken stress manifested itself in a great deal of anti-social and self-destructive behaviour, and in a logjam of strained relationships.

Those people from all levels who weathered the costly decade-long tempest and who finally looked set to reap the rewards of their tenacity and resourcefulness were then confronted by a merger with another company. I have never seen a corporate merger that worked; each one I have experienced from either the inside or the outside has resulted in a takeover rather than a merger, with the executives from one of the amalgamating entities dominating the process and steadily eliminating actual and potential rivals from the other side.

The people from the corporation in this story fared very badly, particularly at the executive level. However, all of them at least moved on to more financially-rewarding positions with other organisations. Middle managers and the rank and file did not always experience the same good fortune. A small number thrived in the new environment, but most, having survived years of uncertainty, now found the pressure had returned. Good people who had persevered through tough times, always serving the corporation well, were treated with scant appreciation or respect, and must have looked back on the previous ten years in complete disillusionment. Sadly, this corporation was in no way an exceptional case, and it seems eerily portentous that as I write this, I have just read an article from the *Economist* dated 10 October 2009, examining the issue of unhappiness in the workplace. The one thing in the article that surprises me is the weight given to the current recession as the major cause of the escalating rates of clinical depression; I have witnessed the trends for the past thirty years, and while the downturn obviously intensifies the stresses, no economic recovery will eradicate them. An excerpt from the article is revealing:

'A spate of attempted and successful suicides at France Telecom — many of them explicitly prompted by troubles at work — has sparked a national debate about life in the modern corporation. One man stabbed himself in the middle of a meeting (he survived). A woman leapt from a fourth-floor office window after sending a suicidal e-mail to her father: "I have decided to kill myself tonight...I can't take the new reorganisation." In all 24 of the firm's employees have taken their own lives since early 2008 — and this grisly tally follows similar episodes at other pillars of French industry, including Renault, Peugeot, and EDF. There are some parochial reasons for this melancholy trend. France Telecom is making the difficult transition from state monopoly to multinational company. It has shed 22 000 jobs since 2006, but two-thirds of the remaining workers enjoy civil service-like job security. This is forcing it to pursue a toxic strategy: teaching old civil servants new tricks while at the same time putting new hires on short-term contracts...America's Bureau of Labour Statistics calculates that work-related suicides increased by 28 percent between 2007 and 2008, although the rate is lower than in Europe. And suicide is only the tip of an iceberg of work-related unhappiness.'

That last point is most important. The suffering being endured by many more people than those who commit suicide underlines the fact that post-modern corporate life is inimical to human fulfilment generally (the exploiters and manipulators are impacted negatively too). Statistics from all over the Western world have shown for many years that workplace stress is costing national economies billions of dollars annually — and in human terms that translates into enormous suffering for workers and their families. Charles Handy in *The Hungry Spirit*, written in 1997, presented some startling statistics which confirm that the issue raised in the *Economist* is not a recent development.

'In a 1993 survey of managers by the Institute of management, 77 percent considered their hours were stressful, 77 percent worried about

the effect on their family, and 74 percent about their relationship with their partner. By 1996 it had got worse. Stress, the Institute said, costs Britain forty million working days a year and £7 billion in health care. A study by the Massachusetts Institute of Technology calculated that depression at work was costing America $47 billion a year, roughly the same as heart disease.'

When I first read Handy's book ten years ago I found it consistent with my own experience of corporate life. In the decade since, working closely with many people in many different fields, my impression has been that matters have steadily worsened. Handy himself echoed the concerns of earlier writers — for example, Romano Guardini and Daniel Bell — when he predicted that the wide public acceptance of neo-Darwinian principles would bring increasing distress in business.

'Businesses sometimes relish this sort of thinking. They like to see themselves as economic entities in the grip of forces greater than themselves. They are what they have to be in order to survive in the Darwinian world of economics. Such a philosophy allows them to exploit their customers or their suppliers, or even their employees as long as they can get away with it. Geraniums have short but often sunny lives. So it is with many get-rich-quick businesses who think that the idea of a contribution to society is just a lot of woolly wish-wash, about as relevant to them as grace before meals.'

Things have deteriorated further since Handy wrote *The Hungry Spirit*. The number of hard-working professionals I know personally who are suffering from stress-related illnesses, or who are emotionally at the end of their tether, or who are simply deeply disillusioned, is quite shocking. The same Economist article quoted earlier provides a useful description of the management mindset that is sponsoring the suffering:

'A second source of misery is the drive to improve productivity which is typically accompanied by an obsession with measuring performance. Giant retailers use 'workforce management' software to monitor how many seconds it takes to scan the goods in a grocery cart, and then reward the most diligent workers with prime working hours. The public sector, particularly in Britain, is awash with inspectorate and performance targets. Taylorism, which Charles Chaplin lampooned so memorably in 'Modern Times', has spread from the industrial to the post-industrial economy. In Japan some firms even monitor whether their employees smile frequently enough at customers.'

Earlier today I received an e-mail from an acquaintance — an intelligent, dedicated professional woman with a tough, no-nonsense approach to her work. She is on the point of handing in her resignation due to her exasperation at the refusal of her immediate superior to address serious issues threatening the personal and professional well-being of her people, as well as the efficiency and reputation of their department and the corporation itself. And he also refuses to let her address them. The fact that these very issues impact negatively on the annual performance reviews of all concerned is grossly unjust. However, this seems to be par for the course in corporate life, where human resources tools are employed as weapons of control and coercion rather than valuable feedback and coaching opportunities.

This all reminds me of the words of Steven Berglas of Harvard Medical School, a clinical psychologist and a specialist in executive stress, who was quoted in *Fortune* magazine in September 1997 as saying:

"The biggest lie in business life today is that the boss wants honest feedback. CEOs say, 'I want the truth,' because they know they won't get it."

NO PLACE TO HIDE

Looking at the example above of the corporation that restructured repeatedly and then was swallowed in a merger, it is all too easy to slip into one of the two established ideological camps — either arguing that government regulation and workers rights should be increased, or asserting that management has to be cruel to be kind and that many more would suffer if corporations failed to move decisively with the times. People who unthinkingly occupy these default positions have been hurling mud at one another for many decades. Each side claims to hold a moral high ground which demands sacrifice from all except themselves. These ideological poles rest on a belief that their proponents have the exclusive formula for a socio-economic Utopia, and that all problems will be solved by the mere application of their template.

However, life is never that simple. To lay out the complexities of the cited organisation's case alone would require a thick, heavy volume all of its own, and the evidence in my files emphasises the bewildering tangle of complications and contradictions involved in dealing with people. Placed in the context of hundreds of other equally unfathomable personalities, the complexity of each individual is greatly multiplied.

But a leader is called to address this complexity; there is no place to hide — the choice in every situation is leadership or misleadership – or else abdication of one's responsibilities as a human being.

The corporation had no shortage of expertise and experience, but the organisation and deployment of that expertise and experience was cut back and restructured in response to changing socio-economic realities. That the corporation had the intellectual capability to meet the challenge was never in question and, indeed, for nearly a decade before the merger it appeared to have steadily and very successfully transformed itself into an entity that would flourish in the years ahead. However, the ongoing loss of jobs, poorly managed workloads, and a persistent training backlog, meant that undue levels of stress were a commonplace and the character of individuals was constantly under siege.

Contrary to popular opinion, human beings are not able to compartmentalise their lives, keeping home, community, and work separate, like non-interactive parallel universes. Stress at work may affect family and social relationships, and vice versa. Consequently, many of the psychological issues encountered in the workplace are brought in from the outside, and exacerbated by the pressures of the environment into which they are introduced. A woman who has had an argument with her husband over family finances may well take her pain and frustration with her into the workplace, where her emotional state is subjected to the usual mix of pettiness, rivalries, misunderstandings, cynicism, and whinging, as well as the operational demands of her work. Without leadership, the situation is hopeless. And that raises the question of how leadership impacted this case, and where it may have made more of a difference.

The CEO was one of the better corporate heads I have encountered. A man of vision, energetic and confident, who time and again demonstrated genuine compassion through his support for people who had suffered misfortune, he had a decisive vision for the corporation and worked hard to ensure that his executive team and the workforce understood where he was taking the ship and what was required of all on board. No one could have credibly complained that the reality was not defined for them from the start. Moreover, he backed his vision consistently with bold investment in people and new technology.

However, like chief executives generally in the post-modern corporate world, he was in no position to act with a completely free hand and this led to the development of a blind spot. Though he was strongly supported by the Board of Directors, the incessant pressure to deliver on financial goals (driven by voracious shareholders) prompted him to turn up the heat on his divisional heads in an effort to produce levels of profitability which, in some areas of the business, were simply not possible in the short term. The divisional heads were for the most part intelligent and experienced executives, and I remember all of them as compassionate people, but they found themselves caught in the vice-like grip of the profit imperative, and their response was too often short-term and mechanical rather than creative. Though they bore a heavy burden themselves, largely as a result of reverting to a management mentality rather than a proactive leadership stance, the real cost was carried by the middle managers and the people at the coalface.

It would be simplistic to see the board, the CEO and the executive team as the villains, and the middle managers and the workforce as the victims. The reality is that every person in any enterprise has a contribution to make in terms of leadership. First of all, there is the universal responsibility for self-leadership — defining reality to oneself and others, always standing firm on principle, being accountable, being empathetic, and supporting those around you. Secondly, there is the crucial need in any organisation to coach upwards — constantly providing feedback, insights, and suggestions, and expressing reasons for concern. Where this leadership from below does not occur, leadership from above is proportionately compromised. For the suffering that afflicted so many in that corporation for so many years, all involved must shoulder some measure of the blame, from the Board of Directors and shareholders to the workers on the factory floor.

Yet in the end, it was the leadership of the corporation that carried the responsibility for its people and its performance. They held aloft a vision that they pursued at great cost to many, only to see the dream frustrated. There is simply no place to hide for leaders.

The frustration of viable corporate visions is a sad feature of the business world. The media is full of it, as are the pages of history. It is a constant reminder to all of us that life is hard, even though the prevailing worldview in the West pretends that it is meant to be easy. Success is elusive and there are no win-win solutions. Improving human and material circumstances involves hard work, perseverance, sacrifice, and suffering; and mutually rewarding human relationships require empathy, self-control, love and forgiveness. In every human endeavour the risk of failure and of people being hurt is always a possibility — but only the cynic says that we should therefore proceed with the predicted collateral damage factored in. The human response, the leadership imperative, is to seek the best for all people, and to look after those who need support for whatever reason.

KNOW WHERE TO TURN

And so the question persists: Quo Vadis? In difficult times, when you need to know where you are going, and when there is no going back, no place to hide, and no easy answers, it helps to know where to turn.

The Mel Gibson movie *Braveheart*, the Hollywood version of the struggle of the Scots against King Edward I of England, started an avalanche of public interest in its hero, William Wallace. In spite of the shortcomings of the movie as a historical record, I was heartened by the fact that people all over the world had been introduced to an engagingly told, classic tale of loyalty, commitment, sacrifice, and creative genius — of leadership.

The story of William Wallace is inspiring for leaders who want to know where to turn when things look bleak. In the last decade of the thirteenth century, Edward I was making a determined effort to subdue Scotland once and for all. His ruthless sacking of the merchant city of Berwick and the slaughter of thousands of its citizens broke the spirit of almost all the Scottish nobles heading the resistance to English hegemony. John Balliol, the King of Scotland, abdicated; he submitted, as did most of the prominent nobles, to an English administration. It was a dark hour for Scotland. Winston Churchill, another courageous and decisive leader in a time of national calamity, captured the greatness of Wallace in *A History of the English-Speaking Peoples:*

> 'It has often been said that Joan of Arc first raised the standard of nationalism in the Western world. But over a century before she appeared, an outlaw knight, William Wallace, arising from the recesses of South-West Scotland which had been his refuge, embodied, commanded, and led to victory the Scottish nation. Edward, warring in France with piebald fortune, was forced to listen to tales of ceaseless inroads and forays against his royal peace in Scotland, hitherto deemed so sure. Wallace had behind him the spirit of a race as stern and as resolute as any bred among men. He added military gifts of a high order. Out of an unorganised mass of

valiant fighting men he forged, in spite of cruel poverty and primitive administration, a stubborn, indomitable army, ready to fight at any odds and mock defeat. The structure of this army is curious. Every four men had a fifth man as leader; every nine men a tenth; every nineteen men a twentieth; and so on to every thousand; and it was agreed that the penalty for disobedience to the leader of any unit was death. Thus from the ground does freedom raise itself unconquerable.'

Wallace won many stunning victories through his ingenious strategy and tactics, and his inspirational devotion to the cause. Though he was later defeated by sheer weight of numbers and resources, the flame he had lit refused to die, rising triumphantly once more at Bannockburn under Robert the Bruce. At a time when despair had tormented the nation, and its would-be ruling class had buckled under the pressure, Wallace had stepped forward and held up the ideal of Scottish independence. While the lords who the people looked to for leadership discarded their principles and froze, Wallace turned to his principles and took decisive action. In the face of overwhelming odds, he thought as Mother Theresa did when she said (as quoted in *USA Today*):

"I am not called to be successful; I am called to be faithful."

Great leaders such as Churchill and Lincoln knew the central importance of decisive action, in moving swiftly to do what needs to be done in line with one's clearly defined principles. That is the very ground on which integrity is built. Churchill knew well that the price of greatness is responsibility, and in typical bulldog fashion, he affirmed an essential truth about leadership: that having enemies means that at least one has stood for something.

Popularity and success are the supreme values of the post-modern utilitarian society, and notions such as standing on principle and observing points of honour are often ridiculed as archaic and inapplicable in today's world. Yet question the personal integrity of any of the meretricious myrmidons who scoff at principle and honour, and they will be deeply offended, failing to understand that their lack of principles will always be exposed, sooner or later. Integrity without principle is impossible; leadership without integrity is a lie. This is the root of our current leadership crisis and it explains the prevalence of misleaders — utilitarian nihilists prepared to do whatever works for them, and principles be damned.

Sadly, increasing numbers of people despairingly take the abdication-of-responsibility option. The human failure of shrinking into inertia in the face of daunting challenges has afflicted civilised societies from the very beginning of history and was given its classic expression in Shakespeare's *Hamlet*. The Prince of Denmark, tormented by his indecision following the murder of his father and the hasty marriage of his mother to the chief suspect, voices the existential angst of all mortals confronting the seemingly ambiguous crises of life:

"To be, or not to be: that is the question;
Whether 'tis nobler in the mind to suffer
The slings and arrows of outrageous fortune,
Or to take arms against a sea of troubles,
And by opposing end them?"

Today this weakness threatens to overwhelm us, even as politicians, scholars, media commentators, and comedians loudly proclaim our innocence and victimhood, caught as we are in the snare of intricate structures that defy our comprehension. The unseen and often unscrupulous influence of lobbyists and special interests in our severely wounded democracies, and the crushing burdens thrust on businesses by government, the financial sector, unions, and their own boards of directors and shareholders, come on top of labyrinthine organisational and legal structures, and a dizzying confusion of agendas. Short of nuclear war or the total collapse of civil society, these structures will not be easily dismantled. But far from being an excuse for cynicism and resignation, this is a call for leaders at every level to stand up and contest the ground currently dominated by misleaders.

Fortunately, there are signs of hope, and what follows are just two of the many examples of principled action I have encountered on my leadership programme. Both are of leaders from the same organisation and they demonstrate the very different possibilities open to people who lead like they mean it.

The two were operational managers at an internationally-reputable consultancy which has in recent years undergone a significant measure of change, both structural and cultural. While few would dispute that the reorganisation was long overdue, there was quite naturally resistance to the form and spirit of some of the changes. The two managers in question, both highly-respected professionals to whom their colleagues looked for guidance and inspiration, independently identified aspects of the restructuring that they considered detrimental to the company and its people. They individually articulated their concerns to senior management, but though each man received a respectful hearing, the CEO was disinclined to make anything more than minor concessions in his drive to achieve his own objectives.

Over the next year, as the company made solid gains but left many of its people chafing under the tight constraints of the restructure, the careers of the two managers took dramatically different turns. One accepted a position on the senior executive team, working closely with the CEO; the other resigned.

The remarkable thing is that both men provided outstanding examples of leadership in the contrasting choices they made. Each is without question well-qualified for senior management, though the one who resigned would probably not have accepted such a position had it been offered to him. The man who was promoted predictably made an immediate impact on the performance of the organisation, and his energy, enthusiasm and infectious confidence drew spontaneous approval from all sides. With clarity, tact and persuasive eloquence, he continues to define reality for the CEO, his peers, and the people who report to him, and it seems certain that he will strongly influence the direction of the company for the foreseeable future. His personal integrity enabled him to make a principled decision that is yielding rich fruits for all concerned.

His former colleague followed a path neither more nor less challenging when he submitted his resignation. He chose to leave the company, not in pique but on principle, believing that corporate policy and procedures made it impossible for him to perform his operational role to the best of his ability and to help his team members to be the best they could be. Senior management was obviously disappointed to lose a man of this calibre, but they too took a stand on principle, feeling that the conditions he stipulated for staying with the company were incompatible with what they were trying to achieve. The resignation sent shockwaves through the company, but everyone benefited from seeing a leader turn to his principles in a challenging situation and act decisively in accordance with them.

In any crisis other than one involving a mathematical problem, there is no simple formula or quick-fix response. Turning to your principles and taking decisive action is the correct leadership response, but in an age scornful of principles, this is easier said than done for many people.

KNOW THYSELF

A few years ago, I was invited to speak to an audience drawn from a variety of different business categories on the subject of the impact of values in the commercial world. The feedback that I received after the talk made it clear that people had been surprised to hear me saying things that were not only politically incorrect, but which were also a provocative challenge to both managers and workers to take an honest look at the way they did things.

The most startling response came from a young woman who thanked me for opening her eyes and told me that she was returning to her place of work to resign. Even though I had set out to be controversial, I was stunned by such a radical response. Sensing my unease, she explained that she had been uncomfortable for some time with the way employees and customers were treated by the company and that my talk had put things in perspective for her. For better or worse, she had made a decision based on her personal principles, and I was quite certain that her employers would be the losers, unless of course her sudden defiance shocked them into examining their own attitudes.

With relentless logic, the Socratic imperative to know thyself and Kant's three questions are raised again, as they must inevitably be in the life of any person who seeks to know the truth about themselves. What you stand for and what you will not stand for ultimately determines who you are, and the choice is nobody's but your own. Those foundational principles, your worldview, provide the framework that determines the form and quality of your culture — that is, your self-driven education, which is essentially what equips you for leadership; any inadequacy or perversion sets the scene either for abdication of responsibility or for misleadership. Personal integrity can only be built on solid principles.

I have no intention of proposing a particular worldview, though the humane criteria according to which your principles may be evaluated were laid out in Chapter Four, and the core attitudes that should flow from them were detailed in Chapter Eight. Those criteria and core attitudes have a trans-cultural currency that makes the brotherhood and sisterhood of humankind an unshakeable reality, even if many people choose to ignore it. They have enabled me to find common ground with friends, colleagues, and acquaintances from America, Australia, Argentina, Brazil, Canada, China, Columbia, England, France, Germany, Greece, Holland, Italy, Israel, Iraq, India, Japan, Lesotho, Malaysia, Malawi, Mexico, New Zealand, the Philippines, Romania, Russia, Singapore, South Africa, Taiwan, Turkey, Venezuela, Zambia and Zimbabwe. Among those hundreds of people have been Muslims, Buddhists, Jews, Christians, Hindus, Confucians, secular humanists, and one Zoroastrian, a Parsee from Mumbai.

The difference between principled and unprincipled people is seen in the quality of their domestic, professional, and civic relationships, just as the gulf that divides principled and unprincipled organisations and societies shows itself in the way people (particularly the most vulnerable) are treated. We are known by our fruits, so each of us should be aware of the impact we have on the lives of others and strive to make sure it is positive.

In seeking to know yourself, it is your principles and your integrity that provide the surest guide, and as you come to a greater understanding of who you are, so your understanding of the reality outside of you will progressively fall into place.

KNOW REALITY

The first and obvious fact about reality is that there is simply too much to know, which is why education is the adventure of discovery that should continue throughout life. For all of us, especially in this age of radical specialisation, this means that ignorance is a large part of our lives, and something we must wrestle with constantly.

Naturally, human beings have mental strategies to help smooth out some of life's complexities. While it is extraordinary that we can make sense of reality and even manipulate it through these intellectual manoeuvres, what is even more astonishing is our ability to recognise their limitations. Sadly, in an age when education has been impoverished, this aptitude for discrimination is not common.

The power of the human mind to generalise — that is, to place things in mental categories in order to evaluate and understand them — is the foundation of rational thinking, but it can also give rise to lazy and superficial thinking which distorts our view of the world. This is seen in silly judgments such as: "blondes have more fun", "Asians are bad drivers", "accountants are boring" and "Catholics cannot think for themselves", and people who make judgments like these unwittingly place themselves in the more rationally constituted category of bigoted fools. Nonetheless, even superficial categories are sometimes not merely useful, but are actually necessary to make sense of the complexities of this life that we share.

For example, distinguishing between cultures is necessary if one wishes to treat all with proper respect, but to accuse all the people of a particular culture of being 'thieves' when you have been defrauded by only one of them is to be guilty of prejudice. Likewise, different generations can be better understood when one considers the socio-economic, technological, and cultural influences that have crowded their lives. But again, to claim that all members of Generation Y have a deficient work ethic on the basis of even several experiences is to be badly misguided. No one's character is determined by their year of birth.

Two cultural categories of particular significance for leaders are *Classic* and *Romantic*. In *Classic, Romantic, and Modern* (an insightful study of these classifications and of the modern mindset that emerged from their interplay) Jacques Barzun shows how academically shallow histories and superficial criticism have impoverished our understanding of these enduring cultural dispositions and how they affect our world today.

Typically erroneous is the view that Classicism is objective, rational and realistic, while Romanticism is subjective, emotional and idealistic, or in other words that people of a Classical bent are cool, calm and collected, while those of a Romantic temper are passionate, wild and given to flights of fancy. A careful study of the lives and work of the scientists, artists and writers of the Classicist Enlightenment, and those of the period of Romanticism that followed, reveals far too many anomalies in both eras for these superficial judgments to be taken seriously.

However, when the categories are more accurately defined, the light they shed on the human condition in any time or place is most enlightening. Classicism, according to Barzun, elevated the ideals of peace, serenity, order and control, and in pursuit of these it resorted to repression, formalism and a preference for abstract theorising. Barzun's description of the flaw of Classicism is instructive:

'It had supposed society to be static, emotions compressible, and novelty needless. It had selected what had seemed to it best and truest and most eternal — monarchy, orthodoxy, courtly etiquette, mathematics, and rules of art and of morality so simple that their universality could be deemed self-evident.'

Barzun's understanding of Classicism can easily be applied to many corporate, professional, and political examples today. Classicism is alive and well, though grappling feverishly with a new Romanticism.

Barzun's description of the Romanticism of the last third of the eighteenth century and the first half of the nineteenth is also useful for leaders in our own era. The common characteristics of the very diverse personalities that make up the ranks of the Romantic painters, poets, and writers, were what one would expect from people setting out to renew their world after the failure of the old socio-political models and the exhaustion of Classicist themes and styles in the arts.

These very different people all demonstrated passionate commitment, a propensity for action and creative licence, and a work ethic that resulted in voluminous output. They understood that action is the only test of true emotion. The record proves that the label often attached to the Romanticists, of sentimentality — that is, emotion without personal cost — is more appropriately applied to their Classicist predecessors. The Romantic protagonists defied convention and the narrow ideological constraints of Classicism, looking for inspiration in history, tradition, nature, and religion — wherever they could find it.

Today's Romantic spirits can be seen in those philosophers, scholars, columnists, bloggers, teachers, scientists, software developers, and creative business people who sincerely work against the increasingly sanitised and controlled corporate and political environment that keeps insisting that "there is no alternative" (TINA). This Classicist TINA is being confronted by the Romanticist NITA that proclaims "new ideas through action".

Neither Classicism nor Romanticism is wholly right or wrong; both express real human needs. Ironically, older Romantic cultures tend to harden into Classicist models, necessitating yet another creative revolution. As complex human beings, we all have both Classicist and Romanticist predispositions in some degree. No one is entirely rational, and everyone is prey to their emotions; to talk glibly about right-brained thinkers and left-brain thinkers is to deny their full humanity and potential. We are a mix that is determined by life's experiences, education and culture, and while some people may be more prone to intuitive and passionate responses, this hardly means they are incapable of discursive reasoning.

Society and all human organisations need both action-oriented creative minds as well as proponents of order and discipline, because it is in the dynamic interplay between them that human progress is achieved, not in mere change for change's sake. History shows that the human propensity for throwing the baby out with the bathwater leads to the exaggerated swings between sterile authoritarianism and destructive utopianism. The geniuses of Classicism — like Descartes, Bernini, and Swift — and those of Romanticism — like Goethe, Beethoven, and Wordsworth —demonstrated great self-control as well as groundbreaking creativity in their work, and all were strongly influenced by tradition.

The lessons for political and business leaders today and indeed for parents and teachers as well, are clear. We must jettison the crude templates which objectify people in order to manipulate and control them. It is time to take up the enduring challenge made to every generation to balance the legitimate claims of civility and order with the equally legitimate demands for creative action in dismantling dead structures and devising fruitful alternatives.

But here's the rub: none of this can be done unless the trust that has been eroded in Western society over many decades is somehow restored. Promiscuity, family breakdown, the exploitation of innocents, political betrayal, callous corporate corruption, spiralling private greed, and an epidemic of deceit have all conspired to undermine trust and to place in jeopardy relationships of every sort. And that is all society is — a complex web of relationships. Destroy them and you destroy civil society, leaving a void that can only be filled by totalitarian tyranny or a barbarous anarchy, both of which are live possibilities in our world.

This is where we clearly see the indestructible link between truth and freedom. Albert Camus, in the *Myth of Sisyphus*, noted that:

'Thinking of the future and setting goals presupposes a belief in freedom.'

It goes without saying that to use such words as 'thinking', 'future', 'goals', 'belief'', and 'freedom' would be meaningless if there was no such thing as truth. And without truth, trust itself has no meaning.

A world without trust is a world set up for misleaders, because control can then only be imposed by violence and the lie. As is shown in Figure 11.1, in order to elevate freedom, both culture and character have to move in the direction of trust. To the extent that they shift towards a climate of mistrust, they necessarily elevate the need for control to be imposed.

The ever-increasing regulation, compliance, and constraint that are crowding out our civic and democratic freedom are inversely proportionate to the trust draining out from our society. One does not have to be a doctrinaire conservative to appreciate Edmund Burke's dictum in his letter to a member of the National Assembly:

'Society cannot exist unless a controlling power upon will and appetite be placed somewhere, and the less of it there is within, the more there must be without.'

The choice is always the same for the individual and society: on the one hand, self-control; on the other, authoritarianism or anarchy. We are motivated by love, or we are constrained by law. This is why the five criteria for a humane worldview and the seven virtues are indispensable. Whatever the shape of a positive future we may wish to build in a business or society, they are the conditions for mutual trust, the essential ingredient for mutually fulfilling relationships. And that is the reality the leader of today has to address.

Elevating freedom

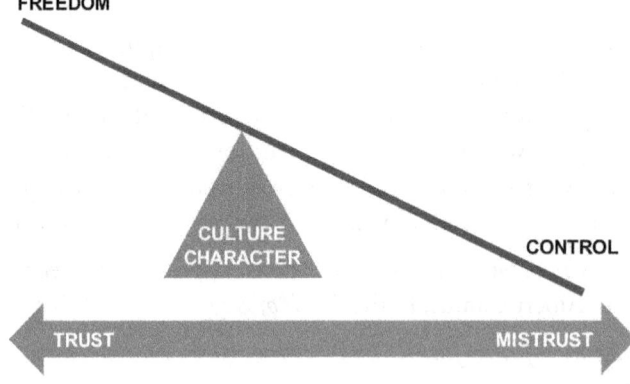

Figure 11.1

Know what to do

Quo vadis? It has been the theme of this book that leadership is about helping people to be the best that they can be, and that the first step has to be sincere acceptance of the need for personal transformation through ongoing education. On that basis, even though it is a life-long journey, your development as a leader should bear significant fruits from the first day. I have deliberately avoided providing anything substantial by way of skills tool-kits for the simple reason that I am convinced that living the aforementioned principle alone will make you an effective leader, acquiring new skills as you go and polishing old ones in the process. Conversely, without that personal transformation, no amount of skills training will be of any real value.

However, it would obviously be reasonable for even the convinced reader to still ask the question: "In a nutshell, what should I do now?" And so at the risk of appearing to slip into the formulaic approach of 'How to succeed' books, let me spell out what you must actually do to lead like you mean it:

- Constantly evaluate your worldview and your personal integrity in line with the criteria suggested. You no doubt keep a regular check on your physical health; your mental health is even more important.
- Audit your attitudes daily and cultivate the seven virtues. In purely practical terms, you will be infinitely more effective in building relationships, and you will be surprised at how much more effective you are in everything you do. It is always your own free choice what you make of yourself. Hamlet's advice to his mother was:

  "Assume a virtue if you have it not... for use can almost change the stamp of nature."
- Drive your own education daily in accordance with the guidelines provided in Chapter Six
- In every situation, define reality to one and all, starting with yourself, especially in clarifying your vision. In communicating with others, always be guided by the seven virtues, showing empathy with their human weakness, their anxieties, and aspirations.
- In your role as leader, actively demonstrate that you want the best for everyone, monitoring their progress and well-being, and promoting their development. Unleash their creativity, giving

them recognition in success, and encouragement in failure. As Epictetus said in his *Discourses*:
"*It were no slight attainment, could we merely fulfil what the nature of man implies.*"

- Be decisive and action-oriented — always! Unleash your own creativity in identifying goals and finding the best ways to reach them. And remember, the only bad decision is the decision to make no decision.

- Take stock daily, always asking "Have we made progress today?", "Where next?" and "Is there a better way?". This reflection time obviously relates closely to the first guideline concerning your principles and your personal integrity

KNOW THERE IS HOPE

Men and women who pick up this gauntlet will certainly make a real difference by doing "what they can, with what they have, where they are"; and in this perilous historical nexus, they are the only ones who will help humanity find a better way forward. There are those who will accuse me of painting too bleak a picture of the world and the apparent poverty of leadership, but in surveying the data that flows constantly across my desk, I am more concerned that I have not stated the case forcefully enough.

Nonetheless, it is heartening to be able to acknowledge that there are increasing signs of hope. I am encouraged by the number of women, young and not so young, coming to the fore, bringing more compassion and creativity into the workplace, eschewing the aggressive, arrogant, adversarial masculine model slavishly imitated hitherto by too many of their peers. I am encouraged by an almost uniformly positive reception given to the message concerning integrity and principled leadership by people from every demographic grouping. I am encouraged by the increasing anger at political and corporate misleadership, and the growing propensity for principled action in opposition. I am encouraged by the growing realisation that the world is on the cusp of a major socio-economic revolution with inevitable political overtones, and the resultant hunger of people for knowledge as opposed to propaganda. Ironically, I am even encouraged by the clumsy machinations of those who seek to exploit the worldwide crisis of culture by imposing more rigid controls, because they actively parade the bankruptcy of their ideas as they seek refuge in misleadership.

In the complexities of any age, it is the principled, creative action of leaders in homes, schools, communities and workplaces, as well as in the corridors of power, that helps the world move forward. It is my great privilege to witness daily the extraordinary difference ordinary people can make. Of course, it is easy to dismiss this kind of thinking as idealistic and impractical, but what could be more practical than making a decisive change for the good of all by ordering your own life according to the principles of love and respect? But that is precisely why it is so hard — because it has to start with you.

THE END

Leaders and Misleaders

About Andre van Heerden

Since studying Law and History at university, Andre has been a teacher, a soldier, a policeman, a refugee, an advertising copywriter, a creative director, an immigrant, an account director, a marketing consultant, a professional speaker, a corporate coach, and an expert on leadership. Andre's career in advertising saw him work with multinational blue-chip brands like Toyota, Lexus, Ford, Jaguar, Honda, Renault, American Express, Kodak, S. C. Johnson, John Deere, Kimberley-Clarke, TDK, Canon, and Motorola. The ***Power of Integrity*™** corporate learning program he now provides has involved working with leading New Zealand organisations engaged in the dairy industry, food production, retail, the financial sector, real estate, advertising, print production, governmental services, education and training, accountancy, and legal services.

Drawing on the perspectives of history and philosophy, and a wealth of business experience, Andre demonstrates the impact of leaders and misleaders on business, making plain the psychologies of progress and regress. He shows how corporate culture determines performance, and how leadership or misleadership determines corporate culture. His highly successful ***Power of Integrity*™ *Leadership Program*** has earned enthusiastic praise from almost 500 corporate leaders over the past eight years.

Andre is available to speak about Leadership and Misleadership.

Contact Andre van Heerden on +64 9 535 8932
or via email: amd@xtra.co.nz

www.powerofintegrity.com

Bibliography

Albacete, Lorenzo, *God at the Ritz* (Crossword 2002)

Arendt, Hannah, *The Portable Hannah Arendt* (Penguin 2000)

Asser, *Life of Alfred the Great* (Penguin 1983)

Adams, Henry, *The Education of Henry Adams* (BNP 2007)

Adler, Mortimer J., *Intellect – Mind over Matter* (Macmillan 1990)

-----, *How to think about the great ideas* (Open Court 2000)

-----, *Six Great Ideas* (Touchstone 1997)

-----, *Ten Philosophical Mistakes* (Touchstone 1996)

-----, *The Great Ideas – a Lexicon of Western Thought* (Scribner Classics 1999)

-----, *The Paideia Proposal* (Touchstone 1998)

Aristotle, *The Politics* (Penguin 1981)

Bartlett, Robert, *The Making of Europe* (Princeton 1994)

Barzun, Jacques, *Begin Here* (Chicago 1992)

-----, *Classic, Romantic, and Modern* (Chicago 1975)

-----, *From Dawn to Decadence* (Perennial 2001)

-----, *The Culture we Deserve* (Wesleyan 1989)

-----, *The House of Intellect* (Perennial 2002)

Becker, Ernest, *The Denial of Death* (Free Press 1997)

Bell, Daniel, *The Cultural Contradictions of Capitalism* (Basic Books/Harper 1978)

Bell, Madison Smartt, *Toussaint L'Ouverture* (Vintage 2007)

Belloc, Hilaire, *The Servile State* (Liberty Fund 1977)

Berdyaev, Nicolas, *The Destiny of Man* (Harper Torchbooks 1960)

Blanning, Tim, *The Pursuit of Glory* (Viking 2007)

Brown, Peter, *The Rise of Western Christendom* (Blackwell 2001)

Buber, Martin, *Good and Evil* (Charles Scribner's Sons)

Burleigh, Michael, *Earthly Powers* (HarperCollins 2005)

-----, *The Third Reich* (PAN 2001)

Butterfield, *Christianity and History* (Bell 1954)

-----, *The Whig Interpretation of History* (Norton 1965)

Caldecott, Stratford, *Beauty for Truth's Sake* (Brazos Press 2009)

Catton, Bruce, *A Stillness at Appomattox* (White Lion 1975)

-----, *Never Call Retreat* (Gollancz 1977)

-----, *Terrible Swift Sword* (Gollancz 1978)

-----, *The Coming Fury* (Phoenix 1988)

-----, *This Hallowed Ground* (Wordsworth 1998)

Chesterton, G. K., *Collected Works: Volume I* (Ignatius 1986)

-----, *Collected Works: Volume II* (Ignatius 1986)

Churchill, Winston S., *A History of the English-Speaking Peoples* (Cassell 1980)

Confucius, *The Analects* (Wordsworth 1996)

Conquest, Robert, *Reflections on a Ravaged Century* (Norton 2001)

Conrad, Joseph, *Heart of Darkness* (Penguin 2000)

Dalrymple, Theodore, *Life at the Bottom* (Ivan R. Dee 2001)

-----, *Our culture, what's left of it* (Ivan R. Dee 2005)

-----, *In Praise of Prejudice* (Encounter Books 2007)

-----, *Not with a bang but a whimper* (Ivan R. Dee 2008)

Damon, *Greater Expectations* (Free Press 1996)

Daniels, Aubrey C., *Bringing out the Best in People* (McGraw Hill 1994)

Dawson, Christopher, *Dynamics of World History* (ISI Books 2002)

-----, *Medieval Essays* (CUA Press 2002)

-----, *Progress and Religion* (CUA Press 2001)

-----, *Religion and the Rise of Western Culture* (Image/Doubleday 1991)

-----, *The Crisis of Western Education* (Franciscan University Press 1989)

-----, *The Making of Europe* (CUA Press 2003)

De Lubac, Henri, *The Drama of Atheist Humanism* (Ignatius 1998)

De Soto, Hernando, *The Mystery of Capital* (Black Swan 2001)

Dostoevsky, Fyodor, *The Brothers Karamazov* (Penguin 1982)

-----, *The Devils* (Penguin 1971)

Eliot, T. S., *Christianity and Culture* (Harcourt 1976)

Faulkner, Robert, *The Case for Greatness* (Yale University Press 2007)

Ferguson, Niall, *Empire* (Penguin 2008)

Fox, Robin Lane, *The Classical World* (Basic Books 2006)
Frankl, Victor, *Man's Search for Meaning* (Washington Square Press 1985)
Gamble, Richard M. (Ed.), *The Great Tradition* (ISI Books 2007)
Gatto, John Taylor, *Dumbing Us Down* (New Society Publishers 2008)
Gergen, Kenneth J., *The Saturated Self* (Basic Books 1991)
Gilson, Etienne, *The Unity of Philosophical Experience* (Ignatius 1999)
-----, *Being and Some Philosophers* (PIMS 1952)
Gimpel, Jean, *The Medieval Machine* (Barnes and Noble 1976)
Goleman, Daniel, *Emotional Intelligence* (Bloomsbury 1996)
Greenberg, Daniel S., *Science, Money, and Politics* (Chicago 2001)
Guardini, Romano, *The End of the Modern World* (ISI Books 2001)
Goodwin, Doris Kearns, *Team of Rivals* (Simon & Schuster Paperbacks 2006)
Handy, Charles, *The Hungry Spirit* (Arrow 1998)
-----, *Understanding Organizations* (Penguin 1999)
Himmelfarb, Gertrude, *On Looking into the Abyss* (Vintage 1994)
-----, *The New History and the Old* (Belknap/Harvard 2004)
-----, *The Roads to Modernity* (Vintage 2005)
Hirsch, E. D., *The Knowledge Deficit* (Houghton Mifflin 2006)
Hitchens, Peter, *The Abolition of Britain* (Quartet Books 2000)
Jaki, Stanley L., *Means to Message* (Eerdmans 1999)
-----, *The Purpose of it All* (Scottish Academic Press 1990)
Johnson, Paul, *A History of the Modern World* (Weidenfeld Paperbacks 1984)
-----, *A History of the American People* (Weidenfeld & Nicholson 1997)
Kierkegaard, Soren, *Fear and Trembling* (Penguin 1985)
Kotter, John P., *Leading Change* (HBS Press 1995)
Lasch, Christopher, *The Culture of Narcissism* (Norton 1991)
Lewis, Clive Staples, *The Abolition of Man* (Collier Books 1955)
Livy, *The Early History of Rome* (Penguin 2002)
McClellan & Dorn, *Science and Technology in World History* (The Johns Hopkins University Press 2006)
MacIntyre, Alasdair, *Dependent Rational Animals* (Open Court 2006)
Marcus Aurelius, *Meditations* (Penguin 1964)
Ohmae, Kenichi, The Mind of the Strategist (McGraw-Hill 1991)

Orwell, George, *Homage to Catalonia* (Penguin 2001)

-----, *Selected Writings* (Heinemann 1965)

Paul, Annie Murphy, *The Cult of Personality* (Free Press 2004)

Pernoud, Regine, *The Crusaders* (Ignatius 2003)

-----, *Those Terrible Middle Ages* (Ignatius 2000)

Pieper, Josef, *A Brief Reader on the Virtues of the Human Heart* (Ignatius 1991)

-----, Abuse of Language, *Abuse of Power* (Ignatius 1988)

-----, *In Defence of Philosophy* (Ignatius 1992)

-----, *Leisure – the Basis of Culture* (St. Augustine's Press 1998)

-----, *Only the Lover Sings* (Ignatius 1990)

-----, *Scholasticism* (St. Augustine's Press 2001)

-----, *The Four Cardinal Virtues* (Notre Dame 1966)

Plato, *Republic* (Penguin 1986)

Plato, *Phaedrus and Letters VII and VIII* (Penguin 1973)

Plutarch, *Makers of Rome* (Penguin 1965)

Rose, Jonathan, *The Intellectual Life of the British Working Classes* (Yale University Press 2002)

Sacks, Jonathan, *The Politics of Hope* (Vintage 2000)

Safire, William, *Lend Me Your Ears* (Norton 1992)

Sayers, Dorothy L., *The Mind of the Maker* (Harper Collins 1979)

Schama, Simon, *Citizens – a Chronicle of the French Revolution* (Alfred A. Knopf 1989)

Scruton, Roger, *Culture Counts* (Encounter Books 2007)

-----, *Gentle Regrets* (Continuum 2005)

-----, *Modern Culture* (Continuum 2005)

-----, *Philosophy: Principles and Problems* (Continuum 2005)

Semler, Ricardo, *Maverick* (Arrow 1994)

Southern, R. W., *The Making of the Middle Ages* (Yale 1953)

Stark, Rodney, *The Victory of Reason* (Random House 2006)

Stern, Sol, *Breaking Free* (Encounter 2005)

Tacitus, *The Annals of Imperial Rome* (Penguin 1996)

Tartaglia, Louis A., *Flawless* (Eagle Brook Morrow 1999)

Thompson, J. M., *The French Revolution* (Blackwell 1966)
Tooley, James, *The Beautiful Tree* (Cato 2009)
Trilling, Lionel, *Sincerity and Authenticity* (Harvard University Press 1973)
-----, *The Moral Obligation to be Intelligent* (FSG 2001)
Turgenev, Ivan, *Faust* (Hesperus 2003)
Vaillant, George L., *Aging Well* (Little, Brown 2001)
Vitz, Paul, *Psychology as Religion* (Eerdmans 2002)
Vitz & Felch (Eds.), *The Self – beyond the post-modern crisis* (ISI Books 2006)
Weaver, Richard M., *Ideas Have Consequences* (Chicago 1984)
West, E. G., *Education and the State* (Liberty Fund 1994)
Williams, Walter E., *More Liberty Means Less Government* (Hoover Press 1999)
Yunus, Muhammad, *Banker to the Poor* (Public Affairs 2007)
Yakovlev, Alexander N., *A Century of Violence in Soviet Russia* (Yale University Press 2002)

INDEX

A

Abelard 182
Adair, John 54
Adams, Henry 21, 119
Adcock, Colin 192
Ad hominem 93
Adler, Mortimer 17, 102, 121, 147
Admiral Nelson 137
Aeneid 112
Aitmatov, Chingiz 133
Alaric 204
Albacete, Lorenzo 137
Albania 62
Alexander the Great 16, 29, 46
Alfred the Great 44-45
Amazon.com 192
America 62, 137
American Declaration of Independence 140 - 142
American Revolution 28
Analogy 197
Apartheid 81
Aquinas, St. Thomas 91, 95, 120, 152, 155
Aragon, Katherine of 14
Arendt, Hannah 39
Argumentum ad numeram 94
Aristotle 90, 92, 99, 103-104, 112, 120-121, 141
Arnold, Matthew 110
Aspiration 154
Attila 62
Attitudes 144 - 148, 150, 152 -153, 155
Augustine, St. 63, 117

Augustulus, Romulus 204
Aurelius, Marcus 23
Auschwitz 117
Austen, Jane 187
Averroes 104
Avicenna 104
Aztec 159

B

Balliol, John 213
Bangladesh 192
Barrie, J. M. 69
Bartlett, Robert 117
Barzun, Jacques 86, 112, 219
Becker, Ernest 124
Beethoven 221
Belfast 117
Belgian Congo 144
Belgium 160
Belief 125
Bell, Daniel 209
Belloc, Hilaire 76
Bellow, Saul 59
Bennis, Warren 24, 55
Berdyaev, Nicolas 167, 171
Berglas, Steven 210
Berkeley 120
Bernini 221
Bible 112, 137
Bismarck 159
Black-market economy 184
Blake 112
Blood Diamond 137
Blood feud 175
Bloom, Allan 205

Boethius 65
Boleyn, Anne 14
Bolt, Robert 13-15
Bonhoeffer, Dietrich 7
Bonjour Paresse 8
Boudicca 182
Brainstorming 197
Britain 62
Browning 112
Bryson, Elizabeth 111
Buber, Martin 124, 127, 130
Burke, Edmund 222
Butterfield, Herbert 160-161
Byron 193

C

Caesar 29, 46
Cahokia 159-161
Calhoun 59
Cambodia 117
Camus, Albert 63, 72, 76, 221
Carlyle, Thomas 111, 192
Carrel, Alexis 133
Carroll, Lewis 93
Carton, Sydney 137
Catton, Bruce 112
Cellini 193
Chamberlain 76
Chaplin, Charles 209
Chaput, Archbishop 75
Character 150
Charles 75
Chaucer 111, 180
Cherokee 59
Chesterton, G. K. 13, 108, 118, 154, 186, 189, 200-201
China 62
Churchill, John 25
Churchill, Winston 13, 25, 27, 76, 110, 213-214

Cincinnatus 21, 60
Cinderella Man 137
Civil War 137
Classicism 219, 220
Clausewitz 196
Clynes, J. R. 111
Cold War 195
Columbus 27
Common Law 183
Compassion 174
Confidence 149, 153
Confucius 23, 71, 72
Congolese 161
Conquest, Robert 76, 87, 110, 134
Conrad, Joseph 111, 159
Constantine 204
Cookson, Catherine 111
Coppola, Francis Ford 187
Corruption 183
Courage 151-153
Cox, Baroness Caroline 116
Crankshaw, Edward 134
Crash 137
Creativity 179, 185, 195
Crusades 132
Cynicism 178

D

Daedalus 179
Dalrymple, Theodore 128
Damon, William 155
Daniel-Rops, Henri 204
Dante 180
Darfur 117
Dawkins, Richard 132
Dawson, Christopher 76
De Bono, Edward 186
Dell, Michael 192
Delphic Oracle 119
De Pree, Max 17

Derrida 79
Der Spiegel 183
Descartes 221
Dessalines, Jean-Jacques 29
Development aid 183
Dewey, John 113
Dhuoda 182
Dickens 137
Dilbert 8
Dinka 116
Diocletian 204
Disney, Walt 54, 192
Dominican Republic 27
Donne 111
Dostoevsky 112, 137
Douglass, Frederick 97
Drucker, Peter 19, 54
Dryden, John 73
Duke of Marlborough 25
Duvalier, Papa Doc 29

E

Early History of Rome 112
Eastman, George 192
Economist 208
Edward I 213
Edwards, Betty 193
Egypt 184
Eichmann, Adolf 39
Eilmer 179
Einstein, Albert 51, 90, 110, 131, 203
Ekman, Paul 148
Eleanor of Aquitaine 182
Eliot, T. S. 76
Elizabeth I 16
Emerson 145
Emotional appeals 94
Emotions 146, 147, 148, 149
Empathy 173, 198
Epictetus 29

Erasmus 111
Eritrea 183
Escher 109
Ethnic cleansing 81
Euclid 104
Extras 79

F

Facebook 84, 162
Faith 153
Faithfulness 176
Fatalism 88, 178
Federer, Roger 113
Feiner, Michael 16
Ferguson, Niall 196
Fitz-Gibbon, Bernice 186
Flew, Anthony 90
Flight of the Conchords 79
Forgiveness 175
Formulae 188
Formula, Trust in 87
Foucault 79
Franklin, Benjamin 21, 110
Frankl, Victor 37
Frederick II 158
Frederick the Great 46, 192
Free will 124
French Revolution 28, 105, 107, 161
Frost, Robert 186

G

Gandhi, Mahatma 23, 27, 71
Gatto, John Taylor 81
Gauguin 193
Gergen, Kenneth J. 127
Gertrude of Helfta 182
Gettysburg 140
Gheddo, Fr. Piero 116
Gibbon 110, 111
Gibson, Mel 213

Gimpel, Jean 196
Gladstone 46
Goethe 150, 221
Goleman, Daniel 147
Goodwin, Doris Kearns 46, 196
Gore, Al 83
Grameen Bank 192
Grand Torino 137
Great Wall of China 180
Guardini, Romano 76, 209
Gulag 117

H

Haber, Fritz 69
Haiti 27, 184
Hamilton 21
Hamlet 175
Handy, Charles 208
Harold 179
Harvard Business Review 198
Hastings 179
Havel, Vaclav 82
Hawking, Stephen 131
Heloise 182
Hempel, Hendrik 183
Henry VIII 13-15
Herrad of Landsberg 182
High Noon 175
Hildegarde of Bingen 182
Hitchens, Peter 206
Hitchins, Christopher 132
Hitler 19, 39, 75
Hobbes 120
Holyfield, Evander 139
Honda, Soichiro 192
Hope 153
Hotel Rwanda 137
Hubris 163-168, 172-175, 184, 194-195, 198
Huff, Darrell 90
Hugo, Victor 137

Human genome project 188
Hume 120, 141
Humour 175
Huxley, Aldous 76
Hyderabad 190

I

Identity 123
Inca 159
Information overload 84
Inhofe 83
Intellect 124
Iraq 62
Israel 137

J

Jacobin 'Reign of Terror' 61
Jaki, Stanley 49, 91
Japan 137
Jardine, Neil 191
Jefferson 21
Jericho 180
Jihad 132
Joan of Arc 23, 213
Job 152
Jobs, Steve 192
Johnson, Paul 59
Jonas, Hans 130
Jones, Reverend Jim 118
Julius Caesar 112
Justice 152-153
Justinian 182, 204

K

Kamprad, Ingvar 192, 193
Kant, Immanuel 68, 69, 81, 96, 120, 131, 140, 217
Kearsney College 187
Keats 169
Keeler, Christine 137

Keller, Helen 43
Kenya 144
Khmer Rouge 120
King, Martin Luther 140
Kipling 112
Kotter, John 16, 18, 20, 24, 48, 55
Krier, Leon 187
Kyi, Aung San Suu 71

L

Lancaster schools 59
Langland 180
Language 125
Lasch, Christopher 89, 162, 171
Lauder, Estee 192
Lewis, C. S. 172
Lincoln, Abraham 13, 23, 46, 47, 140, 157. 214
Lippmann, Walter 27
Livy 112
Loaded words 94
Locke 141
Logical Positivist School 138
Longfellow 112
Lord Chesterfield 111
L'Ouverture, Toussaint 27
Love 149, 153-154, 168, 194-195
Lysistrata 175

M

Macbeth 107
Machiavelli 29
Macmillan, Harold 137-138
Mandela, Nelson 23, 71, 137
Manzoni' 79
Mao 19
Maritain, Jacques 90
Marshall 21
Marxist-Leninist 161
Masefield 112

Maslow, Abraham 65
Maugham, W. Somerset 115
Mau Mau 144
May, Rollo 65
MacIntyre, Alasdair 130, 157
Media mushroom 83
Mexico 184
Mill, John Stuart 71
Milne, A. A. 56
Minogue, Kenneth 34
Mintzberg, Henry 55
Modernism 79
Modigliani 187
Monroe, James 59
Montesquieu 141
Moonie cult 118
More, Sir Thomas 13-15
Morita, Akio 192
Mother Theresa 13, 16, 214
Mugabe, Robert 77, 184
Mussolini 75
Myers, Dr. David G. 146
Myhrvold, Nathan 56
My Lai 117
MySpace 162

N

Nanking 117
Napier, Sir Charles 81
Napoleon 16, 20, 21, 29, 46
Narcissism 168
Nelson 137
New Zealand 111
Nietzsche 120
Nigeria 62
Nihilism 168
NITA 220
Nominalism 120
Norman 117
Nyerere, Julius 77

O

Ockham 120
Ohmae, Kenichi 196
One and the Many 171, 172
Oracle, Delphic 119
Orwell, George 76

P

Pascal, Blaise 85, 119, 154, 181-183
Pastiche personality 127
Pauketat, Timothy 159
Peck, M. Scott 43
Pernoud, Regine 182
Perpetuum Jazzile 187
Personality 171
Peru 184
Petitio principii 94
Philippines 184
Pieper, Josef 80, 84, 101, 150, 170
Pirie, Madsen 90
Plato 61, 80, 95, 101, 103, 107, 112, 120-123, 127, 149, 205
Plotinus 91
Plutarch 25
Poisoning the well 94
Poland 137
Political correctness 82
Politics 112
Pope Gregory 45
Postman, Neil 83
Post-modernism 79
Post-modern mindset 78
Problem 188
Prodigal Son 137
Profumo, John 137-138
Prudence 151-153
Ptolemy 104
Pyramids 180

Q

Quintilian 107

R

Ralph Waldo Emerson 145
Reframing the question 197
Reign of Terror 61
Relationships 125, 157-158
Relativism 80
Religious intolerance 81
Renaissance 181
Republic 112
Rhodesia 62, 76, 99, 143, 144, 191
Richter, Jean Paul 175
Robert the Bruce 214
Robespierre 61
Rochefoucauld, Duc de la 14
Roddick, Anita 192
Rogers, Carl 65
Roman Law 183
Romanticism 219, 220
Ronaldo, Christiano 188
Roosevelt, Teddy 20, 109
Rorty 79
Rose, Jonathan 110-111
Rousseau 120
Royce, Josiah 17
Russell, Bertrand 188-189
Rwanda 117

S

Sartre, Jean-Paul 127, 132, 158
Sayers, Dorothy 179
Scientific Revolution 181
Scramble for Africa 159
Scruton, Roger 36, 176
Seinfeld 79, 175
Self-consciousness 123
Semler, Ricardo 192

Serbia 62
Shackleton, Ernest 170
Shakespeare, William 25, 110-112, 215
Shapiro, Harold T. 101
Sharpeville 117
Simon, Paul 187
Sistine Chapel 194
Slavery 81
Smartt-Bell, Madison 29
Smith, Adam 120, 141
Socrates 23, 72, 80, 92
Solidarity 137
Solution 188
Solzhenitsyn, Alexander 72
Sophists 80
Sorokin, Pitirim 111
Soto, Hernando De 184
South Africa 62, 137
Specialisation 85, 105
Stalin 19, 75, 133
St. Augustine 63, 117
Stein, Edith 137
Stonehenge 180
STORM 55, 57
St. Paul 137, 154
Strategy 195
STRETCH 114
St. Thomas Aquinas 91, 95
Subjugation of women 81
Swift 112, 221
Syrus, Publilius 55
Szent-Gyorgyi, Albert 186

T

Tartaglia, Louis 164
Taylorism 209
Temperance 152-153
Tennyson 112
The Golden Rule 164
Theodora 182

The Office 8
There-Is-No-Alternative 88, 220
Thermopylae 133
The SWOT Analysis 198
Thomas Carlyle 161
Thomas Jefferson 110
Thompson, J. M. 61
Thouless, Robert 90
Tocqueville, Alexis de 120
Tolkein, J. R. R. 31
Tolstoy, Leo 46
Tooley, James 190-191
Totila 205
Toussaint 28, 29
Toyota 192
Trilling, Lionel 166
Truth 169
Twin Towers 117
Twitter 84, 162
Tyler, John 110
Tyson, Mike 139, 140

U

USSR 195
Usury 193
Utopia 15

V

Values clarification 168
Vendee 61, 117
Victimhood 89
Victor Hugo 137
Virgil 112
Vocational training 105

W

Wallace, William 213
Walton, Sam 192
Washington, George 21

Wehrmacht 131
Weil, Simone 72, 76
Wilde, Oscar 166
William of Ockham 120
Williams, Walter E. 108
William the Conqueror 179, 206
Windschuttle, Keith 81
Wordsworth 112, 221
World War II 195
Wright brothers 95

Y

YouTube 84, 162, 187
Yunus, Muhammad 192

Z

Zaleznik, Abraham 16
Zambia 100
Zhivkov 62
Zimbabwe 62, 76, 77, 184